AL-QAEDA 2.0

DONALD HOLBROOK

(*Editor*)

Al-Qaeda 2.0

A Critical Reader

With a foreword by
Cerwyn Moore

OXFORD
UNIVERSITY PRESS

OXFORD
UNIVERSITY PRESS

Oxford University Press is a department of the
University of Oxford. It furthers the University's objective
of excellence in research, scholarship, and education
by publishing worldwide.

Oxford   New York

Auckland   Cape Town   Dar es Salaam   Hong Kong   Karachi
Kuala Lumpur   Madrid   Melbourne   Mexico City   Nairobi
New Delhi   Shanghai   Taipei   Toronto

With offices in

Argentina   Austria   Brazil   Chile   Czech Republic   France   Greece
Guatemala   Hungary   Italy   Japan   Poland   Portugal   Singapore
South Korea   Switzerland   Thailand   Turkey   Ukraine   Vietnam

Oxford is a registered trade mark of Oxford University Press
in the UK and certain other countries.

Published in the United States of America by
Oxford University Press
198 Madison Avenue, New York, NY 10016

Library of Congress Cataloging-in-Publication Data is available
Donald Holbrook.
Al-Qaeda 2.0: A Critical Reader.
ISBN: 9780190856441

Printed and bound in Great Britain by Bell and Bain Ltd, Glasgow

CONTENTS

Preface   vii
Foreword by Cerwyn Moore   ix
Glossary   xiii

Introduction   1

PART 1

AL-QAEDA AFTER THE ARAB SPRING

The Noble Knight Dismounted—Ayman al-Zawahiri, May 2011   21

Message of Hope and Glad Tidings to Our People in Egypt,
Part 8—Ayman al-Zawahiri, December 2011   33

Support for Islam Document—Ayman al-Zawahiri, August 2012   47

General Guidelines for the Work of Jihad—Ayman al-Zawahiri,
September 2013   51

Scent of Paradise: A Study on the Most Honourable Sacrifices of
Worshippers; Death and Martyrdom Campaigns (2nd edn)—Ayman
al-Zawahiri, November 2013   59

Emancipation from the Cycle of Failure and Frivolity—Ayman
al-Zawahiri, February 2014   73

PART 2

AL-QAEDA AND THE SYRIAN *FITNA*

The Seventh Interview with Sheikh Ayman al-Zawahiri: Reality Between
Pain and Hope—Ayman al-Zawahiri and Al-Sahab, May 2014   99

CONTENTS

Testimony to Preserve the Blood of the *Mujahidin* in Al-Sham—Ayman
al-Zawahiri, May 2014   135

PART 3

AL-QAEDA AND THE "ISLAMIC STATE"

Friday Prayers and Sermon in the Grand Mosque of Mosul—The "Islamic
State", featuring Abu Bakr al-Baghdadi, presented as "Caliph Ibrahim",
July 2014   147

Indeed, Your Lord is Ever Watchful—Sheikh Abu Mohamed Al-Adnani
Ash-Shami, spokesman for the Islamic State, September 2014   153

Support your Prophet—peace and blessings be upon Him—Ayman
al-Zawahiri, March 2015   169

The Islamic Spring, Part 1—Ayman al-Zawahiri, September 2015   185

The Islamic Spring, Part 2—Ayman al-Zawahiri, September 2015   203

The Islamic Spring, Part 3—Ayman al-Zawahiri, September 2015   219

The Islamic Spring, Part 5—Ayman al-Zawahiri, September 2015   231

The Islamic Spring, Part 6—Ayman al-Zawahiri, September 2015   239

Let us unite to liberate al-Quds [Jerusalem]—Ayman al-Zawahiri,
November 2015   247

Sham [Syria] is entrusted upon your shoulders—Ayman al-Zawahiri,
December 2015   253

March forth to Sham [Syria]!—Ayman al-Zawahiri, May 2016   263

We shall fulfil our pledge—Ayman al-Zawahiri, June 2016   269

Notes   275
Index   283

PREFACE

On 16 June 2011, three days away from his sixtieth birthday, Ayman al-Zawahiri was declared the new leader of the Al-Qaeda organisation. Osama bin Laden, his predecessor and long-time colleague, had been killed in a raid by US special forces on his compound in north-east Pakistan six weeks earlier. Zawahiri, as documents taken from bin Laden's home later revealed, was inheriting an organisation that was far removed from its operational heyday in the late 1990s or the zenith of its political impact in the aftermath of the 9/11 attacks in 2001. The network was fractured and dispersed, affiliates were unruly and autonomous and many questioned Al-Qaeda's continued relevance or indeed its ability to carry out large-scale attacks matching atrocities committed in New York, Washington, London, Madrid and elsewhere. Zawahiri had been involved in jihad for decades, and longer than bin Laden, but he lacked his predecessor's ability to capture the imagination of his followers or indeed the attention of the world's media. He had sacrificed his family, career and personal well-being for the sake of jihad, but never attracted the same level of romanticised celebration that was so often associated with bin Laden.

Yet he was faced with some of the greatest challenges that Al-Qaeda, as a political entity, has ever faced; challenges that unquestionably threatened the very existence of the group, which risked disappearing into oblivion as it was overtaken by events following the 'Arab Spring' revolutions in the Middle East and North Africa, the civil war in Syria and the emergence of the Islamic State organisation, a mutation of its former affiliate in Iraq, as an enormously resolute competitor that accentuated Zawahiri's powerlessness and isolation.

Zawahiri's response to these crises has followed a familiar pattern of authoring statements that are posted online. Much like his own position in the jihadi universe, Zawahiri's often lengthy and repetitive diatribes seemed dated and outpaced by IS's vast propaganda machinery, which included everything from textbooks to mobile phone applications and a strong interactive component on social media. The Islamic State, understandably, has received much more attention.

But, as I argue in the Introduction, Zawahiri's discourse as leader of Al-Qaeda—spanning the aftermath of bin Laden's death, the Arab Spring and the dawn of the Islamic State—forms an essential part of our understanding of the way in which global jihadism has evolved. It sheds light on the way that Al-Qaeda, in a position of weakness, has responded rhetorically to some of its greatest challenges. Understanding how terrorist leaders react, rhetorically and publicly, once their power and influence has been diminished is no less important than exploring this discourse during their ascent or at their peak. Furthermore, during this period we have seen arguments that have always existed within this space about the boundaries of legitimate warfare and the 'correct' way in which to organise political protest and rebellion being brought to the fore. They are very much part of the public discourse. These debates highlight the heterogeneity of the jihadi universe. They shed light on the extent to which individuals split into opposing camps and—despite the rhetoric about unity among brothers—join different groups and alliances and other manifestations of 'man-made' political activism, where each cohort claims to offer the 'authentic' way in which to emulate the Prophet's legacy and fight for the religion.

This book provides the reader with a collection of professionally translated communiqués covering Zawahiri's first five years as commander of Al-Qaeda. Zawahiri, as always, has been prolific during this period, so the collection is not exhaustive in terms of his output; but the statements contained here have been selected to be illustrative of the way in which he has approached these debates. I introduce each statement with a brief assessment of what I feel are some of the key issues raised that explain why I wanted to include the communiqué in the book, but each individual statement is provided here in full as readers with different backgrounds and from different disciplines may well be interested in different parts of the text. These were tumultuous times for Zawahiri and his perceived constituents, so he touches upon a vast range of issues: such as the Arab Spring revolutions, the formation of political parties and political representation more broadly, constitutional reform, conflict and conflict resolution, the regional economy and involvement of external actors—including states and international organisations—in addition of course to the rise of the Islamic State group and the organisation of jihad. This is a sourcebook for those interested in Al-Qaeda's take on these topics after Ayman al-Zawahiri became its leader.

FOREWORD

Although greatly weakened, Al-Qaeda continues to hold sway over militant networks despite the death of one of its founders and former leaders, Osama bin Laden. In a bid to retain influence, bin Laden's successor, Ayman al-Zawahiri, has sought to realign the organisation and reshape the wider jihadi milieu. However, al-Zawahiri has been faced with multiple challenges, including the continued military campaign to destroy the organisation, political upheaval in parts of North Africa and the Middle East, and the burgeoning appeal of other extremist networks associated with the Islamic State (IS). As scholars, researchers and analysts, we should ask how the leadership of Al-Qaeda has responded to these challenges.

The public pronouncements contained in this volume offer the first open-source record of the ways in which Ayman al-Zawahiri has appealed to activists, mobilised ideology and addressed new challenges. What has happened to the broader militant movement of which Al-Qaeda is a part? And how can we assess both the intellectual content of the arguments al-Zawahiri raises, and the ways in which Al-Qaeda has sought relevance in contemporary extremist theological debates? We might also ask what rhetorical, theological and intellectual arguments al-Zawahiri has deployed in a bid to retain influence as leader of Al-Qaeda. This book will help answer some of these questions.

Debates take place between organisations and their enemies, but struggles also occur inside movements and networks. The ways in which communiqués are created and delivered, translated and disseminated are a form of public—indeed global—communication and messaging. Exactly how communiqués are produced, the ways in which leaders are able to stitch together coherent messages in order to mobilise followers, or the ways in which ideological discourse can splinter are all fruitful areas of research touched upon throughout the book. Untangling the different threads of these debates, putting arguments in context, is valuable in and of itself.

The communiqués and statements presented in this volume also offer insight into the ways in which Al-Qaeda has sought to respond to the theological challenge of the Islamic State (IS). It is widely known that considerable efforts have been made to produce and disseminate information about the Islamic State, drawing on a vast array of messaging strategies and outputs. These efforts have involved a mixture of spectacle, theatre and violence—tailored for specific audiences. The pronouncements contained herein are part of a dynamic public interaction between Ayman al-Zawahiri and Abu Bakr al-Baghdadi.

To this end, the collection includes a selection of statements by key leaders from the Islamic State. These statements illustrate how younger leaders such as Abu Bakr al-Baghdadi presaged followers to establish a caliphate, emphasising activism as a duty, by focusing on the local struggle in Iraq and Syria. In making the announcement at the Grand Mosque in Mosul, Abu Bakr al-Baghdadi rejected the authority of Ayman al-Zawahiri. In contrast Ayman al-Zawahiri has relied on doctrinal issues, and a wider reading of history, in an attempt to bolster his credibility. In essence, he seeks to position himself as an experienced, legitimate leader who can authoritatively lead a worldwide jihadist movement. In this way, the statements highlight the very different leadership styles of Abu Bakr al-Baghdadi and Ayman al-Zawahiri.

Ayman al-Zawahiri's leadership style is, though, also very different from that associated with Osama bin Laden. In this sense, the volume illustrates how al-Zawahiri has sought to respond to various crises as a secessionist leader. The political upheaval in the Middle East and North Africa created considerable difficulties for al-Zawahiri—who responded through a series of communiqués. In order to justify the position of Al-Qaeda and respond to these events, as Holbrook notes, al-Zawahiri sought to emphasise continuity. The book offers comment on these different leadership styles, while also acting as a resource and a contribution to debate.

Other questions come to mind when looking over the collection of pronouncements. Perhaps we should be asking which methods can be used to analyse communiqués and statements effectively? We might also ask whether statements in isolation or a corpus of communiqués offer a more robust platform for analysis. Indeed, many researchers who draw on statements often do so in piecemeal or selective ways. This volume is comprehensive. It includes a useful timeline to help plot the evolution of themes in the statements and thus offers a more rounded understanding of debate in the jihadi universe. Taking the corpus as a whole will enable researchers to tackle familiar problems from a new perspective. How militant leaders seek to proselytise—to inspire activism—based on beliefs is one issue; another may be that authority figures seek to restrain or redirect action. In other words, situating the statements in context also provides a fuller or more complete way of understanding how ideological arguments have changed over time.

However, the book addresses other aspects of inquiry too. It offers scholars and researchers the opportunity to study primary source material—which is all too often lacking in the analysis of terrorism. In part, research on ideology and discourse is reliant on the statements by leaders, but this collection illustrates that those very same leaders communicate with their own audiences in nuanced and subtle ways. Despite being less central to arguments, the poetry associated with communiqués has significance, and is deserving of attention from analysts and scholars. This is especially the case when seeking to understand how leaders demonstrate credibility, or reach out to audiences with little knowledge of doctrinal debates. In essence the poetry is more than context— it serves to embed the doctrinal issues in a wider set of emotional narratives which resonate in different ways to ideological discourse.

In this impressive volume, Donald Holbrook—a leading analyst of extremist ideologies—sheds light on the battle of dogmas and doctrinal struggles within Al-Qaeda. And it is good for scholars and researchers alike to be reminded by him of the continued significance and threat posed by the extremist organisation. By looking closely at Ayman al-Zawahiri's communiques and statements, we can perhaps start to learn how Al-Qaeda has changed after the death of bin Laden.

Cerwyn Moore   University of Birmingham

GLOSSARY[1]

al wala wal bara	loyalty to God and the Muslims, disavowal of the disbelievers
ansar	supporters, referring initially to the group of people who supported the Prophet Mohammed and his flock after he arrived in Yathrib (later Medina) from Mecca in 622 CE. In the transcripts this sometimes refers to the "locals" in Syria and neighbouring regions.
dawa	call, benediction, prayer
deen	faith, religion
fitna	sedition, strife, dissensus, infighting
IED	Improvised Explosive Device
ISIS	Islamic State of Iraq and Syria, sometimes referred to as ISIL (Islamic State of Iraq and the Levant), a translation of the Arabic acronym (*Da'esh*) used to refer to the Islamic State organisation, usually before it was declared a 'caliphate' in June 2014, when it changed its name
kufr	unbelief, disbelief, minor or major abrogation of what God prescribed
Majlis Al-Shura, or Shura	advisory or consultative council
manhaj	method, methodology or way of life, used in this context to refer to the true Islamic method (e.g. method of the pious predecessors or method of the Prophet)
muhajiroun	emigrants, those who went out or emigrated.

	Referred initially to those who followed the Prophet Mohammed from Mecca to Yathrib (Medina) in 622 CE. In the transcripts it sometimes refers to those who arrived in Syria from abroad.
mujahid (pl. *mujahidin*)	fighter in religious wars, those who engage in jihad
Nusayriya	derogatory term referring to the Alawi Shia sect
PBUH	Peace Be Upon Him
Rafida	rejectionists, usually a derogatory Sunni term for the Shia
sahwa	awakening, revival, term used to refer to a collection of Sunni militias and resistance groups in Iraq combating Islamist militants
salaf	ancestor, in this context this usually refers to the "*al-salaf al-salih*", the pious predecessors that comprised the first three generations of Muslims
sura	chapter in the Quran
takfir	excommunication, declaring someone an unbeliever
tawheed	the principle of monotheism, the "one-ness" of God
ummah	nation, community (of believers)

INTRODUCTION

Osama bin Laden, may God have mercy on him, went to his Lord after he achieved what he desired. He was aiming to incite the ummah *[nation or community] to Jihad, and his message reached from East to West and all over the world. The Muslims answered it, as did all the oppressed on the face of the earth.*

Ayman al-Zawahiri, June 2011

I advise those who care about or are keen on knowing the reality of the mujahidin *releases and words, either from among the supporters or the enemies of the* mujahidin, *to depend only on the complete texts of the releases of the* mujahidin, *which they publish on the internet.*

Ayman al-Zawahiri, April 2013

Terrorism is all about communication. The purpose of the violence is to propagate a message, promote a cause, affect publics and decision-makers.[1] Terrorists throughout the ages, therefore, have always sought to develop discourses that communicate their agendas. Many terrorist organisations have created specific sub-units devoted to these tasks, and exploited the latest technological innovations to expand their communicative reach.

Following the 9/11 attacks there was a burst of interest, both from the public as well as scholars and students, in the beliefs and ideas that the Al-Qaeda leaders were conveying. The organisation had been responsible for one of the most catastrophic terrorist attacks in modern times, so people naturally asked: What motivates this group? What are they fighting for?

The attention, at the time, was mostly on Osama bin Laden, the charismatic leader of the group who had been interviewed by the mainstream press and whose pointed speeches and statements often attracted worldwide attention from the media. Behind the scenes, and attracting much less attention, was the dour Ayman al-Zawahiri, a veteran jihadist who had known bin Laden for many years and acted as his deputy in the Al-Qaeda organisation.

Zawahiri was born in a middle-class area of Maadi, an upmarket suburb of southern Cairo, on 19 June 1951. Both his parents belonged to prominent Egyptian families, and many relatives were senior medical professionals, politicians and religious figures. Ayman himself graduated as a surgeon in 1978, later earning a PhD in Pakistan. He is invariably described as having been studious, shy and deeply religious from a young age. According to Montasser al-Zayyat, who met Zawahiri in prison in 1981, the young Ayman would "not spend time with children his age or play or watch television, but rather read books on religion and Islamic jurisprudence as a pastime." Growing up, he had "strong opinions", but "has always been humble, never interested in seizing the limelight of leadership".[2] Zawahiri became involved in Islamic activism in high school, joining what he described as a "religious cell" in 1966, one of several that formed in Egypt during Gamal Abdel Nasser's reign, consolidating and in some cases radicalising during the presidency of Anwar Sadat.[3] Zawahiri and his associates were appalled by the secularisation of society in Egypt and abroad, outraged by the failure of pan-Arabism—highlighted by its inability to crush Israel—and disillusioned by the attempts of the moderate establishment of the Muslim Brotherhood to achieve religious reform through compromise and appeasement. The solution, as the chief ideologue of this movement, Sayyid Qutb (d.1966 CE), argued, was armed jihad against the ruling class, in order to dismantle the areligious order and bring the masses out of the slumber of secularism.

After a stint in prison between 1981 and 1984, Zawahiri travelled to Jeddah, Saudi Arabia, and then on to Peshawar, Pakistan, joining Egyptians and other Arabs in the contingent of foreigners who had travelled to the area to support the jihad against the Soviet Union in Afghanistan. After the war ended, he was determined to continue his violent struggle against secularism in Egypt, which he saw as key to wider Islamisation of the region, orchestrating numerous attacks through his Al-Jihad organisation, mostly from his haven in Sudan and later Afghanistan.[4] It was through his association with bin Laden that Zawahiri's agenda internationalised and became more focused on the United States and its allies as the principal foe, seen as the linchpin of corrupt regimes in the Muslim world.[5] In February 1998 he entered the global stage, literally, joining bin Laden on a panel of jihadis who assembled in front of the media to announce the creation of the "World Islamic Front" declaring worldwide jihad against the US, Jews and the modern crusaders. Whilst Zawahiri formally merged his local Egyptian jihadist outfit with bin Laden's Al-Qaeda in early 2001, therefore, he had been part of bin Laden's cohort for much longer.

Zawahiri has always been a prolific writer and ideologue. In addition to a memoir titled *The Knights under the Prophet's Banner*, he has authored numerous books on topics ranging from the Muslim Brotherhood and other developments in Egypt, several works on the interpretation and implementation of religious concepts such as separation between believers and disbelievers, constitutional reform and martyrdom, as well as publishing extensive rebuttals of those critiquing the methods adopted by Al-Qaeda.

As a member of Al-Qaeda's inner circle, he has published a vast number of communiqués on behalf of the group, frequently in the form of lengthy diatribes delivered as filmed speeches or recorded audio lectures. Starting in 2005, Zawahiri began conducting mock "interviews" with Al-Sahab, Al-Qaeda's premier media outlet, which offered opportunities to delve into great detail regarding his stance on current events, that were invariably traced back to historic grievances. The most recent of these interviews is included in this book. Whilst bin Laden invariably offered pithy and topical addresses focusing on particular issues that were pertinent at that given moment and—importantly—likely to grab headlines, Zawahiri has always been prone to offer more detail. He delivers laboured justifications for the substantive argumentation in support of his position, focusing particularly on the perceived interconnectedness of ailments that are affecting the Muslim world. A keen amateur historian, Zawahiri has always placed great emphasis on establishing continuity in what he sees as the deliberate subjugation of Muslims at the hands of Western hegemony and the geopolitical power plays of secular regimes underpinning a false international order.

In the first major communication from Al-Qaeda after the initial Arab Spring revolutions in early 2011, for instance, Zawahiri began by expanding in great detail on the way in which the current situation in Egypt could be traced back to repeated cases of foreign interference: dating from Napoleon's intervention in 1798, the British imperial presence, the creation of Palestine and—as he very frequently mentions—the British-French "Sykes-Picot agreement" of 1916, which divided post-Ottoman provinces into spheres of influence between the two colonial powers.

Zawahiri is not alone, of course, in tracing the current predicaments of the Muslim world to colonial interference, or indeed to present depictions of a current Western "crusade" as a mere continuation of past crusades,[6] but these themes are particularly prominent in his output.

By 2005, Zawahiri had surpassed bin Laden in the number of statements issued on behalf of the group, although the latter continued to attract much more attention worldwide. It was one of Zawahiri's internal documents from this time, however, that ultimately became far more prominent and important for what has since become a major predicament of Al-Qaeda, its allies and foes. This was a letter dated 9 July 2005 which Zawahiri wrote to Al-Qaeda's ally in Iraq, Abu Musab al-Zarqawi, which was subsequently uncovered by the US intelligence community and published. In it, Zawahiri voiced his concerns regarding the brutally violent and sectarian tactics that Zarqawi's recently formed subdivision of Al-Qaeda in Iraq had adopted since Zarqawi pledged allegiance to the Al-Qaeda leadership in the aftermath of the 2003 US-led invasion of the country. The disproportionate and sectarian nature of Zarqawi's targeting, Zawahiri warned, would jeopardise Al-Qaeda's mission. He wrote:

> Indeed, questions will circulate among *mujahidin* circles and their opinion makers about the correctness of this conflict with the Shia at this time. Is it something that is unavoidable? Or is it something that can be put off until the force of the *mujahid* movement in Iraq gets stronger? And if some of the operations were necessary for self-defence, were all of the operations necessary? Or were there some operations that weren't called for? And is the opening of another front now in addition to the front against the Americans and the government a wise decision? Or does this conflict with the Shia lift the burden from the Americans by diverting the *mujahidin* to the Shia, while the Americans continue to control matters from afar? And if the attacks on Shia leaders were necessary to put a stop to their plans, then why were there attacks on ordinary Shia? Won't this lead to reinforcing false ideas in their minds, even as it is incumbent on us to preach the call of Islam to them and explain and communicate to guide them to the truth? And can the *mujahidin* kill all of the Shia in Iraq? Has any Islamic state in history ever tried that? And why kill ordinary Shia considering that they are forgiven because of their ignorance? And what loss will befall us if we did not attack the Shia? And do the brothers forget that we have more than one hundred prisoners—many of whom are from the leadership who are wanted in their countries—in the custody of the Iranians? And even if we attack the Shia out of necessity, then why do you announce this matter and make it public, which compels the Iranians to take counter measures? And do the brothers forget that both we and the Iranians need to refrain from harming each other at this time in which the Americans are targeting us?[7]

The letter is now seen as a precursor to the bitter confrontation between Al-Qaeda and the Islamic State (IS) organisation which grew out of Zarqawi's outfit in Iraq. This concern about the limits of legitimate combat, the defini-tion and consequences of excessive violence and the role of sectarian dimen-sions constitutes a central theme in the communiqués contained in this book. These issues, and the problem of protecting the Al-Qaeda "brand" and reining in affiliates, were revealed to be a major preoccupation of bin Laden and other Al-Qaeda leaders, according to documents found in his compound in north-east Pakistan following the raid by US special forces on 2 May 2011 in which the Al-Qaeda leader was killed.[8] In the months leading up to bin Laden's death, Zawahiri had begun to warn publicly against the consequences of what he saw as excessive, uncontrolled and unsanctioned acts of violence commit-ted by jihadists, including Al-Qaeda's allies, in public places, particularly in Pakistan, that resulted in large civilian casualties. With the emergence of IS as a distinct entity, this narrative became less internally focused and more directed towards Al-Qaeda's former ally.

Zawahiri as leader of Al-Qaeda

With the death of bin Laden, the mantle was passed to Zawahiri, who contin-ued his practice of relying predominantly on the spoken and written word—disseminated online—to communicate the message of his group.

And there was plenty to talk about. Zawahiri's tutelage of Al-Qaeda coin-cided with the gravest crises the group had faced since losing its haven in Afghanistan in 2001. These were not isolated incidents that could be addressed through targeted initiatives, but rather more gradual developments, where one event merged with the next and all combined to create a toxic and potentially fatal combination of events that threatened Al-Qaeda's relevance and existence. Three key issues stand out.

First, bin Laden's death itself, of course, was a great shock, as was the feeling that the central leadership was increasingly being marginalised by other jihadi entities, including those that operated in Al-Qaeda's name.[9]

The second major shock came with the initial wave of Arab Spring revolu-tions in the Middle East and North Africa, where the Islamist voice was initially muted and where Al-Qaeda's view of the world seemed increasingly dated, its leaders too removed from the experiences of their perceived constituents.

The third crisis evolved from these Arab uprisings as protests spread to Syria, which had a history of dealing with public uprisings through brutal oppression. Syria collapsed into full-scale civil war in 2011, creating a power vacuum that jihadists eventually managed to exploit. Al-Qaeda's troublesome

Iraq franchise, virtually obliterated by Iraqi and coalition efforts to subdue it, sprang to life again and expanded its programme of ethnic slaughter and religious purification to provinces in Syria. It openly contradicted Zawahiri's edicts, disobeyed his orders and eventually split from Al-Qaeda, creating a new transnational jihadist force with far greater material power than Al-Qaeda, after seizing territory in Syria and Iraq, and declaring a new caliphate under the auspices of the "Islamic State". This group would now compete with Al-Qaeda for attention and status as the world's premier Islamist militant entity. It would, like Al-Qaeda, seek not only to orchestrate, direct and organise violence, but also to inspire and incite acts of violence across the globe.

Zawahiri has sought to respond to these challenges through his public statements. His task has been to convince his audiences that the momentum of Al-Qaeda will continue after the death of bin Laden, that Al-Qaeda will remain relevant in the rapidly changing political landscape of its heartland in the Middle East/North Africa (MENA) region and that its mode of jihad offers sounder, more sustainable solutions to the region's problems and its populations than those presented by its new competitor, the Islamic State organisation.

These statements were not issued at a time when Al-Qaeda alone enjoyed universal notoriety as the world's predominant global jihadi force, something it experienced in the aftermath of the 9/11 attacks, for example. These statements do not convey the confident, unwavering resolve of an enormously popular jihadist leader, as did bin Laden's output at that time. They do not represent the discourse of a near unipolar global jihadist realm, but a voice in what is now a much more contested and fragmented universe.

The obvious question to ask, therefore, is why should we dedicate a book to conveying this discourse to those interested in politics and counterterrorism? Why should anyone care? The answer is that it is precisely *because* Al-Qaeda has been weak during these years, *because* Zawahiri is faced with enormous challenges to which he has had to respond through his statements that this body of content is important to explore and understand.

Zawahiri's statements during this period offer opportunities to study the way in which the leader of a global terrorist movement responds, rhetorically, to the dangers of being sidelined, marginalised, forgotten. They show us how a particular path is laid for Al-Qaeda and its followers that is distinct from the Islamic State group and its followers. They show us how different forces within the Islamist militant realm that have always clashed and caused acrimony have burst onto the public stage in unprecedented ways. Ultimately, the statements offer opportunities to explore an aspect of political violence that will be of central interest to those who study it or are charged with responding to it: namely the way in which a group seeks to regain strength and prolong its life. Amid all the conversations about counter-narratives aimed at reducing the appeal of the extremist discourse, we have here a counter-narrative, of sorts, communicated by a veteran terrorist leader seeking to undermine and rebuke an alternative narrative from another terrorist group, re-establishing the authority and credibility of his preferred method.

For Zawahiri, the Islamic State group, which declared its independence from Al-Qaeda in 2013, ruptured the apparent order that was supposed to exist within the hierarchy of transnational Islamist militancy by severing links with Al-Qaeda and the Afghan Taliban whose "emirate" had offered asylum to Zawahiri, bin Laden and their associates in 1996, allowing their group to flourish. The disorder sapped the militants' energy, Zawahiri cautioned, and elevated pointless sectarian slaughter and mayhem above calculated strikes against the United States and its cronies who constituted the real threat. When, in June 2014, the Islamic State of Iraq and Syria (ISIS) announced the creation of an Islamic State (IS), Zawahiri argued that this went against the advice of the wise scholars and indeed the legacy of the prophet himself. It was a move that ignored religious protocol—the immutable principles of theocratic literalists—and was driven by greed and a thirst for power. Ultimately, Zawahiri warned, IS's tactics undermined the public support that would be key to the success and survival of the jihadist movement. Presenting IS as excessive and extreme and Al-Qaeda as the legitimate alternative, therefore, has been a central theme in Zawahiri's rhetorical strategy countering the former. Measurement of public opinion in this regard, of course, is inherently difficult, but there is some logic behind this strategy. Whilst IS has attracted thousands of Arab volunteers, for instance, polling among young Arabs suggests that they view the group's rise as the greatest obstacle facing the region, above other concerns such as unemployment. Of participants in the Arab Youth Survey, 13 per cent claimed to be prepared to support a less violent version of the group.[10]

IS, of course, has responded. In its propaganda, Zawahiri has been described as "senile and deviant",[11] a man who led Al-Qaeda to "the bottom of the pit".[12] Purported former members have described how Zawahiri apparently paid lip-service to Sharia law, tolerating and even respecting tribal customs which IS has prided itself in expunging. Refuting Zawahiri's notions of hierarchy, IS has accused the Afghan Taliban, including its most prominent leader, the late Mullah Mohammed Omar, of "dangerous shar'ī violations"[13] and pointed out that Afghanistan when under its command flirted with the forms of "man-made" heresy such as UN recognition and collaboration with secularised states that IS would exorcise. In undermining Zawahiri, however, IS has sought to tread a careful path whereby it pays homage—and presents itself as the proper heir—to bin Laden, who remains widely respected. Bin Laden in turn, and no doubt partly for this reason, remains prominent in Zawahiri's communications, both through citations and through footage of the late leader that is often used to frame Zawahiri's video releases.

Zawahiri has thus been keen to display a sense of continuity, logic and order running through the lifetime of Al-Qaeda, connecting his tutelage of the group seamlessly with the epoch defined by bin Laden. In this version of events, the current manifestation of Al-Qaeda is a naturally evolved form of the group that blossomed under the Afghan Taliban in the 1990s, that shaped world politics in the aftermath of 9/11 and pioneered global jihad. In this narrative, the fragmentation and disorder inflicted by the usurpers in the Islamic State organisation become accentuated. This of course is a very complex history to which I do not purport to do justice here. To aid the reader in situating Zawahiri's narrative as leader of Al-Qaeda in the broader context of these developments, however, I have placed some of the key milestones of this story on a timeline in Figure 1.

The statements

This book contains translations of eighteen statements issued by Ayman al-Zawahiri, from the moment he announced the death of bin Laden to his efforts to influence the shaping of translational jihad two years after IS declared a caliphate. The period thus covers the first five years of Zawahiri's leadership of Al-Qaeda. The statements do not, as noted above, represent an exhaustive library of Zawahiri's publications during this time, when the Al-Qaeda leader has authored a large number of statements, edicts, tracts and speeches, often issued as multipart series, and extensive books that would be far too voluminous for a collection like this.

Additionally, two key statements of the Islamic State organisation are included in the volume: these are the Friday sermon from the group's leader, Abu Bakr al-Baghdadi, delivered at the Grand Mosque in Mosul shortly after IS captured the city in June 2014; and a statement from the group's spokesperson, Abu Mohammed al-Adnani, titled "Your Lord is Ever Watchful", which

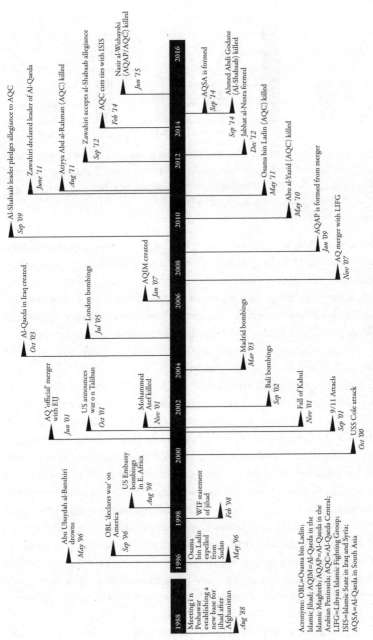

Figure 1: Selected milestones in the history of Al-Qaeda

Acronyms: OBL=Osama bin Ladin;
Islamic Jihad; AQIM=Al-Qaeda in the
Islamic Maghreb; AQAP=Al-Qaeda in the
Arabian Peninsula; AQC=Al-Qaeda Central;
LIFG=Libyan Islamic Fighting Group;
ISIS=Islamic State in Iraq and Syria;
AQSA=Al-Qaeda in South Asia

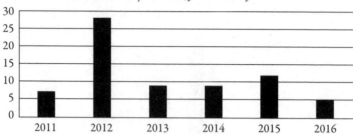

Publications by Zawahiri, June 2011 to June 2016

Figure 2: Presents an overview of Zawahiri's communiqués since taking over as leader of Al-Qaeda in June 2011. I have taken care to select statements that are representative of the challenges Zawahiri has had to face during his tenure as leader of Al-Qaeda and that are illustrative of the way in which he faced them.

sets out IS's strategic agenda for indiscriminate and mass-casualty violence. The purpose of including these two texts is to add context to the part in Zawahiri's output that is almost entirely devoted to refuting and undermining the Islamic State group. This is not, of course, intended as a representative sample of IS's discourse, which—as noted above—is vast, comprehensive and easily accessible online. The aim is to allow the reader to appreciate the different ways in which these alternative discourses are constituted and the extent to which Zawahiri's message is different.

The transcripts were all provided by Linguassist,[14] a British-based translation service specialising in translation tasks for courts and government departments, which translated the publications from the Arabic original. They include all the content of Zawahiri's publications as well as important contextual matter that adds to the substance which Zawahiri has sought to convey. Zawahiri often uses poetry in his statements, especially in eulogies, and whilst it is very hard to convey the original meaning, which often relies on opaque metaphors, this poetry is included in the transcript and specifically identified where it appears in the text. Quranic verses are identified too, with reference to the specific chapter and verse provided in brackets after the quotation.

I have added clarifications regarding particular matters in the text (such as names and dates) in square brackets embedded in the transcripts. More substantial explanations of events that Zawahiri references are offered in the footnotes.

I secured the original publications from the websites archive.org, justpaste. it, youtube.com and dailymotion.com. Most of these are well-known commercial websites that are frequently exploited by terrorist organisations. Archive.org, however, is a non-profit online repository which, again, is frequently used to store terrorist publications. The specific web address of the source is provided in Table 1, although it should be noted that most of these may since have expired since material is frequently removed from these sites.

Half the publications were initially translated from their original audio/ video format, but seven of these were also reviewed against the written transcript that Al-Qaeda's media body later provided online.

The dates of publication are sometimes approximations, based on the time the article appeared to have been uploaded in cases where the statement itself offered few details beyond the year of publication according to the Islamic calendar.

Table 1 provides a brief explanation of why the particular publication was chosen for this book, whilst the individual introductions prior to each transcript offer some further thoughts on the significance of the communiqué and the wider context in which it is offered.

Zawahiri's responses to the Arab Spring and reshaped realities in the aftermath of the self-declared Islamic State were delivered in multipart series ("Messages of Hope and Glad Tidings" and "The Islamic Spring", respectively) where I have chosen only particular parts that are representative of the whole to avoid excessive repetition. Another multipart series, a set of reflections from Zawahiri's time with bin Laden titled "Days with the Imam", is not included in this volume since, whilst interesting and often more personal in tone than is common for Zawahiri, it offers less of the geopolitical nuance that I am trying to convey in this book.

Outline

The book is divided into three parts, with transcripts arranged chronologically. The first part looks at Zawahiri's initial period as leader of Al-Qaeda, where he seeks to come to terms with the tumultuous events of the Arab Spring revolutions, striving to influence the scope and direction of translational jihadi rebellion in a very different political landscape. Some of the themes that then continue to appear in subsequent periods feature prominently here too, such as the need to limit the extent of violence used in order to avoid alienating potential supporters. The second part focuses on the *fitna*, chaotic infighting, that has erupted between Islamist combatants in Syria, whereby Zawahiri seeks publicly to express his desire to establish unity among fighters and—of course—his legitimacy as overall leader of transnational jihad within the framework established by bin Laden. The third part focuses on the rift between Al-Qaeda and the Islamic State; this part begins with two transcripts from the IS leadership, its leader Abu Bark al-Baghdadi and the group's spokesperson Abu Mohammed al-Adnani, setting the scene for Zawahiri's subsequent and laboured rebuttals, where Al-Qaeda's leader again seeks to set out his vision for the future, placing Islamist militancy on what he feels is a sustainable footing.

Table 1: Overview of transcripts

Date	Title	Speaker	Why is it included?
May 2011	The Noble Knight Dismounted	Ayman al-Zawahiri	Zawahiri's eulogy of bin Laden and official recognition of his death. It contains a rallying call to Muslim fighters across the globe and a summary of the issues they should be combating. It reflects upon the legacy of bin Laden and highlights the points that Zawahiri wishes to emphasise in recognising bin Laden's contribution to the issues affecting them and the way in which this struggle should be shaped in the future. *Source:* https://archive.org/details/retha_001
Dec. 2011	Message of Hope and Glad Tidings to Our People in Egypt, Part 8	Zawahiri	This was part of an extensive 11-part series of communiqués surrounding the Arab Spring revolutions. This eighth part of the series is one of the more comprehensive of this particular cohort of statements. Zawahiri talks especially about events in Egypt, Palestine and Libya, touching upon issues that have remained prominent as part of this discourse, such as the release of prisoners. Zawahiri re-emphasises the need to establish an Islamic State, which is important for what comes after, given his opposition to the way in which ISIS eventually sought to realise that goal. *Source:* https://archive.org/details/resala_08
Aug. 2012	Support for Islam Document	Zawahiri	One of the two most prominent documents from Zawahiri during this period, setting out the four key problems with the international order that need to be addressed and seven steps to replace that order. *Source:* https://archive.org/details/nusrat-islam

| Sept. 2013 | General Guidelines for the Work of Jihad | Zawahiri | The second major document released during this period. Zawahiri, in the wake of the creation of ISIL, sets out the guidelines that he urges the *mujahidin* to adopt, stressing the need to limit sectarian conflict and bloodshed. Zawahiri sets out in very clear terms what—in his view—should be the priorities of what he calls 'military work' and how rules of engagement should be constituted.

Source: https://archive.org/stream/JihadGuidelines/guidelines_djvu.txt |
| Nov. 2013 | Scent of Paradise: A Study on the Most Honourable Sacrifices of Worshippers; Death and Martyrdom Campaigns, (2nd edn)—Introduction | Zawahiri | Whilst not a prominent publication, the introduction to *Scent of Paradise*, a book initially published in 2004 and re-issued as a 2nd edition in 2013, offers very important insights regarding Zawahiri's concerns about sectarian and mass-scale targeting of protected people. It is a crucial source in relation to debates about targeting and justifications for murder more generally. This transcript includes introductions to both editions of the book. The 1st, from 2004, is replete with references to the apparent glory of the 9/11 hijackers; whilst the 2nd version, issued during the civil war in Syria and the emergence of ISIL, offers a far more cautionary approach, emphasising the limitations that need to be respected in combat.

Source: https://archive.org/details/Rih.2–20 |
| Feb. 2014 | Emancipation from the Cycle of Failure and Frivolity | Zawahiri | This is Zawahiri's reflection on how events unfolded after the Arab Spring, where he appeals for unity and resolve in order to replace a secular order with religious governance in Egypt and neighbouring regions. He urges believers to look to Chechnya as an example of religiously-sanctioned rebellion, and sets out his concerns about developments across the Middle East and North Africa.

Source: https://archive.org/details/Tampering |

May 2014	The Seventh Interview with Sheikh Ayman al-Zawahiri: Reality Between Pain and Hope	Zawahiri

Here, Al-Sahab—Al-Qaeda's media arm—revisits a mode of communication that it had adopted throughout the past decade, in issuing 'interviews' with Zawahiri to 'discuss' important events. It is the first time that Zawahiri talks at length—sometimes explicitly, sometimes implicitly—about his reaction to the emergence of ISIS, which by this time had been officially renounced, and the dangers that lie ahead if their mode of jihad becomes adopted.

Source: http://justpaste.it/fb61

May 2014	Testimony to Preserve the Blood of the *Mujahidin* in Al-Sham	Zawahiri

Here we get more details regarding Zawahiri's public stance on Syria and ISIS. He declares the latter 'a branch subordinate to Jamaat Qaeda Al-Jihad [the Qaeda Al-Jihad organisation]'; speaks directly to the ISIS leadership and urges Syrians to end the turmoil and infighting and sets out guidelines to achieve this.

Source: https://archive.org/details/shehadaemam

July 2014	Friday Prayers and Sermon in the Grand Mosque of Mosul	Abu Bakr al-Baghdadi

This is Abu Bakr al-Baghdad's major sermon at the seized Grand Mosque of Mosul in northern Iraq which had become the second major base for IS operations. Baghdadi is introduced as the new 'Caliph Ibrahim', commander of the believers, demanding that all Muslims follow him. It is this position of authority and apparent legitimacy that Zawahiri has spent so much effort through his communiqués trying to refute.

Source: https://archive.org/details/kh6bh_9lang

Sept. 2014	Indeed, Your Lord is Ever Watchful	Abu Mohammed al-Adnani al-Shami

This statement from IS's spokesperson sets out the group's strategic framework for an indiscriminate policy of 'shock and awe', promoting acts of violence against non-combatants on an unprecedented scale in the West and in areas under IS's control. The call comes at a time when Zawahiri, by contrast, has sought to temper the force that the *mujahidin* are urged to display and adopt.

Source: https://archive.org/details/kalemahde1

Mar. 2015	Support your Prophet	Zawahiri	Moving away from the Syrian scene, temporarily, Zawahiri praises the *Charlie Hebdo* attack in Paris and urges fighters to respond to further 'threats' against the sanctity of the Prophet and other aspects of religion that are seen as part of Western colonialism. The statement serves as an important reminder of the fact that grievances and justifications for violence are based not only on issues to do with foreign policy and conflict, but also more cultural, less tangible events that cause anger in the population. *Source:*http://ia601307.us.archive.org/30/items/onsrou-tafriq/onsoronabeyakom.pdf
Sep. 2015	The Islamic Spring, Part 1	Zawahiri	In March 2015 Zawahiri began to compile his series on the 'Islamic Spring,' and the first communiqués began to drift online in autumn that year. Here, Zawahiri sets out his grand vision for an alternative to the turmoil and anxiety inflicted not only by the Arab Spring—and government responses to those revolutions—but also the emergence of the Islamic State group. Zawahiri repeatedly seeks to refute and undermine the authority and legitimacy of the latter and sets out an alternative agenda for the creation of an Islamic State as a society respecting his vision of divine religious social justice. The series had reached eight iterations at the time of writing, but the editions presented here represent the most significant parts where the above issues are raised. *Sources:* https://www.youtube.com/watch?v=ZkXQJkGuKrM; http://www.dailymotion.com/video/x36msal:https://www.youtube.com/watch?v=qmcHTFX34QY&nohtml5=False;https://www.youtube.com/watch?v=6ivAfYZRZis&nohtml5=False; https://www.youtube.com/watch?v=sAc5qKu2_aU&nohtml5=False https://justpaste.it/all-rabi3islami
Sep. 2015	The Islamic Spring, Part 2	Zawahiri	
Sep. 2015	The Islamic Spring, Part 3	Zawahiri	
Oct. 2015	The Islamic Spring, Part 5	Zawahiri	
Oct. 2015	The Islamic Spring, Part 6	Zawahiri	

Nov. 2015	Zawahiri	Let us unite to liberate al-Quds [Jerusalem]	During periods of turmoil, the issue of Palestine has always been treated as a potent rallying call with which to unite disparate communities and audiences. Here, Zawahiri asks for unity to respond to the crisis of the Palestinians, whereby Al-Qaeda's vision is presented as more successful—of course—and more likely to succeed than those offered by competitors. In fact, Zawahiri uses the opportunity to reflect upon the achievements of Al-Qaeda and the extent to which it has managed to display its resolve through attacks in the United States, Spain, the UK and beyond. *Source:* https://archive.org/details/Abu_263
Dec. 2015	Zawahiri	Sham [Syria] is entrusted upon your shoulders	In this short talk, Zawahiri discusses the wider regional political implications of the civil war in Syria, focusing on the alleged failure of Saudi Arabia to protect Islam, which he traces back to colonial times and weaves into existing accusations regarding the treachery of Abu Bakr al-Baghdadi, who is now denounced in very explicit terms as being even worse than the Kharijites. *Source:* https://archive.org/details/sham_amana
May 2016	Zawahiri	March forth to Sham [Syria]!	Here Zawahiri issues renewed calls for unity in Syria, which are used to sharpen the distinctions between the Nusra Front and Zawahiri's method on the one hand, and IS on the other. The statement was released just weeks before the Nusra Front announced it was splitting from Al-Qaeda. *Source:* https://www.youtube.com/watch?v=PUF0OhHc4cU
June 2016	Zawahiri	We shall fulfil our pledge	We end with Zawahiri's pledge of allegiance to the new leader of the Taliban, Mawlawi Haibatullah, who took over after his predecessor was killed in a drone strike. Zawahiri uses the opportunity to highlight the importance of true allegiance, which he claims all contemporary stalwarts of jihad have respected, as a fundamental condition of successful militancy. *Source:* https://www.youtube.com/watch?v=6jy__RPde0c

PART 1

AL-QAEDA AFTER THE ARAB SPRING

THE NOBLE KNIGHT DISMOUNTED

MAY 2011

Ayman al-Zawahiri

We begin with Ayman al-Zawahiri's first statement as leader of Al-Qaeda. Issued weeks after Osama bin Laden was killed by US special forces in his Abbottabad compound in north-east Pakistan, Zawahiri seeks to combine his eulogy of the fallen leader—heavily reliant on poetry—with his vision regarding the challenges the ummah *[nation or community] is facing and how to address them. He reiterates bin Laden's "oath", promising to inflict casualties on the oppressors as long as they make the Muslims suffer. Reflecting on bin Laden's objectives, he argues that the late leader had been successful in rousing the* ummah, *which he claims was his principal goal. The statement was issued in the early days of conflict in Syria and during the ongoing fallout from the Arab Spring revolutions. In sharp contrast with what came later, Zawahiri recognises the achievements of his allies in the Islamic State of Iraq and urges other regions, such as Pakistan, Yemen and Libya, to join those who challenged their governments in an uprising against a US-dominated secular order.*

Al-Sahab Media Productions May 2011

[The video begins with a clip of Osama bin Laden saying:] *"I swear by God the almighty who raised heaven without support that neither America nor the people who live in America can dream of peace before it becomes reality in Palestine and*

21

before all the disbelieving armies withdraw from the lands of Mohammed (PBUH). God is the greatest; glory be to Islam! Peace and blessings be upon you."

[Recital of the Quran] *"Think not of those who are killed in the Way of God as dead. Nay, they are alive, with their Lord, and they have provision. They rejoice in what God has bestowed upon them of His bounty, rejoicing for the sake of those who have not yet joined them, but are left behind that on them no fear shall come, nor shall they grieve."* {Sura 3 (The Family of Imran), 169–172}

[Nasheed entitled "So the Noble knight dismounted":]

> *Farewell, O hero!*
> *Eyes cried for your loss*
> *The whole world mourned your departure*
> *And so did the ruins*
> *Even if our bodies depart, our souls stay in touch*

[Zawahiri's full speech:]

Dear brothers, peace and blessings be upon you. God the almighty says, *"Permission to fight is given to those (i.e. believers against disbelievers) who are fighting them, (and) because they (believers) have been wronged, and surely, God is able to give them (believers) victory. Those who have been expelled from their homes unjustly only because they said: "Our Lord is God." For had it not been that God checks one set of people by means of another, monasteries, churches, synagogues and mosques, wherein the Name of God is mentioned, much would surely have been pulled down. Verily, God will help those who help His (Cause). Truly, God is All-Strong, All-Mighty."* {Sura 22 (The Pilgrimage), 39–40}

The Prophet (PBUH) says, "There will always be a group, triumphant in fighting for the truth, until the Day of Resurrection."

I announce to the Muslim *ummah* [nation or community] of creed and monotheism, jihad and martyrdom seeking, generosity and sacrifice, migration and *ribat* [fortification] the news of the martyrdom of the *mujahid* Imam, *mujaddid* [renewer; i.e. one who renews or revives the religion], migrant, steadfast, noble Amir and experienced leader, abstinent worshipper, who stands above the unworthy attributes of worldly life; the front-line heroic fighter, leader of jihad against the communists and later on the crusaders, leader of jihad in the current era against America, inciter of the *ummah* and symbol of its pride and dignity, and its refusal of humiliation and subordination, Abu Abdullah, Osama bin Mohamed bin Laden, May God bless his soul with His great mercy and allow him to enter the highest level in Paradise, with the Prophets, their first followers, the martyrs and the righteous *"and how excellent these companions are!"* {Sura 4 (The Women), 69}

> *A glorious man! He is from glory and for the glory*
> *Glory to him has become in sight*
> *The bequest of prides has ended with him forever*
> *He was alone in this and it wasn't shared with anyone else*
> *How surprising, all the people agreed on a man*
> *Who bended the pride of old age to the hailstones of honour*
> *Osama who doesn't care about the noises of cowards*
> *There is a wrangler for every caller of jihad*
> *What is his sin if he submitted to [jihad] easily?*
> *When they didn't move for fear of slanders*
> *Have you criticised him for being proud?*
> *Who refused to live the life of chickens after he lived the life of honour?*
> *He could, like others, shut his eyes and surrender to*
> *The easiness of life and not roughness*
> *He could dwell in the life and status of lowliness*
> *As a master with entourage enjoying wealth*
> *But Osama the lion, who even if the people reconciled with the enemy, he will not*
> *Saw the shackles of America on the necks of his people*
> *Lovingly with them, he loathed the stinking place*
> *Don't ask Al-Aqsa and what they did to it*
> *And who will retaliate and avenge Baghdad*
> *They revived the crusaders and on their crosses*
> *We crucified Salahaddin on the day of weakness*
> *Terrorise God's enemy with steeds and blood*
> *Destroy New York and bury Washington*
> *Flatten the Pentagon and the Congress*
> *And make them in the palm of the kneader*
> *Bring down their planes and confound their shrewdest leader*
> *Without the strength of [God] there is no victory*
> *He guaranteed a good outcome and He was generous with the guarantor*

He [Osama bin Laden] went to his Lord with the bloodstains of his martyrdom, the man who said "NO" to America. The man who took an oath and God released him from his oath and He will, God willing, release him from what he said when he said: *"I swear by God the almighty who raised heaven without support that neither America nor the people who live in America can dream of peace before it becomes reality in Palestine and before all the disbelieving armies withdraw from the lands of Mohammed (PBUH)."*

> *O you the hawk, the warrior!*
> *No one rejoiced in his misfortune but the cowards*

O with whom our hopes are revitalised!
When harm reached him
Your generous hand, how could we deny it
God forbid! From those who have denied
Who is that? The world has gazed its eyes
Looking dazzlingly at his awe and reverence
That is bin Laden! What thunder has echoed
In the world of silence exploded
When he called for generosity
Comply! There is neither trouble nor hardship
He didn't show an excuse for those who asked
But he was good to them and justified it
The flow of those who arrived in his battlefields
Followed his path in groups and groups
If the swords were panting from thirst
Lower those who disbelieved to be beheaded
He didn't achieve opulence from his insistence
With his determination he didn't disappoint the unthankful ones
He climbs the peaks of glory proudly
As if they are slopes to him
He loved jihad even though the opponents
Ridiculed the mention of jihad and its people
He who has deep determination
That only heads to the fields of sacrifice
From the land of Kashmir which they occupied
To the mountains of Kabul which they captured
To the heroes' prisons in Yemen
For the war in Sudan is deployed
He gazes at Al-Quds and its battlefields
Towards that tough path
And says to Al-Aqsa the caravan has started
In spite of those who sold it off

He went to his Lord with the bloodstains of his martyrdom, the man who was often mentioning the saying of our master Assim bin Thabet[1]—may God be pleased with him—on the day of non-seasonal fruits:

What is my defect and am I a firm archer?
The bow has a long arrow
Death is the truth and life is false
If I didn't fight you then my mother will be bereaved

He was often mentioning the saying of our master Abdullah bin al-Zubeir[2]—may God be pleased with him—on the day of his killing:

Not on our backs the wounds bleed
But on our feet blood is coming down

The noble knight has gone, who loved Palestine, a love that filled his heart and said to its people: to our brothers in Palestine, we say to them: *"The blood of your sons is the blood of our sons and your blood is our blood. Blood is blood and destruction is destruction. I testify to God almighty that we will not desert you until victory is achieved or we taste what Hamza bin Abdul-Muttalib (may God be pleased with him) tasted."* The generous, forgiving, cheerful, polite and lively has gone; everyone who knew him acknowledged his high morals, decency in speaking, good manners, modesty and integrity:

He is relaxed but he is feared
His beauty is defined by two characters, his good manners and his qualities
He carries the great weight of the nation
He is good-natured and always affirming

He went to his Lord with the bloodstains of his martyrdom, the abstinent and content who threw the world with all its adornments behind his back although it came to him amenably. But he chose the life of jihad, migration and abstinence in the cause of God, so God changed him for a love that filled the hearts of tens of millions. The abstinent one has gone, who lived the life of modesty in his own house and showed generosity to his visitors and followers.

He endures hunger and is exhausted by it
His generosity flows among the people
Like the martyr who dies of thirst
Squeezing generosity from his veins

He went to his Lord with the bloodstains of his martyrdom, the man who never surrendered until his last spark of life and was killed amongst his family and children. Abu Abdullah Osama bin Laden was killed like Abu Abdullah al-Hussein (may God be pleased with him) was killed among his family and children. The scream of honour which was voiced by Abu Abdullah al-Hussein in Karbala when he said: *"How impossible, disgrace!"* Abu Abdullah Osama bin Laden repeated it in Abbottabad: *"I wish disgrace for America, I wish disgrace for the crusaders' arrogance and I wish disgrace for Pakistan's being a lackey."* How impossible, abusing the nation's sanctities and its dignities.

Osama and his glories are outstanding
Came one after another that cannot be counted
Tears pour down from the eyes when you are mentioned
O dear soul! The cheeks are bleeding
Although today the world is filled with great people

You are among them the most outstanding
You used to kill hopelessness in us
You took us to every pinnacle and were still going
You looked from the victim's point of view
And for revenge no shackles could chain you
Your acuteness in the hand of destiny is a sword
Your method in the hand of Islam is a banner
Your followers on the day calamities roared
They responded by raiding death
They filled themselves with great nobility
And filled their chests with strong determination
The banners of jihad in Tora Bora
Where the lions rose up
May calamities come upon America
And its towers are destroyed
How many lands lasted for decades?
Wiped out by earthquakes
You declare it a war on Islam
And gather against it troops and forces
O dearest, go to jihad, go to jihad!

There is no escape without mounting terror

He, Osama bin Laden (may God have compassion on him), went to his Lord after he achieved what he wanted. He was aiming to incite the *ummah* to jihad, and his message reached the east and west of the world and all Muslims and every oppressed one on the earth responded to it. Osama bin Laden emphasised, very often, that our task is inciting the *ummah* and referred to what God almighty says: *"Then fight (O Mohammed) in the Cause of God, you are not tasked (held responsible) except for yourself, and incite the believers (to fight along with you), it may be that God will restrain the evil might of the disbelievers. And God is Stronger in Might and Stronger in punishing."* {Sura 4 (The Women), 84}

Today, praise be to God, America doesn't face an individual or group or sect, but a nation in revolt that has woken up from its slumber to a jihadi uprising that challenges America wherever it is. In the last decade America has faced four catastrophic blows: First, the blessed attacks in New York, Washington and Pennsylvania, where the hawk-like self-sacrificing bombers destroyed the symbol of the American economy in New York and the American military central command in the Pentagon. These represent all their military, economic and psychological losses.

The second blow: their defeat in Iraq at the hands of the *mujahidin* and, especially, the Islamic State in Iraq. They withdrew from there after they lost their money and military equipment and the life of their sons. Then the third blow was in Afghanistan, where America is sinking in the mire of defeat and its losses are continuing. It was forced to declare that it will withdraw next July, despite admitting that the *mujahidin* of the Islamic Emirate control most of Afghanistan.

The fourth blow is the fall of America's corrupt cronies in Tunisia and Egypt and the shaking of their seats [of power] in Libya, Yemen and Syria. America has tried to turn on the popular uprising, and after some hesitation it announced its support for the people's revolutions. But the popular movement in each of Egypt and Tunisia directed the slap to America, when the revolutionary youth in Tunisia demonstrated against Hillary Clinton's visit and in Egypt they refused to meet with her.

He went to his Lord, the man who emphasised that our biggest victory over America lies in revealing its decadence and defeat in the field of morality and principles. God almighty willed to reveal America's mendaciousness, vileness and decadence when they killed Osama bin Laden. America alleged that after they killed Osama bin Laden (may God have compassion on him), they threw his body, according to the Islamic practices, into the sea. What kind of Islam is this? America's Islam or Obama's Islam, who sold his father's religion and became a Christian and performed the Jewish prayer to satisfy the big criminals? This is the Islam that America wants to bring to us, a deceitful, permeated and fabricated Islam, which is subordinated to the power of the oppressors, and which doesn't know loyalty nor disownment and not commanding good and forbidding evil and neither jihad.

America threw a sea of glory (i.e. Osama) in the sea of Arabs, witnessed by Arabs and non-Arabs. America refrained from granting a grave to the *mujahid* hero, but his grave is in the hearts of millions. America revealed with its vileness that it does not know honour in hostilities, and from where could they have known it when they lack honour anyway? America, which signed the Geneva conventions to protect civilians and prisoners, was the first to violate them in Vietnam, Iraq, Afghanistan, Pakistan, Guantanamo and its secret prisons in the world. While America was abandoning the treaties they signed, they were obliging others to follow the decisions of the International Criminal Court. And while they were arrogantly alleging that they are committed to them, they remained ignorant of bin Laden's honour in battle.

While America was doing that time after time [violating the laws of war], Osama bin Laden (may God have compassion on him) cared about complying with what he agreed to. In Tora Bora, after agreeing to a ceasefire, about a hundred of the hypocrites fell in the ambush of the *mujahidin*. He just needed to order the *mujahidin* to open fire on them and kill them, but Sheikh Osama bin Laden ordered his brothers to let them out of the ambush and not to shoot a single bullet. After agreeing to a ceasefire, some of the *mujahidin* attacked the hypocrite's position and took some spoils. The Sheikh [Osama] ordered them to return what they took.

What a big difference! He went to his Lord as a martyr, the man who terrorised America when he was alive and who is terrifying it when he is dead. They are even shaking from giving him a grave because they know that millions of people love him. He is terrorising them even when he is dead to the point that they cannot publish the pictures of his body, because they are aware of the Islamic popular outrage against them and their crimes.

Sheikh Osama bin Laden—with God's permission—will continue to be a terror, fear and dread haunting America and Israel and their crusader allies and their corrupt cronies. His famous oath will—with God's permission—make them sleepless: *"You will not dream of security until we live it in reality and until you get out of the Muslim lands."* The love of Sheikh Osama bin Laden— may God have compassion on him—has grown in the hearts of the Muslim people, who went out after his killing to show their love for him and hate for America, from Manila to Cairo passing by Gaza, Pakistan, Lebanon, Somalia, Yemen and Sudan.

I would like here to express my gratitude and the gratitude of my brothers to everyone who took part in this epic [show of affection] and to those who prayed the prayer of absence on the martyr of Islam in the Islamic world and for those who praised the Sheikh—may God have compassion on him—and his jihad. I mention for example, but not exclusively, Sheikh Hafiz Salama, Mufti Kifaytuallah and Sheikh Hassan Awis, Ismael Hania and many others, may God reward them.

O our dear and valuable people, the Sheikh—may God have compassion on him—went to his Lord as a martyr, as we consider him to be, and we have to continue to work on the path of jihad to expel the occupiers from the lands of Muslims and cleanse them from oppression and oppressors. We, therefore, renew the pledge of allegiance to the Amir of believers, the *mujahid* Mullah Mohammed Omar—may God protect him—and we promise him to obey and listen whether in the time of ease or hardship and to continue jihad in the cause of God, establishing Sharia and supporting the oppressed ones.

We also send a message of support to all the *mujahidin* in Afghanistan, Pakistan, Iraq, Somalia, the Arabian Peninsula and the Islamic Maghreb and we encourage them to try harder to fight the crusaders and their aides. We hold the hands of the *mujahidin* in the stolen Palestine and we confirm to them and to the strong and steadfast Muslim people in the environs of Jerusalem that we will sacrifice selves and valuables until we deprive America of security and until it becomes a reality in Palestine. We thank them for their honest feelings that they expressed in support of the Sheikh—may God have compassion upon him—and for their rage and hatred towards America.

I also encourage the masses of the Muslim *ummah* in Pakistan to rise against the military and the bribed politicians, who control their destinies and who transformed Pakistan into an American colony, killing whoever they want, imprisoning whoever they want and destroying whatever villages they want. Those politicians and military sold off the honour and dignity of Pakistan for a bunch of dollars. O Muslims of Pakistan, rise up as your brothers in Tunisia, Egypt, Libya, Yemen and Syria have risen up. Dust off the humiliation that covers you and remove those who sold you in the slave market to America.

I advise my brother *mujahidin* everywhere to unite with the masses of the Muslim *ummah*, to care about serving them, defend them and protect their peace and sanctities and to avoid any action that would put them in danger in shops or mosques or crowded places. We haven't left our homes and countries but to defend them [the Muslim masses] and their dignities. We confirm to all the Muslim people that we are their soldiers and we will not save any effort to liberate the occupied places in Kashmir, Philippines, Afghanistan, Chechnya, Iraq and Palestine. We support their blessed uprisings in Tunisia, Egypt, Libya, Yemen and Syria and we promise that we will wage one war together with them against America and its aides. We call upon the masses of the Muslim *ummah* in beloved Syria to continue the struggle, strife and jihad against the criminal and corrupt regime that sheds the blood of its people.

> *The youth has died for its lands in order to live forever*
> *They vanished so that their people will remain*
> *You stood between life and death*
> *If you aim for the comfort of a long life you must do the unbearable*
> *Who could face and be faced with death*
> *If not the free men*
> *They don't build kingdoms in mornings*
> *They don't usurp rights [...]*
> *May the almighty reward you*
> *O the sons of Damascus*
> *The most honourable of the East is Damascus*

We assure the beloved people of Yemen, the Yemen of reinforcement and of faith and wisdom that we are with them in their uprising against the crony corrupt oppressor Ali Abdullah Salih and his gang. We advise them not to be deceived by the tricks of politics and the Gulf aides of America, who want to derail their blessed revolution in order to change one oppressor for another and one American crony for another. They have to continue with their sacrifices and wrath until the crony and corrupt regime vanishes and a righteous regime will be installed in its place to rule with Sharia, with fairness, respecting consultation, distributing funds justly, spreading equal rights between weak and strong, uprooting corruption and expelling the Americans and their tails from the honourable and dignified Yemen.

As for the jihadi and steadfast people of Libya, we say to them: O the children of the *mujahidin*, be the best descendants of the best antecedents. Your forefathers fought in order for the word of God to become the highest. So don't forsake this trust and don't accept humiliation from a disbeliever like Qaddafi and not from the crusader NATO alliance. Don't let the crusader NATO compromise your freedom, honour and beliefs in return for their bombardment of Qaddafi. Get ready, be equipped and save weapons and ammunition so that no one can dare to impose conditions on you or chain you.

Our active brothers for Islam everywhere, we say to them that we extend our hands to you and open our chests to you to cooperate. That is to make the word of God the highest and to make Sharia in the land of Islam sovereign and not subordinated, commanding and not commanded, no other legitimacy can crush it and no other authority can share with it. And we stand shoulder to shoulder to liberate the lands of Muslims from every assaulting occupier and every corrupt crony and to support every oppressed one in the world.

My brothers engaged for Islam, the gates in the rising Tunisia and stronghold of Egypt have opened with the fall of the two corrupt tyrants. Cooperate, assist and support one another and encourage the Muslim nation to engage in a comprehensive popular movement and in a general invocatory rise to make Sharia the sovereign and not subordinate. Rise to cleanse the [two] countries from the corruptors and thieves, end the ordeal of the oppressed prisoners; divide the wealth justly and all types of political and social oppressions will disappear. Return your countries to be the two bastions of Islam, supportive of Muslims in Palestine and everywhere else.

The last word is for Obama, America and their allies. You were pleased when you entered Kabul with the hypocrites, but this didn't last long as it turned to a disappointment in Tora Bora and a defeat in Shahi Kut and disasters come upon you in a historical crisis, from which your only way out is to flee.

The *mujahidin* of the Islamic Emirate are still giving you lessons, one after another, and whenever you lied they revealed your lies. You claimed that you would cleanse Marjah [in Afghanistan], and the liar Obama claimed that he was following the situation very closely, but it turned to a disgraceful defeat. You also claimed that you were training the Afghan army and police, but the *mujahidin* of the Emirate attacked the Kandahar prison for the third time.

After the martyrdom of the Sheikh [Osama], they [the Taliban] attacked Kandahar and killed the mayor and attacked its security centres and cut off the roads leading to it to prove to the whole world the extent of the failure of all your plans. You were pleased again when you overthrew Saddam Hussein and [George W.] Bush arrogantly declared the end of the main military operations in Iraq. Your happiness turned into unstoppable attrition of blood, money and equipment until you had no choice but to withdraw, leaving Iraq to the *mujahidin*. Today you are pleased by the martyrdom of the renewer Imam, the hero Osama bin Laden—may God have compassion on him. So, wait for what will happen to you after every happiness.

Woe unto America, woe unto its people
I with Al-Qaeda get prepared
For an unpleasant day like Tuesday when
We shed the blood of the disbelievers and it will be so

Our last prayers praise be to God the Lord of the universe and peace and prayers be upon our master Mohammed and on his family and companions. Peace and God's compassion and blessings be upon you.

MESSAGE OF HOPE AND GLAD TIDINGS TO OUR PEOPLE IN EGYPT, PART 8

DECEMBER 2011

By *Ayman al-Zawahiri*

The Arab Spring revolutions undermined the relevance of Al-Qaeda, as forces that were anathema to the group—nationalism, pluralism, areligious mass mobilisation— had materialised to topple secular regimes, which otherwise had always been a central objective of Al-Qaeda and Zawahiri in particular. The latter thus responded, seeking to exploit disillusionment in the fallout of the revolutions and reframing the events according to Al-Qaeda's agenda. The mainstay of this public relations initiative was his "Message of Hope and Glad Tidings" series, aimed predominantly at citizens of his native Egypt, but with dedicated messages to peoples across the Arab world. In the series, Zawahiri railed against democracy, secular rule, foreign interference, exter- nally-induced division, subjugation and corruption, seeking especially to turn a local- ised narrative into one that reiterated the need to target foreign enemies, predominantly the United States. He warned against the emergence or empowerment, particularly in places like Tunisia and Egypt, of political parties that purported to display Islamic credentials, but failed to be guided by the creed. He warned against the complacency of the masses, urging publics to continue the uprising in order to uproot the colonial order: including the imposition of borders and nationalities, free Palestine, and achieving legislative and judicial reform based on the complete implementation of Sharia law as opposed to the cosmetic lip-service payed to its 'principles' in the exist- ing constitutional regimes.

In this eighth instalment of the series, we thus dip into an ongoing debate where Zawahiri continues in his attempts at reframing the revolutions, presenting the uprising in Egypt as a protest against areligious laws and treaties and against the peaceful relations with Israel, underpinned by American interference. He sets out the parameters of success for the revolutions, highlighting adherence to religious law. Turning to more specific current events, Zawahiri discusses the situation of Coptic Christians in Egypt at length, which have suffered oppression and violence after the revolution, recognising their right to reside within the country.

Al-Sahab Media Productions presents:

A Message of Hope and Glad Tidings to our Families in Egypt, Part 8
by the *mujahid*, Sheikh Ayman al-Zawahiri Dhu al-Hijja 1432 AH
In the name of God. Peace and prayers upon the Messenger of God, his kin and companions and those who support him.

Muslim Brothers everywhere: May peace and God's blessings be upon you.

This is episode eight of the message of "Hope and Glad Tidings to Our Families in Egypt". If our dear viewers will excuse me, I would like to move out of its context again, so that I can focus on what has happened in Cairo, the clashes between the army and the Christian Copts. But before I begin my speech, I would like to start off with a greeting and two messages of congratulations, then I would like to end it with a message of support and encouragement.

As for the congratulations and prayers, they are for the detainees in Palestine who were granted, by our Lord the almighty, their freedom from captivity and detention. Our thanks go to God for this great gift. I take this opportunity to remind them [the released captives] that they must be very clear in their beliefs that their freedom was granted to them through God almighty alone, and that the reasons that appear are merely tools of God's fate, where God uses them [the tools] as He wishes, and hence they must direct their gratitude, prayers and thanks to our Lord the almighty and be true to Him in their worship openly and discreetly. They must also realise that their release is a new trial for them because just as they had been tried [tested] in bad times, they too shall be tested in good times, they are to be tried in both [good and bad] states. God said, through His Prophet Moses, to his people, *"Perchance your Lord will destroy your enemy and make you successors in the land and, then, observe what you will do."* Gratitude includes words and action. God says, *"Work thankfully, O David's House; for few of My servants are truly thankful."* {Sura 34 (Sheba), 13}

Those who are jihadists or members of an Islamic movement must dedicate what is left of their lives to the service of God's great religion, and they must work really hard seeking, with all that they own, to make God's religion the one that rules in their lands, not superseded by any other legislation or system, and to free every inch of Palestine, and to bear the burden of their nation everywhere similar to how the Muslim nation bears the burden of Palestine. Those [freed] who are under the banner of secularism or nationalism must take this opportunity to review their past and to remember that they will be standing in front of God one day at the end of their long, or short, lives, and then God will ask them about their support of their religion that was delivered by God, so we should follow it and implement it and rule by it.

God says, *"We have not sent forth a Messenger, but that he may be obeyed by God's Leave."* {Sura 4 (The Women), 64} Those freed must not forget that the national and secular forces have deserted most of Palestine and have accepted crumbs; the only ones holding on to it are the Muslims. I also take this opportunity to remind the families of those freed, whose loved ones were granted a joyous return by God, that they must thank God for this privilege by increasing their obedience to Him and to commit to His religion and to increase their worship of Him and to stay clear of disobeying Him, and to cleanse their homes from anything that opposes Islam and to bring up their sons and daughters so that they learn the Holy Book and they continue to pray regularly and to wear the veil and to commit to the principles of Islam in behaviour and dress. I would also like to remind our families in Palestine and all the Muslims across the world that the release of those prisoners did not happen because of negotiations sponsored by the so-called International Law, nor through the National Unity of those who have sold Palestine. Rather, it came through jihad, martyrdom, resistance and sacrifice. That is the way to victory, so let us remain on that path. I ask our almighty God to grant our freed prisoners the ability to obey Him and to thank Him and support His religion. I also ask the almighty to speed up the freeing of all Muslim prisoners soon and to grant us a glorious victory so we can see all the lands of Muslims free from external domination and internal deviation, and then they unite under a single Caliphate: *"And on that day the believers shall rejoice, in God's support. He supports whom He wills; He is the All-Mighty, the Merciful."* {Sura 30 (The Romans), 5}

This was the message of congratulations and prayers, while the greeting is for the heroes who have, for the fifth time, managed to blow up the gas pipes leading to Israel. Those are the heroes that reflect the right to express the pride of the Egyptian Muslims, the steadfast, who defend Islam and Muslims. God greets those heroes, who renew hope in the hearts of their nation, hope that their sons remain on their pledge that they made to God, they do not tire, and will not rest until they see that the Holy Place has been freed from the dirty Zionists and until the Islamic caliphate is established proud, free, glorious and ruling Muslim lands. I ask God to keep the *mujahidin* of Islam steadfast on the path of sacrifice and jihad, and to give them patience and determination despite the hardships along the way, and to accept their good deeds and to reward them for those good deeds now and in the Afterlife. I repeat what I said in my last talk when I said that the mere supply of gas to Israel is a crime, even if it was at a higher market price. So how is it when it is sold to Israel at a lower market price? It is then a compound crime started by Hosni Mubarak and carried on by the ruling Military Council. The Military Council that considered those who attacked the Israeli Embassy[3] as criminals, while they see those trying to keep it open as patriotic. They described those who attacked it as outside the law and international treaties, forgetting that people's revolts are outside the sphere of corrupt laws and treaties and tyrannical circumstances.

Is a revolt not a rebellion against a constant corrupt circumstance? This is the case in Egypt where the biggest sign is their keeping Israel secure and supporting it against our people in Palestine and facilitating its threats against the security of Arabs and Muslims. The Israeli Embassy was an ugly symbol and a rude signpost of all this ugliness. The removal of the Israeli Embassy is a main target of the Egyptian uprising, which happened as a rejection of the tyrannical laws and treacherous treaties. The noble, honourable, popular revolt against the Israeli Embassy and indeed against the submission to American policy and the arrogant Zionists must carry on if the Egyptian uprising is to reach its goals.

The Egyptian uprising will not reach its goals unless the Muslim people in Egypt establish a proud nation that rules through Islam, independent from external influence and free from internal corruption. The people of Egypt must realise their role through history: Egypt and its people are the bastion of defending Islam and Arabs. This is still their responsibility today, and the Egyptian revolution will not reach its goals unless Egypt has prepared for that role.

As for the second message of congratulations, it is for the Muslim nation and the *mujahidin* and our people in Libya, specifically Misrata, for the martyrdom of the Sheikh, the scholar, *mujahid*, steadfast, the wise, mannered, disciplinarian leader who has gathered hearts and forces together. He is with good manners, fine characteristics, shouts out the truth, supports Islam; he investigates things, he is just, he is the honourable Sheikh Abu Abdul Rahman Jamal Ibrahim Ishtwai al-Misrati, also known as Sheikh Atiyyatullah,[4] may he rest in peace and may God allow him into His great mercy and give him generously for his migration, jihad, steadfastness, seeking knowledge, spreading it and making an effort towards it. He was martyred, may he rest in peace, on the 23rd of the blessed month of Ramadan following a bombardment by a spy crusaders' plane. He and his son, Issam, met their maker, may they rest in peace. The Sheikh had already given his other son Ibrahim as a martyr to the merciful God. [That second son] was killed in the second bombardment he was exposed to, after he survived the first one when he was with Sheikh Abul Laith, may he rest in God's great mercy, where Sheikh Abul Laith was martyred but Ibrahim survived. May God have mercy on this journeying family, the *mujahid* and steadfast family that has offered its leader and his two sons as defence of the banner of Islam, monotheism and jihad, proud enough to stop the criminal crusaders from taking control of Muslim lands and countries, where they will spread corruption there, humiliating its sons, forcing them into the slavery of the atheist, deviant, Western system.

The Sheikh sent me a letter that he wrote a few days prior to his martyrdom, regaling a number of joyous victories in Afghanistan, such as the attack on the American base in Wardak, where he told me that no less than 8 Americans were killed, and that [General] Petraeus was forced to come to Afghanistan to inspect the disaster in person. He also described the Chinook helicopter that was destroyed, killing around 30 American soldiers that were affiliated to the unit that took part in the killing of Sheikh Osama bin Laden,[5] may he rest in peace, plus other operations in Kabul and other parts of Afghanistan. He gave me the good news of the near victory in Tripoli by the hands of the *mujahidin*. The night before his martyrdom, the Sheikh stayed up, following the news of the victory in Tripoli at the hands of the *mujahidin* brothers.

Our great Lord so wished that the Sheikh should follow the steps of the Tripoli martyrs, with God's permission and mercy, towards Paradise and rivers in a seat of honesty at the feet of his Able Master. Sheikh Atiyyatullah does not need an introduction. His great life story is widely known. He has spent his life, may he rest in peace, moving between arenas of jihad and migratory journeys, seeking knowledge, guiding others and educating them, plus he held leadership roles. He, may he rest in peace, migrated to Afghanistan during the Russian invasion, and then at the end of that invasion and the appearance of the treachery between the Pakistanis and the Americans where they betrayed the Arab *mujahidin* in Afghanistan, those who took part in freeing Afghanistan and defended the borders of Pakistan, he migrated to Sudan, then Mauritania seeking knowledge, where he took three years of instruction from its wise scholars, then he went to Algeria to participate in jihad with the Armed Islamic Group,[6] where he went through a bitter experience with them, and returned to Afghanistan when the Islamic caliphate was established and worked there teaching in an Arabic school in Kabul. He assisted the Sheikh in his call for jihad and support for the *mujahidin*, deflecting the lies and suspicions directed at them. He also assisted him in the management of issues linked to the *mujahidin* and facilitating their matters. God made him popular among all the jihadist groups in both Afghanistan and Pakistan. The Sheikh used to write and speak in the name he was more often known by, which is Atiyyatullah, during the incidents that occurred in Libya and when many jihadi groups were made up of Muslim Libyan jihadists, who were steadfast in rising against the atheist tyrant Qaddafi, who surrendered to the West.

The Sheikh decided to share his declaration to encourage his family and brothers in Libya, so he published his letter "Greetings to our family in Libya" using his real name, so he could tell his people and brothers and sons in Libya and Misrata that he was with them. *"I am your brother, you are my family, I am of you and you are of me. I had hoped to be with you except for the fact that I am already in a battle, a fight and jihad against our enemies and your enemies and the enemies of Islam and Muslims, the Americans and the crusader NATO."*

He went as a martyr to his God, this immigrant, the steadfast *mujahid*. His last stop on his journey of migration was his migration to his God as a martyr, where the crusaders shed his blood and tore his body apart using their rockets.

They placed your remains as a banner
That overlooks the valley day and night
Woe unto them, they've made a beacon of your blood
That inspires tomorrow's generation to hate
A scar that screams forever and a victim that seeks red freedom
You were given a choice so you chose to live humbly
You did not seek position or gather wealth
The flare of battles did not spare anything greater
You are hit with calamity but the spears do not spare blood
Like the remains of an eagle or a lion that became dust and specks

The *mujahid*, the scholar, disappeared but his influence remains a debt upon our shoulders and the shoulders of any Muslim and the people of Libya and Misrata, a revenge that we take, God willing, from those crusaders, the West, who killed him and his two sons, and who killed hundreds of thousands of our sons, brothers, women and elderly. They occupied our lands and stole our wealth. They forced their agents on us and planted Israel among us as a power for them that protects their interests and threatens our existence and future with its nuclear bombs.

Following those two messages of congratulations and prayers and this greeting, I return to the main topic of this speech which is about the clashes between the army and the Coptic Christians. This is an extremely sensitive and dangerous matter, and in dealing with it we must be wise, strong and honest. I ask God to assist me in doing so. God has blessed the *mujahidin* in making them the most honest in telling the truth openly. They have paid the price of their freedom and honesty and bravery by having to migrate, and being steadfast and in fighting while being separated from their families, countries and money, they had to endure detention and captivity.

Sheikh Osama bin Laden, may he rest in peace, used to remind us that our freedom has no limits, except religion, because we can breathe in the pure oxygen of freedom. This is confirmed through this Quranic verse: *"He who emigrates for the sake of God shall find on Earth many a place of refuge and abundance."* {Sura 4 (The Women), 100}

To start with, I would like to repeat here our stance when it comes to the Christian Copts. We do not seek a fight with them, because we are busy with a battle with a bigger enemy of the nation and also because they are our partners in the nation, a nation where we seek to share living with them in peace and stability. I also think that our position when it comes to the Military Council is not a secret. We have declared it from the first day. It is that the Council is a council made up of Mubarak's men that had been imposed by America in an attempt to absorb the wrath of the Egyptian people. We thank God that during those incidents, the Islamic groups were not involved, indeed, they were stuck between two parties both of which were allies of America. Otherwise, we would have had a funeral held at the Security Council.

Therefore, as I describe what occurred,[7] I shall seek to describe the facts as they are, to warn the nation and make it aware of the great dangers that surround it. To start with, we cannot imagine the truth of what really happened and what is happening and what they want to happen without seeing the larger picture around us in both the Arab and Muslim worlds. We cannot imagine the truth of the incidents without recalling what had happened in [colonial] Iraq and Sudan, and what they are seeking to do in the Arabian Gulf. In fact, what has happened in the last two centuries where the Western powers gradually took bites from the caliphate, then we had the bilateral rule in Sudan and the law of "Closed Areas" there;[8] then we had the Sykes–Picot agreement [1916] which was part of a British–Russian–French agreement to allow them to divide the caliphate following the end of the First World War. Then we had the separation of Bangladesh from Pakistan [1971] and East Timor from Indonesia [2002], while at the same time we see the countries that control the world insisting on keeping Kashmir with India and Chechnya within Russia.

So we are facing a plan of division to crumble the Muslim world. They take advantage of a problem or make it seem bigger than it truly is, or they create a problem, then they use their Western propaganda to cry over any oppression and injustices, then they support separatist movements, then a decision by the biggest dominant criminals in the world comes out through the Security Council for military intervention and the acceptance of the new country. So, before we start talking about the problem of building a church here or destroying a church there, we must go back a little and contemplate the phenomenon of Nazheer Jayed who went on to become Father Shenouda the Third in the early Seventies. Since then he has not stopped seeking to spread his belief that Muslims have occupied Egypt and that they must be thrown out of it just as they were expelled from Andalucía, and that Orthodox Copts have the right to establish their independent state.

He does not tire, through the support of the Copt immigrants and their organisations, of bemoaning tyranny that he claims Copts in Egypt are suffering. For that purpose, he created a state within a state and sometimes above the state. For that purpose, he established alliances with Hosni Mubarak. Who would not forget the support extended by Shenouda and his church to Hosni Mubarak in the last presidential elections, where he reminded people of the alliance of the Church in the Middle Ages with tyrants and kings when suppressing people. Nazheer Jayed was not forced when he allied himself with Hosni Mubarak, in fact, Nazheer Jayed would be the last person in Egypt that could be forced into this. In fact, it is he who forces the state to wave the sword of America every time a crisis appears. So why are we talking about the armies of the National Party and the pillars of the former regime that have corrupted the political life in Egypt; we ask for their resignation and freezing their activities, yet we do not mention Nazheer Jayed? Was he not spreading that corruption, calling for it and supporting it?

The Sheikhs in al-Azhar too were supportive of Hosni Mubarak's corruption. Thank God I do not flatter anyone. The history of the former Sheikh of al-Azhar [Mohammed Sayyid Tantawy] does not need to be repeated; his errors are infamous enough not to need mentioning again. It is the current Sheikh of al-Azhar [Ahmed El-Tayeb] who decreed through a Fatwa prohibiting demonstrations during the Egyptian uprising; it got to the stage where the formal speaker of al-Azhar handed in his resignation in objection to the stance of the al-Azhar Sheikh regarding the uprising. The Sheiks of al-Azhar are no longer Sheikhs of al-Azhar. Al-Azhar has turned into a mouthpiece for the government and a machine for issuing fatwas when required, because the al-Azhar Sheikh is really an employee appointed by the President of the country. He takes action based on his orders, or the orders of the Military Council. Indeed, he sometimes follows orders from officers in the State Secret Service. Here, I must point out the huge and dangerous responsibility thrown upon the shoulders of al-Azhar scholars where they must free their al-Azhar from the grasp of the government and State Security, and that they must insist that they alone choose, from among them, the next Sheikh of al-Azhar, and that they regain control of their religious endowment funds. They must establish their own organised Union, which will defend them against the tyranny of the government in order to allow al-Azhar to lead the nation and utter the bitter truth in such dangerous circumstances. The chance is ripe now for al-Azhar scholars so they are freed from the government, and if they miss this opportunity, then only God knows when it will return.

I return once more to the clashes between the Christian Copts and the military, and I explain that the matter has gone beyond the building or destruction of churches. Shenouda is trying to force the issue by building churches without getting planning permission. He then applies pressure to obtain that permission. No country on Earth allows anyone to build a church or mosque without planning permits. Last year in Australia, a mosque was not allowed to be built in an area where the residents objected to it. Soon we shall mention the dispute over the building of a mosque close to the Trade Centre Towers in New York, which was only settled when the Mayor of New York intervened. But the thing that cannot [be allowed to] happen in America is encouraged by America to happen in Egypt. Had Shenouda been seeking democracy, as he claims, then rather than try to force his churches by the force of reality, and he has already more churches than he needs, then he would have sought to pass a law through parliament that regulates the building of churches, and he would then accept the rule of the majority. Is that not democracy? But Shenouda does not accept any law unless it meets his desires and whims. Shenouda does not care if an uprising occurs in Egypt or not, as he allies himself with the two opposites in order to get what he wishes for, which is the establishment of a Coptic state in Egypt where he rules it and forces upon it his own inquisition and prisons.

If we then spoke about the law of building churches, then we must point to a bigger problem that Nazheer Jayed has. He rejects that a law or constitution in Egypt should be based on Islamic Sharia. Nazheer Jayed is a fierce enemy and a strong adversary of Islamic Sharia, which he will not accept even if the majority of the population chose it. We do not expect Nazheer Jayed to accept Islamic Sharia, but what Muslims do not accept is when Nazheer Jayed fights this Islamic Sharia and uses the Americans for support. What cannot be understood by any reasonable person is that Nazheer Jayed and his supporters demand democracy on the condition that it is based on their whims, not on what the majority want. The problem Nazheer Jayed has with Islam is bigger than the implementation of Islamic Sharia, because he is facing a huge conversion movement within his church for people to convert to Islam. This current movement that Shenouda is suppressing heavily is an extension to continuous waves of conversion to Islam throughout history since the Islamic conquest of Egypt. With God's blessings, the current Islamic awakening has not had its effect on Muslims only, but thanks to God, it has extended to Christians.

Did Wafaa Constantine[9] not mention that one of the reasons she converted to Islam is what she witnessed in the lessons of "Scientific Miracles" by Dr Zaghloul Najjar? Wafaa Constantine and her sisters are victims of Nazheer Jayed's inquisition, who are not mentioned by America or human rights organisations in the West, not even by a single word, for the simple reason that they have taken up Islam. How often have we heard the Christian Copts lament their peers who are killed, always saying that those killed are Christian Copts? Then who killed Wafaa Constantine? Shenouda responds to the question belittling those listening and asking where her body is, and that there is no murder in the cases where no corpse is found. The corpse is with you in one of your churches' cemeteries that the state cannot come near. God knows how many more victims, martyrs and prisoners we would find in those churches and monasteries.

We have heard cries in the last clashes demanding international investigations and international intervention and for a separate state. These are cries that indicate a lack of balance, because looking for external support will only bring disaster along with it. The Americans have been defeated in Iraq and Afghanistan, and it is not expected that they would repeat the same foolish action in Egypt, and if they did then it shall be their last foolish action, God willing.

Therefore, I address the wise among the Christians that they must realise that Nazheer Jayed is leading them to what will only have disastrous consequences. The man is full of ambition and dreams. The Arab poet al-Mutanabbi was right when he said:

Life is bliss for an idiot or the ignorant
In what was and what is to come
And to those who mix the facts and negotiate
Looking for impossibilities, so it becomes greedy

I also call on the Muslims in Egypt to be aware, alert and vigilant. I know some will interpret my speech as threats for forthcoming bombings and assassinations; this is the policy of the media when it comes to Al-Qaeda and the *mujahidin* in general. I am not making threats of bombings or assassinations, but I am saying that they must be ultra-vigilant because the conspiracy surrounding them is big and ugly, and they are to be the targets. Neither am I calling for a battle in Egypt, at the moment. I repeat and emphasise the phrase "at the moment" as only God knows what will happen next. The battle in Egypt now is a battle of propagation, declarations and statements, gathering the nation and raising its awareness so that it would follow the path of salvation and avoid the routes of loss.

The wise ones in Egypt should not leave alone those who wish to seduce them so it is turned into the next Srebrenica or Southern Sudan,[10] because if they did not stop them then disaster shall befall them and those around them.

I see the ends of soot as sparks
For embers that are nearly becoming a fire
A fire gets going from two pieces of wood
And a war starts with words
And if it is not ended by wise men
Then its fuel shall be certain corpses

The Egyptian people generally, and the Islamic movement specifically, should make peace and protect non-Muslims who do not attack Muslims, because God says: *"God does not forbid you, regarding those who did not fight you and did not drive you from your homes, to be generous to them and deal with them justly. God surely loves the just. God only forbids you regarding those who fought you in religion and drove you from your homes and assisted in driving you out, to take them for friends. Those who take them for friends are indeed the wrongdoers."* {Sura 60 (The Woman Tried), 8–9}

They must do so because there is a huge conversion movement among Christians to which we must open our hearts and minds; we must do so because in this we benefit, as we are in the midst of a big battle with America, the West and Israel, and we must not forget that Britain used the excuse of the killing of a Maltese person to invade Egypt. I ask the Lord almighty to protect Egypt from sedition and enemies' deceit, and to allow for a Muslim nation to be established there, one that would rule through Sharia, spreading justice and a consultative system, and frees Muslim lands, protecting the rights of the meek and fighting corruption and the corrupt.

As for the message of support and strength, it is a letter to our prisoners, the soldiers in Al-Qaeda and Taliban, and our female prisoners held in the jails of the Christians and their allies. I say to them that we have not forgotten them, and shall not forget them with God's help, and that in order to have them released we were blessed by God who enabled us to capture the American Jew Warren Weinstein,[11] a former employee who now works for the American government in the American Aid programme to Pakistan, which aims to fight jihad in Pakistan and Afghanistan. Reflecting the way in which the Americans arrest anyone they suspect is linked to Al-Qaeda and the Taliban, even if through a distant link, we have taken this man who has been linked to American aid to Pakistan since the 1970s.

We request the following in order to release him:

1. Complete lifting of the siege that prevents people and products from moving between Egypt and Gaza.

2. An end to all types of bombardments undertaken by America and its allies in Pakistan, Afghanistan, Yemen, Somalia and Gaza.

3. The release of anyone arrested and accused of affiliation with Al-Qaeda and the Taliban, even if he was handed to another country, for example Abu Musab al-Suri, and even if he was a non-Muslim. In addition, relinquishing the charges directed against them and an end to pursuing them legally, sending them to a location of their choosing, full of support and pride.

4. The release of all prisoners in Guantanamo and other secret prisons in America, shutting down the camp and those jails.

5. The release of Sayed Nasir and Ramzi Yousef and those with them; dropping all charges against them and stopping any legal pursuits against them, and sending them to a location of their choice full of support and pride.

6. The release of Sheikh Omar Abdul Rahman, dropping all charges against him and stopping any legal pursuits against him, and sending him to a location of his choice full of support and pride.

7. The release of Sheikh Osama bin Laden's family, ensuring no charges are brought against them, returning them to their countries full of support and pride, and to stop any investigations in relation to them or any legal pursuits against them.

8. The release of all female prisoners that were arrested with the charge of affiliation to Al-Qaeda or the Taliban, such as Aafia Siddiqui,[12] Hasna, the widow of Abu Hamza al-Muhajir, may he rest in peace, and others. Dropping all charges against them, and stopping any legal pursuits against them, and sending them to a location of their choice full of support and pride.

Before I end this speech, I would like to say to the family of that hostage: your government is torturing our hostages but we have not done so to your hostage. Your government has signed the Geneva Convention then threw it away in the bin, while we have not signed the Geneva Convention and yet we look after your hostage well, this is the first point. The second is that I am warning you against Obama's lies and deceit; he wishes for that man to be killed so he would be relieved from the problem. Obama is a liar; he has lied, is lying and shall carry on lying. He may say to you: I have sought the release of your relative, but Al-Qaeda was stubborn. Do not believe him. He may say to you: I have tried to make contact with them but they did not respond. Do not believe him. He may say to you: I am using all my effort to have your relative released, but do not believe him. The third point is that I assure you that your problem is not with us but with Obama. Our demands are just, based on the release of our prisoners and for aggression by your government against us to stop. So continue to apply pressure on Obama if you want to have your relative returned to you. Obama has the authority, ability and power to have your relative released; with a simple signature, he could solve the issue in seconds. Obama can have your relative released and he can keep him in captivity for many long years. Should he do anything foolish, then he can get him killed. So keep the pressure on him, do not stop chasing him and do not believe his lies.

"The hope and glad tidings to our families in Egypt" is furthermore a message of hope and glad tidings to our brothers in captivity.

Our last prayers are that we thank God, our almighty Lord. Prayers for our master Mohammed, his kin and companions.

SUPPORT FOR ISLAM DOCUMENT

AUGUST 2012

By Ayman al-Zawahiri

In this short, but important document, published during Ramadan in 2012 (1433 according to the Islamic calendar), Zawahiri identifies four key issues that are wrong with the current international order (the five permanent members of the Security Council, rule by majority, the legitimisation of usurped land, and subjugation of Muslims) and presents a seven-part pathway to upturning this order, around which he urges co-religionists to unify. The document is an opportunity to reiterate the relevance of Al-Qaeda in a rapidly changing world, both locally and globally.

Al-Sahab Media Productions
Support for Islam Document, Ramadan 1433 AH
Issued by Qaeda Al-Jihad
Written by Sheikh Ayman al-Zawahiri, the *mujahid* May God Protect him
In the name of God, the Most Gracious, the Most Merciful.
In the name of God, and our thanks to God, peace and prayers to the Prophet of God, his kin and companions and those who have supported him.

Our Muslim nation is living through dangerous times, where it is attacked by the worst crusader campaign seen in its history, and where its people have rebelled asking for freedom, pride, glory and independence under the umbrella of Islamic Sharia, and where the secularist and Christian powers have gathered to try and stop those historic changes that are occurring in the Muslim countries.

In such dangerous circumstances, the Muslim nation must unite its word around the word of monotheism. This is why your brothers in the Qaeda Al-Jihad ["Al-Qaeda" translates to "the Base" and so "Qaeda Al-Jihad" is "the Base of Jihad". Zawahiri refers to the organisation by both names] group call upon Muslims and those working in support of Islam and all groups, movements and Islamic figures to support Islam and Muslims, through uniting behind the following aims:

1. Working towards freeing Muslim occupied homes [lands] and rejecting any agreement, covenant or international resolution that gives atheists the right to steal Muslim lands. For example, when Israel took over Palestine or Russia took Chechnya and Muslim Caucasia and India took Kashmir and Spain took Ceuta, Melilla and China took East Turkistan.

2. Using Islamic Sharia for adjudication and rejecting any other ideals, beliefs and laws, whether they are:
   a. The rule of people that gives sovereignty to the people, or
   b. International System Rules that were created by the victorious powers following WWII, and then called the United Nations, where:
   1) Five conceited [states] dominate it and force their will on the rest of the world.
   2) Its members adjudicate in its General Assembly based on [the rule of] majority, rather than Islamic Sharia.
   3) And where its Charter states that we must respect the sovereignty and security of its member states, in other words, to respect how Russia stole Muslim Caucasia and China stole East Turkistan and Spain stole Ceuta and Melilla and Israel stole Palestine.
   4) And where tens of resolutions were passed which allowed attacks against Muslim lands, such as the resolution that allowed the division of Palestine and the resolution that recognised the State of Israel and other resolutions that followed and those that allowed sanctions against Iraq, and resolutions that permitted the crusader invasion by allies in Afghanistan and the Bonn Conference[13] that appointed a collaborating government in Kabul.

   The justification for referring to Islamic Sharia for adjudication and refusing any other is because we seek to make Islamic Sharia the only one that rules in the lands of Islam, not competing with any other laws or any other authority. We refuse to submit to the International System, which represents the most conceited people in the world.

3. Working to stop organised pillaging of Muslim wealth by the hands of the Western Alliance that is occupying Muslim lands, led by America, which is considered to be the biggest thief in the history of humanity.

4. Support and help for Muslim people in their uprisings against their corrupt and oppressive tyrants. Raising people's awareness of the need to rule through Sharia and to stick to the rules of Islam, and to ask the people who have risen to carry on with their revolutions until they uproot the remaining corrupt regimes and cleanse their lands from external humiliation and internal corruption, and to encourage nations that have not rebelled to follow the lead of the others so that the Muslim world will get rid of the "rule of agents".

5. Supporting and helping any oppressed or feeble people on Earth against tyrants and oppressors.

6. Working to establish the caliphate that does not recognise nation states nor national unity nor the borders forced [upon us] by the occupiers. Instead, establishing a wise caliphate state based on the system of the Prophet, which believes in the unity of Muslim lands and brotherly ties that make everyone equal and which remove all borders forced upon them by the enemies, and aims to spread justice through the consultative process, supporting of the weak and freeing all Muslim lands.

7. Seeking to unite all efforts and energy of Muslims behind these aims and to call for them and spread them among Muslims.

These are the goals of the "Support for Islam" document. We call upon anyone who is convinced by it to call for it, support it, and spread it among the nation's people using any possible means for publication.

We only aim to please God through this. He shows us the way. May God pray for the Prophet Mohammed and his kin and companions.

Our last prayer is to thank God, our almighty Lord. Your brothers in Qaeda Al-Jihad.

These are the goals
Your brother Ayman al-Zawahiri.

GENERAL GUIDELINES
FOR THE WORK OF JIHAD

SEPTEMBER 2013

By Ayman al-Zawahiri

In addition to the "Support for Islam" document, Zawahiri frequently referred to his "General Guidelines" on subsequent occasions as key texts defining the way in which he sought—via Al-Qaeda—to chart a sustainable and ultimately successful course for Islamist militancy worldwide. In his Guidelines, Zawahiri sets out his strategic and tactical priorities, emphasising the need to target America as "the head of unbelief". The main focus of the document is to rein in fighters who were seen to have engaged in excessive violence, avoiding the reputational hazards such targeting would incur. The document is thus interesting not only in relation to Al-Qaeda's immediate prehistory at this point, where allies and affiliates had carried out mass-scale attacks against civilians that ultimately undermined Al-Qaeda, but also of course in relation to what came after: where the sectarian bloodshed inflicted by ISIS/IS became a major theme in Zawahiri's attempts to delegitimise that group. Zawahiri referred to his Guidelines on many subsequent occasions, pointing out that had they been heeded more widely, the turmoil and infighting between groups in Syria and beyond could have been avoided.

Al-Sahab Media Productions presents: General Guidelines for the Work of Jihad.

Ayman al-Zawahiri, 2013

First: Preface

1. It is no secret to the brothers that our work at this stage has two parts: first, military; and second, propagational.
2. The targets of the military activities are: first, the world's head of disbelief, America and its ally Israel; and second, its regional allies who rule our countries.
   A. The aim of targeting America is to exhaust and engage it in a war of attrition so that it ends up how the Soviet Union ended up, and retreats as a result of its military, human and economic losses. This will then loosen its grip on our countries and its allies will start to fall one after another. What happened in the Arab revolutions is proof of the dissipation of US clout. As a result of the *mujahidin's* strikes against America in Afghanistan and Iraq and because of the threats on the security of the US since September 2001, America started to create outlets to allow the release of popular pressures and they exploded in the face of their pawns. God willing, the next stage will witness more US retreat and loss of ground, which will shake their allies' authority.
   B. The targeting of America's regional pawns will be different from one place to another, and the rule is to avoid confrontation with them except in those countries in which confrontation with them is inevitable. In Afghanistan, for example, the confrontation with them [the "local" regimes] follows from the fight against the Americans. In Pakistan, the confrontation with them complements the fight against the Americans to liberate Afghanistan and then establish a secure zone for the *mujahidin* in Pakistan, trying, from there, to establish the Islamic system in Pakistan. The confrontation with them in Iraq is to liberate the areas of the Sunni people from America's Safavid [Shia] allies.

   In Algeria, as the American presence is insignificant and unnoticeable, the conflict with the [Algerian] regime is to weaken it and to spread the influence of jihad in the Islamic Maghreb, the Sahel region of Africa and the southern Sahara region. The signs of confrontation in these areas with the US and their allies have already started to appear. The confrontation with them in the Arabian Peninsula is because they are America's cronies. The confrontation with them in Somalia is because they are the spearhead of the crusaders' occupation. In the Levant

[Syria], the confrontation with them is because they don't allow the mere existence of any Islamic entity, let alone a jihadi one. Their bloody history in trying to uproot Islam is well-known. And in the environs of Jerusalem the main and essential confrontation is with the Jews, and with the local rulers from the Oslo treaty patience should be exercised as much as possible.

3. The propagational activities: to aim towards enlightening the nation about the dangers of the crusaders' occupation. Explaining the meanings of monotheism—that judgement is for God alone—and achieving Islamic brotherhood and the unity of the house of Islam as a ground for establishing, with God's permission, the caliphate on the method of Prophethood. This should be focused, at this stage, on two fronts:

First: enlightening and educating the jihadi activists who will carry, God willing, the burden of the confrontation with the crusaders and their cronies until the caliphate is established, with God's permission.

Second: enlightening the masses, encouraging them and trying to motivate them to revolt against their rulers and side with Islam and those who work for it.

Second: Necessary Guidelines

From this introduction we can put forward the following guidelines from the perspective of Sharia politics, seeking to bring about virtues and prevent vices:

1. Concentrating on enlightening the masses to motivate them, and the jihadi activists to form an organised, united, conscious and jihadi doctrinal force that believes in Islam and obligates itself to its laws to achieve glory for the believers and humiliation for the infidels. Hard work should be done to bring out from among the jihadi movement those invocatory scholarly skills, which can preserve our message and ideology and spread the call among the Muslims.

2. Concentrating on military activities to exhaust the world's head of disbelief until it is exhausted in military, economic and human terms and until it shrinks to a stage of retreat and seclusion—soon, God willing. All the brother *mujahidin* must consider hitting the interests of the Zionist and Western crusaders' coalition everywhere in the world as one of their most important duties and try to do that as much as they can. It follows that the brothers must try hard to release the Muslims from prisons by any means, including raiding their prisons or taking hostages for ransom from those

countries which participate in the occupation of the lands of Muslims. Concentrating on the world's head of disbelief doesn't contradict the rights of the Muslim people in waging jihad against their oppressors with word, hand and weapon. The Muslims in the Caucasus have the right to wage jihad against the assaulting Russians and their followers. Our brothers in Kashmir have the right to wage jihad against the criminal Hindus. Our brothers in Eastern Turkistan have the right to wage jihad against the oppressing Chinese. It is the right of our brothers in the Philippines and Burma and everywhere else where Muslims are attacked to wage jihad against whoever attacked them.

3. Avoiding armed confrontation with the [local] regimes unless necessary, for example if the regional regime forms part of the American presence as in Afghanistan, or if the regime fights the *mujahidin* as a proxy of the Americans as in Somalia and the Arabian Peninsula, or it does not accept the existence of the *mujahidin* as in the Islamic Maghreb, Syria and Iraq. However, fighting with them [the local regimes] should be avoided as much as possible. When there is no choice but to fight them, it must be shown that our war with them is part of our defence of the Muslims against the crusaders' campaign. And whenever the opportunity arises to calm down the conflict with the regional rulers in order to exploit that calm for propagation, demonstration, encouragement, recruitment and to collect money and gain supporters, we should then exploit this to its maximum capacity.

4. Our war is long and jihad requires secure bases and reinforcement of men, money and talents. That does not mean we will not make the crony regimes for the crusaders' campaign understand that we are no easy prey, and that every action has its own appropriate response, even if after some time. This matter is implemented on every front according to the situation.

5. Avoiding fighting the perverse sects like the Shia, Ismaelis, Qadiyani, or Sufis unless they fight the Sunnis. If you fight them, the response should be confined to the fighting parties with the explanation that we are defending ourselves. Hitting non-fighters, their families in their houses and places of worship, their festivals and religious gatherings must be avoided. But, disclosing their falsehood and their doctrinal and behavioural wickedness should continue. In the places which fall under the control of the *mujahidin* and their authorities, dealing with these sects should be done wisely; focusing on propagating the message, enlightening, revealing the doubts, commanding good and forbidding evil to avoid greater harms, such as

leading to the expulsion of the *mujahidin* from those places or popular revolt against them or causing a mutiny that could be exploited by their enemies in occupying those areas.

6. Avoiding confrontation with the Christians, Sikhs and Hindus in the Islamic countries. If they launch an assault, the response should be equivalent to the assault, with an explanation that we are not seeking to start a fight with them. That is because we are busy with the world's head of disbelief [America and allies] and we care about living with them [the minorities] in peace and equanimity if the Islamic state is established soon, God willing.

7. Generally, fighting and striking whomever has not raised a weapon against us should be avoided as the essential concentration is on the crusaders' coalition and their regional subordinates.

8. Avoiding killing and fighting civilians—the non-combatants—even if they are the families of those who fight against us, if possible.

9. Avoiding harming the Muslims by bombing or killing or kidnapping or causing damage to their wealth and property.

10. Avoiding targeting the enemy in mosques, markets and gatherings where they mix with Muslims or those who will not fight against us.

11. Looking after and respecting the religious scholars and defending them, because they are the descendants of the Prophet (PBUH) and the leaders of the nation. This applies to those scholars who come out openly with the truth and sacrifice themselves for it. Our confrontation is only with the bad scholars to reveal their scepticism [of faith], publishing definite proof about their cooperation [with the authorities]. They are not to be killed or fought unless they have participated in fighting against the Muslims and *mujahidin*.

12. The stance towards the other Islamic groups:

    A. We cooperate where there is agreement, and we offer mutual advice where there is disagreement.

    B. The priority is to confront the enemies of Islam and its opponents, so for that reason the disagreement with other Islamic groups should not distract us from military, invocatory, ideological and political confrontations with the enemies of Islam and its opponents.

    C. We support and thank them for their every true word and deed and advise them about any mistake emanating from them, discreetly with the covert ones and publicly with the public ones. We take care in the generation of responses and advice by exposing the evidence in a proper scientific manner, removed from personal insults and injuries, as the power is in the proof and not in disparagement.

D. If a group that belongs to Islam becomes involved in fighting in collaboration with the infidel enemy, the response should be limited to stopping its hostility. Thus blocking the possibility of disunity between Muslims or harming those who did not collaborate with the enemy.

13. The stance towards the revolts of the oppressed people against the oppressors: supporting, participating and guiding.

A. Supporting: supporting the oppressed against the oppressor is a religious duty regardless of whether one of them is a Muslim or not.

B. Participating: this is part of commanding good and forbidding evil, which is a duty upon us.

C. Guiding: by explaining that the aim of the human deed is to achieve the Oneness [of God] by abiding by God's commands and implementing His laws and trying to establish the Islamic system and state.

14. Motivating and supporting whoever supports the oppressed rights of the Muslims and stands against those who attack them with words, opinions and deeds. Avoid causing physical harm to them or insulting them with words, since they are supportive and are not hostile to the Muslims.

15. Protecting the rights of Muslims and respecting their sanctity wherever they are.

16. Victory for the oppressed and weak, whether they are Muslims or not, over those who attack them. Supporting and encouraging whoever supports them, even if they are not Muslims.

17. If the *mujahidin* believe that Muslims are accused on false grounds, they have to try to dispel it and disclose the truth. And any wrongdoing that the *mujahidin* believe that they have committed, they have to ask for forgiveness and disown themselves from its doer and try to compensate the victim, according to their ability, as the Sharia requires.

18. We ask all the brothers, the leaders of the entities that are associated with the Al-Qaeda organisation and all our supporters and sympathisers to disseminate these instructions among their followers, leaders and individuals. They are not secret but general instructions and guiding policies.

Our aim is only to fulfil the interests of religion and prevent corruption—at this stage of Islamic jihadi activities—with an individual interpretation that does not contradict the judgements of Sharia and conforms—with the aid of God—to its rules.

God knows the intention and He will guide the way. Peace and prayers be upon our master Mohammed and on his family and companions. Our last prayer is praise be to the Lord of the universe.

Written seeking God's approval,
Your brother Ayman al-Zawahiri

SCENT OF PARADISE

A STUDY ON THE MOST HONOURABLE SACRIFICES OF WORSHIPPERS; DEATH AND MARTYRDOM CAMPAIGNS

NOVEMBER 2013

By Ayman al-Zawahiri
Second Edition

Here we have an introduction to a book which Zawahiri published initially in 2004 on the topic of martyrdom, and martyrdom operations (i.e. suicide attacks) in particular. Written initially in the aftermath of the 9/11 suicide-hijackings, Zawahiri began his first edition with references to the asymmetric qualities of martyrdom operations, which rendered meaningless the material prowess of the West—acquired through treachery. He condemned those who spoke against that tactic, warning against the consequences such criticism would have for the Muslim nation.

Nine years later, Zawahiri's second edition of his book comes at a time when martyrdom operations and the excessive casualties they inflict had become something of a liability. In this edition, therefore, Zawahiri warns against "deviation" and "exaggeration" in the application of the tactic, arguing that some have not respected the parameters defined by proper reading of scripture. The two introductions, therefore, shed interesting light on ongoing debates about the boundaries of legitimate and sustainable militancy from the perspective of public opinion, which is a recurring theme in this discourse.

Ali ibn Abi Taleb said: *"Death is a keen demander, those who seek it are able to get it and those who flee from it cannot escape it; move towards it and do not be tardy, there is no escaping Death. Even when you are not killed, you will [eventually] die; the most honourable death is by being killed. I swear by God it is better to die after a thousand slashes with a sword than to die in my bed."*

Abdul Aziz bin al-Zubair said: *"By God, a sword attack in glory is more preferable to me than a whip lashing at me in humiliation."*

Introduction to First Edition [2004]

Our gratitude goes to God whom we thank, from whom we seek help and forgiveness, and whom we implore to grant us refuge from our evil deeds and souls; those who are guided by God will not be distracted, and those who deviate will not be guided; I attest that there is only one God and that Mohammed is His Messenger.

O believers, fear God as He should be feared and do not die except as Muslims.

O people, fear your Lord Who created you from a single soul and from it He created its mate and from both He scattered abroad many men and women; and fear God in Whose name you appeal to one another, and invoke family relationships. Surely God is a Watcher over you.

O believers, fear God and speak in a straightforward way. He will set right your deeds and forgive you your sins. Whoever obeys God and His Messenger has won a great victory.

At this stage of the Muslim nation's history, the confrontation between the Muslim nation and its jihadi pioneers and between the Zionist crusading enemy is escalating to dangerous levels; the forces of the Zionist crusading enemy are using all the power they have to oppress the Muslim nation; and the battles are at all levels, such as intellectual, behavioural, media and military levels. Enemy forces have fired at us with no mercy or morality in their attempt to steal our wealth, invade our lands and crush our willpower. The crusading and Zionist enemy forces did not spare us when it came to repeating their bombardments by air or with tanks against homes, villages, hospitals and mosques in the name of "War on Terror" and "Defence of Freedom".

At this stage, I say we had to respond because we are the nation of Monotheism, the nation of the most honourable of morals that fights vile deeds, abominations and transgressions; we are the nation of glory that only submits to God and rejects any other foes and partners; we are the nation that places its trust in God and believes that good and bad come from God alone; we are the nation of the Message that must be delivered to people.

And thanks to God, we are proud and refuse humiliation; we read in the Quran: *"Might belongs to God, His Messenger and the believers, but the hypocrites do not know."* {Sura 63 (The Hypocrites), 8}

A poet described us well when he said:

I am from a proud people who increase with
Patience and tolerance whenever trouble appears

We are after all humans in whom God has planted within our nature the instinct of rejecting and resisting tyranny and fighting it. A poet said:

Two humiliating things will elevate us from disgrace
For someone to make our family and weapons worthless
This man is tied totally to his humiliation and
Another is saddened but no one sympathises with him

We had to respond to this hostility while our enemy's crimes were only increasing [with] his arrogance, haughtiness and conceit, showing off his might, numbers and machinery; our enemy was relaxed enough to think that his superiority with military equipment over us and indeed over the whole world will keep Muslims away from him, especially following the fall of the Soviet Union and his exclusivity to dominate the countries of the world.

But our crusading enemy forgot, or chooses to forget, that the Soviet Union fell by the rock of Muslim, steadfast Afghanistan, and that the fall of great powers could happen again by the hands of the poor and weak Muslims, not just once but many times.

The crusading Zionist enemy carried on recklessly with his hostility and attacks, he added to his crimes in Palestine by occupying the Arabian Peninsula and then Somalia and Chechnya.

The crusading enemy organised a group of agents across the Muslim world that would do his dirty work instead of their masters in Washington and Tel Aviv.

And in return for the enemy's attacks, the jihadist awakening began to get bigger in the faces of the crusaders and Jews in Lebanon, Somalia, Chechnya, Palestine, Nairobi, Dar el-Salam then in Aden, and it peaked with the two blessed attacks in New York and Washington which were seen as prominent features in the history of the Islamic—crusader battle and in fact in the history of humanity.

The disparity between our financial capability and that of our enemy was so enormous that it would lead a man who is not a true believer to despair at facing the enemy. It was the same when it came to the disparity between us and our enemy's military machinery and the amount of destruction it could cause, especially its ability to bombard from a distance while their men remain safe and secure waiting for the enemy to surrender after such great losses due to the bombings and due to the deliberate slaughter of civilians.

We have seen their methods in warfare: they bomb from a distance, then they push forward the sheep of hypocrites; they would be unable to do much face to face on the ground if it were not for the aerial bombardments.

We have faced their soldiers on the ground and we have seen the farce called the American military; they are soldiers that are more cowardly than cowardice itself; they care more about life here and materialistic things; they do not trust their leaders, their principles or the cause for which they are fighting.

I say: the difference between us and the crusaders and Jews is in the military power; it was never through the number of men or their determination or faith or certainty in their fair jihad and their trust in what God had promised them. As they were aware of the lack of will in the souls of their soldiers and how determined and certain our jihadist, Muslim men were, they have ensured in every possible way to keep this difference in military might vast and to increase such a gap.

The story of the difference in military power between us and the enemies of Islam is the story of the Muslims' defeat in the last two centuries; and the story of the dominance of the crusaders and the Jews over our lands, and the story of the intellectual, behavioural and educational warfare against us so that they can enforce their lowly values on us and deprive our minds, hearts and behaviour of the faith of monotheism.

Al-Jabriti, RIP, talks about how the Mamlouks belittled the arrival of the [French] ships to the mouth of Alexandria in the month of Muharram 1213 AH[14] and says: *"As for the Amirs, they cared nothing for this, and did not give it a thought as they thought they had the power; they claimed that if all the Franks came they would not stand to face them and that they would trample on them with their horses."*

Then he talks, may he rest in peace, about how the Mamlouks were defeated by the hands of the French at the gates of Cairo in the month of Safar of the same year: *"The Column that moved forward to attack Murad Bey divided in a way known to them during wartimes, and they got closer to the barricades where they then surrounded all the soldiers, front and back, and they beat their drums and started to shoot their guns and cannons; the winds blew strong, and dust flew, and the skies darkened from the dust and gun smoke; people were deafened by the drum beats and people thought that the Earth had moved like a quake and that the skies had fallen; the war and the fighting continued for about three-quarters of an hour and then there was defeat on the Western Front."*

The story of our weak military power compared to our enemies is the story of our weakness and division and internal defeat which grew until it surfaced as a military defeat and the fall of a Caliphate state and the tearing apart of a Muslim state. This is a long story which is not going to be told here, but I wanted to point out the military defeat of a Muslim nation, which has peaked sadly in the military defeat of the final Caliphate state after its edges were worn out, and which was followed by intellectual defeat. The deviation of faith and behaviour started gradually to eat away into the nation's bones; this deviation was in different gradients according to the creeds and sects; some groups rejected Islam and welcomed the new invaders' ideals and considered Islam as something that belongs to history that should not concern us in the midst of the civilisation of science and the age of speed; this group began to be driven by whatever drove the world of the invaders: some chose the Western free values, others chose communism in its variants, others chose socialism in its variants, while others chose pure nationalism; but they all agreed that they must not be religious or show any loyalty to Islam, which they saw as part of history, because Islam was defeated in the competition of military might.

Another group chose to praise the goodness of the rulers, and to accept whatever crumbs they threw at them from their tables, and not to bother themselves with more than earning a wage, and to compete for status and jobs and materialistic things.

Another group claimed that they would not accept defeat and would face it, but they mixed things together and did not focus on the basics of faith, nor did they clarify to their followers who it is that is loyal to God and who are His enemies in the midst of the battle and conflict; they performed well in some instances, but they also lost and with each loss the voice of the weak began to get stronger and the tide of the failures began to spread, and they began to ask us to stop fighting or to lower the tone we used; ignoring the basics of faith began to bear its rotten fruit, and the retreat of faith and the systematic compromises and behavioural withdrawal began until it reached a stage where it was secularism with a hint of Islam, which accepts the rule but not on the basis of arbitration to God's laws and to accept His rights in arbitration, because He is after all the Creator and the Giver and the One Who Helps us and therefore it is only right and necessary that He should be the arbitrator; based not just on this obligatory rule in Islamic faith, but also on other bases and references and legislations sent to us by God and His Might. When the basis of faith was dropped, other falls began to appear. The worst fall seen, and it is the most contradictory and laughable, is when some decreed the permission to fight the enemy whose skin and eye colour do not match our own skin and eye colour and whose tongues differ from our tongues, indeed they permitted martyrdom operations against them, on condition that our own national enemies agree first.[15]

As for our national enemies who share our skin colour and speak in the same tongue as we do, then it is forbidden, forbidden absolutely and totally, to resist or fight them. Some went as far as to say that if our foreign enemy is Jewish, then it is permitted to fight him and to attack him and his establishments and cities and villages and people whatever they are: military or civilians or any other divisions they could come up with; but if the enemy is American, then martyrdom operations against him are contradictory to Islam and corrupting to the propagation [of Islam] and take away their benefits and other similar trivial excuses.

Another group became tired by all the calamities and finally decided to go on the road and flee and to fight not for the sake of Islam or the victory of Muslims but for the sake of their benefits and personal gain; and they moved from the forefront of *mujahidin* to the back end of beggars, and from the purity of the Salafi faith to the myths and falsehood of the secret police. This group did not leave the *mujahidin* alone, minding their own business, but they agreed to enter this suspect game and began to call the *mujahidin* names and to attack them verbally as a way for them to approach and get close to the low people of the intelligence services and the low people of the government agencies.

The events of the attacks on New York and Washington were their chance not to take advice and be cautious, but to collect some of the crumbs and rubbish thrown at them by the thieves and the corrupt.

Another group revived the creed of *Murjea* [those who postpone] so that they were able to keep the might of the rulers of corruption and agents, and to guarantee their wages and status. In his book *The Beginning and the End* (al-Bidaya wal Nihaya), Ibn Katheer, RIP, wrote: *"Ibn Asaker wrote citing Al-Nudhr Bin Shmail and said: I went to see al-Mamoun and he said: How are you Nudhr? I said: Fine, Leader of the faithful. He said: What is* Irjaa *[postpone-*

ment]? I said: A faith that is agreeable to kings, as through it they get what they want from life but they reduce what they have of their faith. He said: you have spoken correctly."

Another group realised that the strength of this religion is in the purity of its faith and unity and in its sons undertaking their duty and letting people know about jihad and propagation and to work to consolidate and strengthen their religion with all that they own, money and life. This group remained steadfast on the basis of pure monotheism; it did not waver or change despite the sedition, the tempest, the violent raids that tried to chase them away and the attacks of huge enemy armies and their constant bombardments.

Ibn Katheer, RIP, said about the Battle of Yarmouk: *"It is said that the first one to be killed as a martyr that day was a man who came to Abu Ubaida and asked: I am ready for whatever comes; do you need anything from the Prophet (PBUH)? He said: Yes, give him our greetings and tell him: O Messenger, we have truly found what God had promised us. He said: So the man went forward until he was killed, may he rest in peace. They said: And the people were steadfast until the Romans were going around like a millstone, and all you could see on that day of the Battle of Yarmouk were a fallen brain or wrist and a flying hand from that location. Khalid then fought with the cavalrymen on the left wing, those who were fighting the Muslims on the right wing, and they moved them to the centre and they killed six thousand of the Romans, and he said: By the God Who has my soul in His hands, they have no patience and endurance left except what you see; I hope that God gives you their shoulders. He then intercepted them, and with a hundred of his knights he attacked about one hundred thousand, and as soon as he reached them, they dispersed and the Muslims attacked them as one man, and they were exposed and the Muslims chased them until they got them.*

That group remained steadfast wherever it was and it tried, where possible, to defend its faith and religion with words, actions and money; and despite the repeated blows that came its way and which spread through the lands of Muslims, and despite the troubles that hit their finances, themselves, their women and children, and despite the isolation, fear, loneliness and friends' condemnation and lack of support, as if the poet al-Mutanabbi had been describing them when he said:

A stranger from among our friends in each country
When the demands grow, the helpers lessen

Despite all the above, this group remained steadfast in its deeds, learning, martyrdom, jihad and propagation, and God rewarded it with victories and aid and support and acceptance by Muslims and the believers which was unprecedented; God rewarded those groups that have scattered and been chased, and the groups that have been oppressed and in trouble, and the groups that have resisted and had been fighting for the sake of Islam and Muslims with the best of rewards; He was pleased with them and He pleased them and He blessed them with steadfastness on the right path that He likes, so that when they meet Him they would be unchanged and unaltered; their eyes can see the victory which is close; their hearts have been calmed with the banners of victorious Islam as they fly in glory over the hills of Mecca, Medina, Jerusalem, Cairo, Damascus, Baghdad, Kabul and Grozny soon with God's Help and Might and Will.

I return to the disparity in the military might that the crusaders and the Jews were preparing for their strong fortress and I say: the *mujahidin* had to destroy that fortress totally so that the enemy would be unprotected in the battlefield and would suffer blows as a punishment for their crimes and to allow the battlefield to become more balanced. This is why the martyrdom operations began, so they would destroy the enemy's imaginary fortresses, restore parity and open the doors wide for the Muslim nation, so it would take part in stopping the crusaders' and Jews' attacks and hit them after they had been unable to do so for a long time. The peaks of martyrdom operations were the two blessed attacks in New York and Washington in the battle against the crusaders and the Jews, and with those two blessed attacks the pioneering jihadist group sent messages to the Muslim nation that cannot be ignored by the atheists or friends alike. The serious consequences of those two blessed attacks have kept coming and will keep on coming, God willing.

The most prominent effects the two blessed attacks had are:

First: bridging the gap in the disparity in the military machine between the Muslims and the crusaders; the crusaders no longer feel safe, nor do they feel protected by their huge military machine, indeed they feel threatened in the middle of their own homes and in their political and economic centres.

Second: the flow of the blood of hope within the exhausted body of the nation, and the revival of a new spirit in the sons of the Muslim nation; this spirit which is spreading through the souls of the jihadists of Islam today as they hurt and beat the crusaders and Jews in Palestine, Iraq, Afghanistan and Chechnya.

Third: the attacks in New York and Washington showed the nation its ability to defend itself and to face the Jewish crusading enemy and that the solution is in its own hands and not in the hands of the rulers that keep increasing our insanity. Following a period of despair that went through our Islamic world, especially after the enemy managed through internal oppression and international harrying to weaken the Islamic resistance in Algeria and Egypt, and after the undecided kept repeating their old but new phrase: We can only join jihad if our governments allow us!! And after a number of Muslim icons had reversed course after a first spell in prison, and after a number had retreated from jihad, claiming that they never wanted jihad but rather they wanted to command goodness and prohibit abomination, and that the calculations of benefit and ruination, including personal benefit, mean we must reconcile with the biggest of criminals and that reconciliation is good; after that, the two blessed attacks came to alert the Muslim nation that it is still a strong nation through its faith, and that it is young and capable and that its enemy is weak because God has decided to make him so; God says: *"Those who believe fight for the sake of God and those who do not believe fight for the sake of the tyrants, so fight the supporters of Satan, the power of Satan is weak."* {Sura 4 (The Women), 76}

The two attacks came to prove that the Muslim nation is able to overcome defeat and the period of loss and humiliation, despite all that has been practised against it through conspiracies and despite the huge gap in military equipment between it and its enemies.

The two blessed attacks came to send the Muslim nation back to the battlefield of jihad and to dust away all traces of exhaustion and tiredness and to push away claims of despair and defeat.

This is what we want to emphasise: the solution is in the hands of the Muslim nation, this is the period of its jihad and the period of its revival; the Muslim nation, with all its creeds and classes, must carry its arms in its own hands and must move forward to fight its enemies.

This is the lesson that we have learnt from the nineteen martyrs, may they rest in peace, that through their loyalty and desire to defend their nation and avenge their friends, the young Muslims have the features, capabilities and ability to do only what God knows. The nation, especially its young jihadists, must now move in that path after the gates have now opened; it must now move as the factors of victory are in its hands and the requirements of victory are within it.

If nineteen young jihadists from the millions of Muslims in the nation have managed to harm the greatest Satan in such a manner, what stops others from doing the same thing, with God's help and support? What is stopping our nation from rebelling against the rulers who have sold them out thousands of times and who have sucked their blood enough to get drunk on it and who stole its resources until they were full of them, and yet they did not defend them even for a single day, but instead they surrendered to the enemy at each battle and knelt in front of the perpetrators in every field.

What is stopping our nation from winning against its real enemy is fear, hesitance and the preference for safety. Our nation must bring back the values of its forefathers, the Salaf, who used to race towards death and so the world opened up for them; our nation must get back what martyrdom means and plant in the hearts of its sons the love of Paradise and self-denial on Earth.

We must be made aware of the seriousness of martyrdom in the fate of the Muslim people; the benefit of martyrdom is not on the Last Day only, which is great in itself, but the establishment and spread of Islam and the dominance of its laws will only happen when people run towards death for the sake of God. We must race towards martyrdom instead of watching to see who would be the first to do so.

The only way our collaborating rulers are oppressing us is through fear and terror; as for them, they are weak and with no power, and if we faced them with the spirit that the nineteen heroes faced America, then they would disappear like flies.

This is why the pioneering jihadists teach their nation the blessings of martyrdom and its great effect on the fate of the Muslim nation; the pioneering jihadists must pay that price and shoulder that burden as this is their fate and their honour at the same time.

The pioneering Muslim jihadists must lead their nation on the two most dangerous fronts that threaten its existence: the crusading Jewish front and the collaborating [local] rulers' front.

The pioneering Muslim jihadists must spread the call to harm the crusaders and the Jews and to throw them out of our countries and to overthrow the collaborating rulers and to establish a jihadist Muslim government, so it becomes the soul that runs through the nation; it will only reach that level when role models are put forward and when the price is paid through the most honourable and noble lives, until the barrier of fear between the nation and victory and consolidation is broken.

This is where the seriousness and significance of the martyrdom operations come from: in the breaking of the arrogance of the Devils of today and in taking away from them the great might of their military machinery that they rely on against us.

This is why opposing martyrdom operations, whether through good intentions or not, can have dire consequences that will affect the future and reality of the Muslim nation and which will have an effect on the existence of the Muslim nation for many years and perhaps centuries under the humiliating influence of the crusading and Jewish powers with all the faith, behavioural, political, military and economic catastrophes that may accompany that fact. I think that mentioning those catastrophes will push whoever objects to martyrdom operations, even if through good intentions, to revise his opinion once more.

Due to the seriousness of this pivotal issue in the matter of the Muslim nation's jihad against its crusading and Jewish enemies, I have asked God for His help and have put together these pages hoping my efforts would be favoured by God; allowing anyone who wishes to publish them to do so, hoping from God reward and acceptance.

God is my ultimate goal from this work; God guides us. May God pray and pass greetings to His Messenger Mohammed and his kin and companions and followers.

Ayman al-Zawahiri
Rabie al-Thani 1425 AH, corresponding to June 2004.

Introduction to Second Edition [2013]

In the name of God, our gratitude to God; prayers and greetings to the Messenger of God and his kin and companions and followers.

This is the second edition of the letter "Scent of Paradise", in which I have edited the first edition as I realised some errors in it and I added a little to it.

This edition is published nine years after the first one, when martyrdom operations appeared to be one of the most important weapons of the Muslim jihadist resistance against the crusading Jewish invasion of our Muslim nation.

But this increase in martyrdom operations has been accompanied by some deviation and exaggeration which must be corrected and admitted to; some of the operations were undertaken under circumstances that did not justify the sacrifice of the life of a jihadist martyr; at times there were no precautions taken to try to protect innocent lives, and at other times the target was the wrong one, or at other times it was not in the general interest to undertake such an operation, either due to the greater damage it would have caused, or because the general public would not understand its reasons and so they would not sympathise with the jihadists, which is our greatest victory, which we must be keen to preserve to achieve victory and to block the path of the enemy which is aiming to isolate jihadists from the general public. This has led many jihadist leaders, both the martyrs and those still alive, to remind and warn of the need to guide martyrdom operations, which are above all one of the most effective weapons of jihad against the enemies of the Muslim nation. But these excesses—which have not affected most or all martyrdom operations—have been greatly abused by the enemy to debase the image of the *mujahidin* and to put people off them.

The first step to deflect those suspicions is not simply to say that the enemy is lying; it is to admit our mistakes first and then to try to reverse their effects at once; then we can show the mistakes of our enemies in enlarging the problem and making our errors and deviations bigger than they are, and ignoring the great effect the martyrdom operations have had in defending our oppressed nation, and ignoring the numerous crimes against innocent people everywhere.

This is why jihadi groups must study carefully any martyrdom operation from the Sharia, political and military viewpoints before they attempt it. And jihadi groups must not underestimate the criticism made against them by their friends or enemies; they must study them well and examine them thoroughly and they must ask themselves why that criticism was directed at them and is there any truth in it, even if minute? The honourable aim is not an excuse to go about it in a bad way; the *mujahidin* must realise that victory is a gift from God alone; God says: *"Victory comes from only God, God is wise and glorious."* {Sura 3 (The Family of Imran), 126}

The *mujahidin* will not win unless God grants them that victory, God says: *"If God supports you, no one will overcome you; but if He forsakes you, then who will be able to support you after Him?"* {Sura 3 (The Family of Imran), 160}

They must realise that sins, disobedience and taking matters lightly in what is forbidden will only bring God's wrath and will delay victory; God says: *"And when a misfortune befell you after you had inflicted twice as much, you said: Whence is this? Say: It is from yourselves. Surely God has power over everything. And what befell you on the day the two armies met was by God's Leave, that He might know the true believers."* {Sura 3 (The Family of Imran), 165–166} And God says: *"Those of you who fled, who fled on the day the two armies met, were made to slip by the Devil, on account of something they had done. However, God has forgiven them; God is indeed forgiving and merciful."* {Sura 3 (The Family of Imran), 155}

We must support God by committing to His religion so He can support us against our enemies. God says: *"O believers, if you support God He shall support you and steady your feet."* {Sura 47 (Mohammed), 7} We must not be arrogant in our power or capabilities or the large support we have, as this will make us neglect what is forbidden in the Sharia, otherwise God will reduce His support since we have large numbers and a wide support base and power. God says: *"God gave you victory in numerous places and on the day of Hunayn when you were pleased with your large number; but it availed you nothing and the land became too strait for you, despite its breadth, whereupon you turned back and fled. Then God sent down His tranquillity upon His Messenger and upon His believers, and He sent down soldiers you did not see and punished the unbelievers. That is the reward of the unbelievers. Then God will pardon thereafter whom He pleases. God is all-forgiving, merciful."* {Sura 9 (Repentance), 25–27}

I repeat again that despite all the mistakes that may occur in any battle, martyrdom operations appear to be the most effective weapons in the hands of the Muslim nation in fighting the heaviest crusading campaign it faces, a campaign that is not just an alliance between the crusaders and the Jews, but also includes the governments of our Muslim world, which are placing all their resources in the service of the biggest criminals in this world; part of those resources are the scholars of the Sultans and the mouthpieces of tyranny and oppression who are spreading the messages of the tyrants not through the media of atheism, secularism and unbelief, but through the tongues and throats of those wearing turbans and who are bearded; holders of degrees given to them by the tyrants and holders of positions appointed to them [by the tyrants] and earning wages and status while accepting bribes. Those who will continue to forbid martyrdom operations until the Jewish crusading enemy feels safe. The same Jewish crusading enemy which is moaning in pain and bleeding due to the martyrdom operations undertaken by the heroes of Islam from the East to the West, North to South; these blessed attacks are what have forced the enemy to withdraw from Iraq and to make plans to withdraw from Afghanistan; they are threatening his security in Jerusalem and Syria and the Arabian Peninsula and in Somalia, the land of resistance and steadfastness, and in victorious North Africa and Chechnya, the land of resistance and defiance. Those blessed attacks which overcame the enemy not only quantitatively but also qualitatively; who can forget the martyred hero Abu Djanah al-Khurasani, RIP, who equipped himself, funded by the CIA, and then tricked them and hit them in the middle of their own home?

May God reward those great heroes who have wiped away the nation's humiliation using their blood and who chose what God has to offer instead of the temporary materialistic things of this Earth. They cannot wait to meet their God and to gain His approval and His rewards as He had promised them. God says: *"And do not think that those who are killed in the way of God are dead; they are living with their Lord, well provided for. Rejoicing in what their Lord has given them of His bounty, and they rejoice for those who stayed behind and did not join them, knowing that they have nothing to fear and that they shall not grieve. They rejoice in the grace of God and His favour and that God will not withhold the reward of the faithful. Those who responded to God's call and the Messenger's after they had incurred many wounds. To those of them who do what is right and fear God, a great reward is in store. Those to whom the people said: "The people have been arrayed against you; so fear them." But this increased their faith, and so they said: "God is sufficient for us. He is the best guardian." Thus they came back with a grace and bounty from God. No harm touched them and they complied with God's good pleasure. God's bounty is great!"* {Sura 3 (The Family of Imran), 169–174}

Our final prayers are that we pray to thank God, the Lord of the Universe, and we ask for His prayers for His Messenger and his kin and companions.

Ayman al-Zawahiri
The month of Muharram 1435 AH, corresponding to November 2013

EMANCIPATION FROM THE CYCLE
OF FAILURE AND FRIVOLITY

FEBRUARY 2014

By Ayman al-Zawahiri

This publication is typical of Zawahiri's "big films". Like a contemporary Hollywood blockbuster, it is repetitive and overlong. Yet it comes at an important time in the aftermath of the toppling of Mohammed Morsi as the Muslim Brotherhood president of Egypt. Here, therefore, Zawahiri moves on from his focus on reshaping or reframing the Arab Spring according to his framework and agenda, to dissecting the reasons for its failure. He presents Chechnya as an example for Arabs to follow, whereby the enclave persevered in protracted conflict against the Russian state. Zawahiri seeks to construct an uninterrupted rhetorical thread where the current struggle of believers echoes that of the first generation of Muslims, including the venerated battles they fought and won during the formative years of Islam. He uses the aftermath of the Arab Spring to re-illustrate the fallacy of the democratic method, reiterating his demand that Sharia becomes that which governs the affairs of men, as opposed to that which is governed by men. He speaks about the Coptic Christian minority in Egypt, warning its leadership against shoring up secular authoritarianism, whilst noting his desire to avoid direct confrontation with normal members of that faith community.

Rabie al-Thani 1435 AH, corresponding to February 2014
Emancipation from the Cycle of Failure and Frivolity
By Sheikh Ayman al-Zawahiri

Production: Al-Sahab Media Productions
Type: Audio-visual
Length: 70 minutes

Publisher: Al-Fajr Media

In the name of God. Our gratitude and thanks to God, prayers for His Messenger and his kin and companions and those who have followed them.

Brother Muslims everywhere, may God's Peace and Blessings be upon you.

Today, I would like to address you regarding the serious crimes that are repeatedly occurring in oppressed Egypt, but prior to that I would like to comment on a piece of news that came out recently; I think my comment on that would be valuable and is linked to the Arab uprisings, even if it does not appear to be so at first. This is about an item published by the BBC; we know that the BBC is the child of the British Intelligence Services. It announced on Saturday 5 October the news of the death of (Vietnamese) General Giap at the age of 102 years; they commented on his military skills and genius. This reminded me of the silence enforced by the West on the heroics of Muslims; the governments of Muslim states and their media and education system match this [silence].

In our contemporary Muslim world, we have *mujahidin* who are more steadfast and heroic than General Giap and who have achieved victories that are greater in size and effect than his victories; an example of that is the first war in Chechnya that was waged in the period between December 1994 and August 1996. If General Giap is the Minister of Defence and the Chief of Staff in North Vietnam, then in Chechnya his counterpart would be Aslan Maskhadov, may God rest his soul. Aslan Maskhadov is not the only contemporary hero in Chechnya; within the Chechen jihadists there are a number of prominent figures such as Dzhokhar Dudayev, Zalim Khan Yandar Payev, Shamil Basayev, Salman Radiev and Khattab, may they all rest in peace. Through a simple comparison, we can see the difference between General Giap and Aslan Maskhadov (RIP); Aslan Maskhadov is one of the greatest heroes in the wars of freedom of our day.

[Commentary from Al-Sahab Media Productions]

The area of Chechnya, which represents the battlefield, is approximately 15,000 square kilometres, compared to Vietnam which is nearly 330,000 square kilometres. Chechnya was totally surrounded by Russian troops while Giap had the luxury of three states that gave him [strategic] depth: Laos, Cambodia and China, his greatest ally. Chechnya has no coastal line, while Vietnam has a coastline that stretches for 3,500 km. The heroism of the Chechen rebels and their leader Aslan Maskhadov is made more signifi-cant when we consider the small Chechen population, which is around 600,000 com-pared to the Vietnamese population, which is close to 8 million. Chechnya had no international support, while Russia and China and all of the Warsaw Pact countries supported North Vietnam.

The troops led by the martyr, as we see him, Aslan Maskhadov in this tight geographi-cal location amounted to two to three thousand jihadists at most. Under such con-straints, the Chechen jihadists led by Aslan Maskhadov faced half a million Russian soldiers, not to mention the Chechen soldiers who betrayed them. In comparison, Giap led the Armed Popular Troops for Freedom, troops that accounted for 2 million, not to mention the fighters in North Vietnam, which was considered to be the fourth largest army in the world and one of the most experienced armies. He was fighting around half a million American soldiers and the army of South Vietnam, which was about 700,000 men. In the last attack in August 1996, which forced the Russians to sur-render, the Chechen fighters were only about 6,000 men; while Giap in his famous Tet offensive in January of 1968 had 58,000 men; with this number he managed to inflict significant losses on the Americans and to stop their attack after a few days. Aslan Maskhadov (RIP) managed to lead the jihadists to victory in Chechnya after 20 months between December 1994 and August 1996, while Giap was unable to lead his troops to victory in 16 years. The Lord almighty smoothed the path for the jihadists to kill 90,000 Russian soldiers, based on numbers confirmed by the Russians themselves, although figures estimated by the jihadists exceed that figure; while the number of Americans killed in Vietnam only reached 58,000 men.

[Ayman al-Zawahiri continues:]

Despite this great victory led by Aslan Maskhadov (RIP), the media did not mention him, nor the Chechen war generally.

And here lies the question: Why do we see all this ignoring of this great war of jihad and the silence regarding the northern [frontier of] Islam for the last four and a half centuries?

The reason lies in the direction the Chechen jihadists are moving towards, which is the establishment of an Islamic caliphate and the desire to be part of that caliphate. In the martyr President Zalim Khan Yandar Payev we can explain this profound understanding of how the jihadists see their role and their role within the Islamic nation. First, who was Zalim Khan Yandar Payev (RIP)?

Zalim Khan Yandar Payev was a Muslim Chechen intellectual, writer and experienced politician; he was the deputy of the martyred President Dzhokhar Dudayev; he was the one who most fervently encouraged Dudayev to declare Chechnya as an Islamic state by the name of the "Ashkerya Republic" where Islamic Sharia would be applied. Following the death of the president, he temporarily took over the president's tasks, and then he became the president of the Chechen delegation of the Islamic Emirate to Afghanistan where he signed the agreement of mutual recognition between the Islamic Emirate in Afghanistan and the Chechen Republic of Ashkerya. He was finally made a martyr when he was assassinated in Qatar by Russian intelligence forces.

This great intellectual wrote a book called *Chechnya: Politics and Reality*. I invite each free Muslim and each free honourable man who is fighting oppression to read it, especially those who are carrying on the fight of the Arab Spring, so we can reach the desired change we seek.

[Commentary from Al-Sahab:]

The President, the martyr, Zalim Khan Yandar Payev says:

"At the start of the war there was no comparison between the two forces; the Russians used half a million heavily armed troops in their attack against the Chechens, supported further by military aircraft, helicopters, cannons and all types of rockets. Yet, despite all these unlimited military resources that were available to the Russians, they were unable to break the resistance of the few thousands of Chechen fighters with their light weapons which they had mainly won through their battles with the Russians. The weapons of the Chechen fighters were light, but their faith was absolute. From that basis, we can explain the challenge posed by the Chechens against this tyrannical power, and how they managed to destroy it. We would also notice how God stood by us in that war where the enemy had prepared a power way above endurance and the enemy waged a war of hatred against Islam.

[...] The victory achieved by the Chechens in the year 1996 and their heroism in those days in the face of those great differences is clear evidence and a sign for our eyes to see that belief in God and staying on the straight path makes everything possible, including the destruction of our enemies, regardless of how much power they have. For Muslims, to have the features of real Islam, and to have confidence in God and trust in His power, makes them fear no one. Returning the Islamic nation to its former glory is a matter that is achievable once we accept what God has decreed for us, and once we agree on the matters that we are able to achieve. The real question is: Are we, as Muslims, ready to follow in the footsteps of the Chechen fighters and enrol in the ranks of jihad in the name of God?

Do Muslims need more proof to believe that the Russian invasion is only part of a Satanic crusade, and that the fight to destroy that campaign is what we call jihad in its full meaning? This is true jihad because it is not just a jihad to free Chechnya, it is also a jihad to defend the Islamic nation.

As for the question of understanding the fight in Caucasus and the Muslim world, we can say that it is understood that jihad is a jihad for all Muslims, while the jihad in Chechnya is part of a great Islamic jihad, which goes back to the era of the Wise Caliphates. This jihad aims to revive Muslim unity, and thus it is the instrument and the way in which the Muslim nation will be freed, indeed the whole world will be freed from the ties of the Devil.

Moreover, as well as Daghistan and Chechnya, the Caucasus is an inseparable part of the Islamic nation and thus jihad today to free states from the occupation of atheists is a duty for all Muslims; we must each do our duty towards God and in God's name.

Jihad in Chechnya is nothing new; it is merely a stage of jihad that goes back in history to the battle of Badr under the Prophet Mohammed's leadership; it goes further back than that to the battle between the Prophet David and Goliath. The fight in Chechnya is another page in the pages of the everlasting history of jihad that is needed to achieve fairness in the name of God."

[Ayman al-Zawahiri continues:]

With this great and noble understanding of Islam and jihad, which is affirmed by the great leader Zalim Khan Yandar Payev (RIP) in the name of his people, the Chechens today have managed to stop the crusading Russian attacks, some of which were communist attacks, for the last four and a half centuries. This is why the international corrupt powers have covered up and silenced stories about their heroism and victories. We could compare the victory of the Chechens against the Russians in the first war (and they will, God willing, win the second war) to the victory of the villagers in the Far Maghreb [north-eastern Morocco] led by the Amir the *mujahid* Mohammed Bin Abdul Karim al-Khattabi against the Spaniards in many battles, the most famous one being the Battle of Annual [1921] where about 1,000 *mujahidin* faced 25,000 Spaniard soldiers, defeating them and killing about 16,000. I am confident that most Arabs and Egyptians have not heard about Annual and have not studied it at school, where they were only taught a history full of errors and deviations. War historians consider it to be one of the greatest wars for freedom from occupation. In fact, Sheikh Abu Musab al-Suri, may he be released from captivity, mentioned in his book where he wrote about the Taliban that Mao Zedong said that al-Khattabi was one of the best military teachers in gang [guerrilla] warfare.

Some may ask, "What is the link between Chechnya and what is happening in Egypt, Tunisia and Libya?" This is the question that I would like to respond to. The link between them is that Chechnya held firm and became victorious. Chechnya did not hold out for one or two years, it held for four and a half centuries. Its case was as clear as daylight: a Muslim nation that wanted its freedom to establish a Muslim state. Is that what happened in Tunisia and Egypt? Did many of those Islamist activists hold out and demand the establishment of an Islamic state?

Fellow Muslims in Egypt and elsewhere: regardless of what was and what is to come, holding firm is the path to victory. If we wish to establish a Muslim state, then we must insist on demanding one and we must not step down from that demand, especially to those who are enemies of Islam and who are hostile towards it. We must not negotiate that demand and we must not meet halfway with those who are fighting it. If, at the start of that road, we negotiated on matters related to the basics of the religion, without which a believer's faith is worthless, then when we are towards the end of the road how shall we be? When I say the basics of the religion, I mean the legitimacy of Sharia as seen in this Quranic verse: *"But no, by your Lord, they will not believe until they call you to arbitrate in their dispute; then they will have no discomfort regarding your verdict and will submit fully."* {Sura 4 (The Women), 65} This is where God has sworn using His great soul when He said: *"But no, by your Lord, they will not believe."*

This demand does not allow negotiations, understanding or compromise, not even meeting halfway, because this demand is the difference between faith and unbelief, atheism and monotheism. So what are we expected to negotiate over? We must make those demands loud and clear, as clear as daylight, sharp as a knife's edge, that legitimacy is for Sharia alone, with no other reference and no higher leadership and no referendums, choices or elections or vote-counting or playing with phrases and formulae. We must demand that Sharia be the ruler and not the ruled, the one who gives orders but does not receive them, it must be leader not the one to be led.

All the previous methods of understanding, playing with words, negotiations and compromise and meeting halfway have failed and are failing now and shall fail in the future because even if we do not know what we want, our enemy certainly knows what he wants. Every time we compromise with our principles and beliefs, our enemy will hold on to his own; and every time we become flexible, he becomes harder and more arrogant and mighty. And whenever we respond to his methods of allowing our whims to rule and to believe in the principle of counting votes, he bares his teeth and directs against us his cannons and machine guns, and he moves towards us to crush us with his tanks and machinery, and he opens his prison doors and detention centres [to imprison us] and releases his dogs to torture and assault us.

We did not deal with them like lions, so they dealt with us like wolves, and we know that the wolves will eat those who do not act like lions. How full Egypt is with wolves and foxes and how satiated they have become with Egypt's fortunes. The famous poet al-Mutanabbi said:

The guards of Egypt have fallen asleep and missed the foxes
For they are satiated and the vines shall not become extinct

My brothers in Egypt: This calamity will end one day, God willing, just like all calamities do; with God's will any problem soon ends, the Lord almighty has said: *"with hardship comes ease"*. But He will send us someone who will call for the continuity of the cycle of frivolity and failure, where some will abdicate from the legitimacy of Sharia and will accept the idol of democracy and will fawn over the elections—which will be falsified at times and corrected other times—and then they win and start writing up a secular constitution so that the seculars will accept them. But seculars will never accept them and they will prepare to fight them using tanks sent via USAid, which will protect the borders of Israel where they will direct their tanks, cannons and machine guns towards us, and they will roll them on top of us, crushing us underneath them, and then they will start from scratch again, just like an addict who is unable to leave his addiction despite being shown a million pieces of evidence on why he should stop.

Sheikh Hassan al-Banna (RIP) entered the elections twice; the first time he dropped out after Britain applied pressure on him. Britain, the democracy protector, had asked [Mustafa] al-Nahhas—whom it appointed as Prime Minister on 4 February 1942—to apply pressure on al-Banna so he would drop out. Another time he decided to enter the elections, and despite Prime Minister Mahmood al-Niqrashi asking him not to, he insisted and so they accused him of falsification and removed his name. In other words, his trying to participate in democracy was met with blackmail, falsification and political pressure. Seventy years later, the same disaster repeats itself but in an uglier picture; when will we learn? Indeed, when will we manage to get out of the cycle of frivolity and failure?

Brother Muslims in Egypt, Libya, Tunisia, Pakistan, Palestine and elsewhere: Any party that is affiliated to Islam and claims that it will govern through secular elections and the acceptance of the whims of the majority because they have the majority, this party is blind to two facts which are quite dangerous when it comes to the battle for Islam; the first fact is the religious dimension in this struggle; the struggle that is ongoing in the Muslim world is not a struggle between agendas and political parties that are vying to govern, it is a struggle between those who want the rule of Islam and those who do not want it; this is the truth, clear and obvious.

Within the ranks of Muslims, there are some who are blind to that fact and it chases them everywhere; every time they try to escape from it, it faces them and they collide. Others find the path [of jihad and propagation] hard and choose the easier route and agree to compromise and to let go of the governance by Sharia in return for a quick fix of power, but they are inevitably faced with a quick expulsion or violent oppression the minute they are close to power. Some try to negotiate over the rule of Sharia with the people who are ruling and have the power, the might of riyals and dollars so that they would use the name of Islam, which they are supposedly serving, for their benefit. They claim this is the best it can ever be and that they are seeking to fool the enemies of Islam and that what was considered yesterday to be forbidden, and in fact renders one an atheist, is today an obligatory duty because such and such a sheikh has decreed it to be so, or some sheikh has given it his own interpretation, or another sheikh has given it his approval. They claim to be assisting the security services in order to give security to the Muslims, and that they have shown how clever they can be in taking the benefits of a revolution they used to forbid others from joining, and that the problem is not in the secularists or the Americanised soldiers or the separatist Christians, but that the problem lies in those who call others atheists who should be eradicated by the army and Mubarak's police. They would accept a secular constitution if it had some references to Islam, and then they claim that this constitution is a victory they have over seculars. It is also acceptable after a very short while that by the orders of al-Sisi that this constitution, which they saw as a victory, is revoked. All those contradictions, which can make us unsure whether to laugh or cry, remind us of the poet al-Mutanabbi's lines:

> What is it in Egypt that causes laughter?
> But it is a laughter that is more like crying

The poet Hafiz Ibrahim said:

> How often in Egypt we have things to make us laugh
> Just like Abu al-Tayeb [al-Mutanabbi] has said.

Whoever counted that secular constitution as a victory, he himself recanted on his way to Sisi's roadmap, and then he went begging for it in the corridors of the Secret Fifty[16] but was met only with refusal and arrogance, for this is the punishment for beggars. These characters, who are laughably sad, have no problem lining up behind Sisi or to his left and indeed behind Sisi's supporters against the enemies of Sisi, to gain Sisi's approval. That is OK because the secularists that have no religion and those who twist the truth and the separatist crusaders and [Mohamed] ElBaradei and Hamdeen Sabahi and Sisi are not those who call others atheists. As for Israel, it is a reality that we must deal with, accept and commit to the surrender agreements we have with it.

Is the reason for religion that we grow our moustaches?
O nation that other nations have laughed at from their ignorance

I want every noble and free man and every wise and reasonable man—considering that wise men understand from mere gestures—I want those men to look at the image of Sisi on the day of his coup and how he lined up the men. Sisi stood at the front, by the podium higher than everybody else; he lined up tightly the worldly people to his right side and the religious people to his left, in order to show how he was separating religion from this worldly life. Then the religious people were divided; those who support him, rightly or wrongly, were lined in two rows: the first row [was comprised] of scholars of evil and clergymen, one of whom was a secularist, a relic from the days of Mubarak, dressed in a cloak and a turban, a supporter of the army wherever and whenever they may be; while the other was a separatist Christian, who claims that the Holy Spirit comes to him so his decisions are absolute, and with that he supported Sisi and claimed that the day of the coup was a historical day, just like his predecessor Shenouda supported Hosni Mubarak in the last presidential elections and forbade any demonstrations against him. This should remind us of the dark history of the Church's collusion with emperors, despite his [Pope Shenouda's] claims about rendering to Caesar that which is Caesar's, and rendering to God that which is God's, but he still came to support our Caesar Sisi and to employ what he calls religion in the service of Caesar.

Behind the row of scholars of evil and the clergymen we find another row: on the right we find the crusaders wearing a cross on their chest that is the size of the clergymen themselves, while on the left we find the representative of the Salafis in a corner right next to the wall.

With this line-up, Sisi has delivered his message, which is that Sisi, the secularist, Americanised military man is higher than everyone else and stands in the forefront, while religion is to his left separated from earthly matters that sit on his right; but both life and religion are there to serve Sisi. While the representative of the "Sisi" Salafis is kept at the back to the left in the midst of the crusaders and the relics from the Mubarak days; this is where he belongs and this is his value, and he should accept that or go to prison instead.

Al-Mutanabbi was right when he wrote:

Humiliated is he who rejoices in a life
Where perhaps death is easier than that life
Any dream that comes without hardship

Is an excuse used by admonishers
Those who compromise will accept disgrace
A cut will not cause pain to a dead man

In contrast to this submissive behaviour seen by the Sisi Salafists, I remember the noble attitude that shows the glory and honour of the Chechen fighters. I mean the well-known stance by President Zalim Khan Yandar Payev (RIP) with the Russian President Boris Yeltsin during their negotiations in May 1996 in Moscow. When the Chechen delegation arrived, Yeltsin arrogantly asked Sheikh Zalim Khan to sit beside him, but he [Khan] replied firmly that as a president of an independent state he would not sit beside him but opposite him, otherwise there was no point in the negotiations. After a few minutes filled with hesitation, Yeltsin backtracked in front of the media and accepted President Khan's condition, may he rest in peace.

If not for hardship, then people would have prevailed
Generosity is impoverished and advancement retreats
God has created some men for war
And other men for porridge and flour [useless men]

Those [men] have existed throughout history, and history records their actions so that the following generations can read about them.

The second dimension, ignored by those who claim they will become rulers through secular ballot boxes and the surrender to the whims of the majority because they have the majority, or because they hope for that majority even if they get it through building some alliance or another with secular forces, is the actual dimension of the struggle.

It is not a struggle between national competing forces; it is a struggle between the Zionists and crusaders on the one hand and Islam on the other. It is not a fair struggle, even if measured through democracy where votes are counted honestly; it is a dirty struggle where any dirty means are used to win those elections. In the West, they have legalised this dirty method through contributions of large conglomerates and sponsors and media corporations to influence the voters, while in our countries the struggle has not yet reached that level of legitimising this dirty way; instead, the influences are not subtle but clear: where America pays out of its pocket its agents in Saudi Arabia and the Gulf states so that they mobilise their soldiers in poor Egypt. Saudi money has many mouths in Egypt and many hands, some of which are tyrannical and some have no religion, while others are bearded but hypocritical and deceptive.

I see the Dirhams in all places
Dressing men in glory and might
They are the tongue to those who want to talk
And they are the spears for those who want to kill

Muslim brothers in Egypt, Libya, Tunisia, Pakistan, Palestine and other places: There are principal matters that I cannot imagine to be Islamic without Islam being a part of them, such as ensuring the rule of Sharia and for it to be above the constitution and the law and the whims of the majority. It needs to be the highest reference that is not parallel to any other. We must not be defeated psychologically. The military defeat of the caliphate state following the First World War has given us a psychological defeat that goes along with the military defeat where we began to demand Sharia through the methods of the enemies of Sharia; we demand Sharia law through laws outside Sharia; we demand Sharia through the dominance of the whims of the majority. It is as if we were asking for alcohol to be banned through converting to Christianity. Is that reasonable?

This psychological defeat has now prominent symbols where this has reached the level of a chronic disease that has begun to affect their behaviour, talk and actions, where they have become disturbed and confused; such as Rashed al-Ghannouchi[17] who left behind the Sharia decades before he ruled. He denied publicly, many times, having ever applied Sharia, in order for the doors of government and power to open to him. Despite this evasion of Sharia, we find him fighting fierce battles to become prime minister and he tries everything possible to let his party remain in power. He would die for the ministry, but leaves behind Sharia as the price to pay. Some examples of his own contradictions that are a result of the deeply seated psychological defeat are how he praises highly the leader of the "Shining Path"[18] in Peru, while on the other hand he denounces the *mujahidin* and describes them as violent and criminal and that they have brought destruction and disasters to the country. In the end, and in order to please the American State Department and the EU and the Gulf states, he started to say that those in the "Shining Path" were heroes, while those fighting jihad against the Western crusading Zionists are criminals.

Those who have a diseased and bitter mouth
Will taste sweet water as if it was bitter
The eye may deny sunlight entering if it is ill
And the mouth may deny the taste of water if unwell

I find it hard to imagine an Islamic movement being Islamic if they did not defend occupied Muslim lands such as Palestine, Kashmir, Chechnya, the

Philippines, Septa [Ceuta] and Malila and others. And I cannot imagine any movement calling itself Islamic if it accepted the occupation of any Muslim land or accepted any agreements that supported that occupation. It is hard to imagine that they would turn a blind eye to those agreements in order to reach power. What were the consequences for Mohammed Morsi when he accepted those agreements of surrender to Israel as a price for him to reach power? The result was his discharge from power. He would have been more honourable had he been discharged from power having condemned those agreements of surrender to Israel, rather than having condoned them.

The third matter without which I cannot accept a movement to be Islamic is the matter of demanding good deeds and prohibiting abomination[19] in all its guises; in other words, removing corruption from the government and society. The Islamic movement must stand behind the poor, the oppressed and those who have nothing and who are being crushed by the Sisi—Sawaris [the Egyptian billionaire] alliance. Sisi wants to return the favour to Sawaris for his "revolutionaries" by financing the Inqaz Movement and the Tamarod Front.[20] He repays the favour by demanding the raising of aid for basic products, so the poor become poorer while the wealthy become even more wealthy due to the suspect deals and the theft of public funds either through legal or illegal methods. The armed forces, police, intelligence services and the judiciary live through the hard work and earnings of the poor, through money that should go to the children of the poor. They use the excuse of the need to defend the country's borders and to secure society, while in truth they are defending the Israeli borders and surrounding Gaza and protecting the corrupt state. They invest people's money in a market in which they are the largest investor, without allowing anyone to ask them: how much are they spending and on what?

We have seen the results of not carrying on with the revolution in Egypt in order to uproot the corrupt judicial system and the military that has been reared by the Americans. We have seen the Ministry of the Interior run by murderers and hangmen; all of them have turned against those who retreated in front of them. We saw the results of saying that we should leave the amendment of the second article of the constitution[21] and not insisting that Sharia law should be the only way to legislate, because, so they claimed, this would lead to non-cooperation with the enemies of Sharia, those crusader separatists and secularists. The result of this is that they have all turned against those who sought to please them; it would have been more honourable for those who have been spurned to have been rejected while holding on to the legitimacy of Sharia, rather than be rejected after they had denounced Sharia.

In any case, we are the children of today and we must make history a lesson that can enlighten our path today and in the future. This is why I invite, and I invite repeatedly, any Muslim and anyone working to support Islam to unite around the word of monotheism so that we can support Islam and its Sharia, and free Muslim lands from occupation and its noble people from corruption, tyranny, oppression and abuse. For the purposes of this noble and generous call to unite Muslims and those working for Islam around monotheism, we have, with God's help, published a document of support for Islam,[22] which we hope everyone will read and make use of in any way they see fit. Please advise us if you think it is not of value: *"I only see reform as much as possible; I only get success through God whom I trust and rely on."* {Sura 11 (Hūd), 88}

Some might ask, "What is the alternative to this cycle of frivolity and failure?" The alternative is the Sunna of the prophets and their followers: propagation and jihad. We must at this stage gather the nation in a propagation uprising that does not calm or soften until it removes this secular Americanised coup and establishes a legitimacy for Sharia and the rule of Islam. We must unite around that aim and not compromise an inch or negotiate about it at all. We must stand strong and not negotiate or compromise on the matter of Sharia being the only legitimate rule in the Muslim world. We must not stop this confrontation simply when Morsi returns to power, nor with the return of the old constitution, as this is not legitimacy. Legitimacy lies in the rule of Sharia. Sadly, some have not only accepted cutting this short once Dr Mohammed Morsi returns, but in fact they have shown their readiness to give up the return of Morsi and the Parliament and the Consultative Council and find it is sufficient to have the mirage they call "Keeping on the path of democracy", and so we spiral downwards in giving up our demands.

On 25 January the uprising of the Egyptian people was stolen from them when their demands were reduced to simply demanding that Mubarak be removed, and we accepted the rule of the military, and negotiations and compromises began and led to the state we got to of criminality, murder, arrests, torture and assaults on women and children. The blessed uprising of the Egyptian people on 25 January was a historic chance for Egypt to return to its leading role in both the Arabic and Islamic worlds, defending the rights of Muslims and any oppressed people in the world and establishing an honest, fair Islamic rule that would kill corruption and tyranny.

[A televised interview with Sheikh Mohammed Al-Zawahiri, Ayman's younger brother, is played]

Presenter: We will show you an image and we ask you to comment on it, please. Please show us the first image on the screen in front of you. This is a picture of the parliament, what is your comment?

Sheikh Mohammed Zawahiri: We ask God kindness and health.

Presenter: When will you enter under the umbrella of this parliament?

Sheikh Mohammed Zawahiri: God willing, we never will, unless that parliament is removed and starts to do its job. What does this parliament mean? Calmly, so that things do not become complicated. A parliament means we have given dominance to someone other than God, we have given it to people, to creatures. This is a system not created by the West, it is created by the Jewish Zionists so that they can corrupt the people of the world. This is a system that contradicts all divine faiths, not just Islam; it conflicts with us as Muslims, and the Christians and the true Jewish faith that all agree that power should only belong to God.

Presenter: But it is possible for it to exist so we can extract religious laws from it?

Sheikh Mohammed Zawahiri: No, if it exists, it is to extract administrative matters. Scholars and not the public should extract religious matters. If it were to make administrative or organisational matters in a way that does not conflict with God's Sharia, they should not speak on matters that have been mentioned in the [Quranic] verses, as in this case they would be...

Presenter: OK, what is the alternative that you suggest, Sheikh Mohammed? I mean, if we cancel...

Sheikh Mohammed Zawahiri: We suggest the Islamic alternative, which has been applied for thousands of years. Muslims have lived happily for 1,400 years, while now, where the occupation is controlling us, we have become....defeat[ed]. Mahmood, the biggest defeat is the intellectual and psychological defeat; they have defeated us to the extent that we no longer believe in ourselves, we have become their followers; we used to dominate the world with the Islamic system, we do not need their system.

Presenter: So what are the mechanisms of action to reach your goal of applying Islamic Sharia? What will you do? Some parties have used the parliament as a method of paving the way, or an attempt to apply part of Sharia. They have done so, but you have not; what have you done for that cause?

Sheikh Mohammed Zawahiri: No, no, we have done more than that. This is like a man who wants to please God by disobeying Him; what does that man want? To apply Sharia, so he does so by letting go of it from the start.

Presenter: That is what is available, and not what is hoped for.

Sheikh Mohammed Zawahiri: Available? All proper methods are available, for example peaceful demonstrations. Who charged Hosni Mubarak? Was it the parliament? It was the popular uprising. Why do we not carry on with the popular uprising? I call everyone now to carry on....

Presenter: *So you are not against demonstrations.*

Sheikh Mohammed Zawahiri: *No, no, I am not against demonstrations that are controlled by Sharia and which have the right aims. We could resort to civil strikes until Sharia is applied. If the previous ruler has agreed to step down and he and his sons were taken to court under pressure from this popular demand, then why can we not demand Sharia? Sadly, the nation is supposed to be led by pioneering scholars. For a nation to be in power, its demands must be requested by the nation's leading intellectuals, the scholars, but unfortunately the scholars were not up to this task. At that time when they said "Life, Freedom and Social Justice" no one said "Islamic Sharia", which should have been said from the start.*

[Ayman al-Zawahiri continues:]

But all the negotiations, the rush and competition to gain things have pushed some to accept the mere removal of the former president and to then deal with the remainder of his regime, starting with the Military Council and the corrupt judiciary system. The outcome was the current calamity where the secularists have shown their ugly face which has brought back all Mubarak's crimes and accepted them joyfully in order to prevent Islamic rule from returning. They did not care about pride or manners; their animosity extended just like that of their predecessors, and they assaulted the women and mosques of Egypt.

The history of Arab secularism is scattered with lack of ethics and with subordination; the worst cases of oppression against Islamic parties were by that party. Here is the Mubarak regime that has killed nearly a thousand Islamic prisoners in its prisons rearing its face again. Arab secularism is willing to be allied with the devil against Islamic movements, just as it always has done, and then it would unmask its face and throw away the mask of democracy and lick the boots of the military. We see it today aligning itself with the separatist crusaders and the leaders of corruption and those who benefit from Islamic action, and they present us with Sisi. Do you know who Sisi is? Sisi is the one who pre-empts all the former secular military disasters from the days of Abdul Nasser to Mubarak; Sisi the Americanised mercenary and live puppet, the evil cheat; what does he have in his life history except social climbing to reach his goal, and hypocrisy, betrayal and cruelty which remind us of al-Mutanabbi's words:

Is it every time the follower of evil kills his master?
Or betrays him we find he has roots in Egypt
The guards of Egypt have fallen asleep and missed the foxes
For they are satiated and the vines shall not become extinct

And in his words:

If you honour a good man you own him
But if you honour a rebel he will rebel more

Arab secularism applies democracy by running after rules based on Sisi's tanks, which claim that they are not against religion, but that they just seek to separate it from the state; this mirage will end with the state taking over religion.

[Commentary from Al-Sahab:]

Following his departure from Marxism and discovering Islam with the help of God, Dr Abdul Wahab al-Masiri (RIP) said:

"*Even if they said it was partial, yet this partial secularism, which is linked to the early stages of the development of the Western secular system, has retreated and become marginalised; whereas the levels of secularism have escalated and have overcome the fields of economy, politics and ideology. Secularism has become an overriding social phenomenon and a deep structural transformation which is now more serious than separating religion from the state, and the matter of social capitalist or socialist organisations, and any other dictionary terms or intellectual ideas with their own limits. There no longer exists a place for a general life that is independent of private lives; the secular state and the educational establishments and those of leisure and the media have entered people's emotions and their dreams and direct their behaviour and their relationships between them and their nuclear families. It is no longer possible to separate the one from the other; indeed, we can no longer talk about the separation of religion from the state, but rather we talk about the dominance of the state over religion.*

From this perspective, the biggest enemy of the world order is not Arab nationalism, which is receding, especially following the collapse of the socialist states and following the Gulf war; it is anyone who stands in the path of global consumerism, which is Islam as a global human ideology and a system of values. From the perspective of Islam, we did not enter this world in order to buy and sell; we came here to demand good deeds and prohibit abominations. The values of pride and honesty have a place in the minds of a Muslim; Islam is a vision that makes it hard for a person to hide behind the two base activities, their economic and sexual identities; those are merely products of their material nature. A Muslim is not a human with a single dimension; he is the complex person to whom God has gifted a human nature, so that he will build on it and use it for his own benefit and the benefit of generations to follow, God willing.

In this confrontation of faith, Israel will get back its historic role that it has nearly lost, and instead of being a base for capitalist Western occupation, it can be the representative of the modern Western secular civilisation in both its aspects: the capitalist and the former socialist; a great wall that represents the West in the East and stands in the way of the Eastern chaos, according to Herzl. We now have the former Islamic Soviet states

which nearly had their independent dynamics threatened by Islamic movements; and
there are also some Arab regimes that see this Islamic movement as a threat to them."

[Ayman al-Zawahiri continues:]

Arab secularism and military secularism and their allies today are the front for
the old, new occupation project. The military secularists use an army of hypocrites who use their so-called religious features to fight religion and prevent
Sharia rule. This is why the Sheikh of al-Azhar, follower of Mubarak, spoke
against Sharia rule, and he and his followers insisted on not changing article
two where the wording "principles of Sharia" remains, rather than be replaced
with "rules of Sharia". This is why we saw this follower of Mubarak, Sheikh of
al-Azhar, stand behind Sisi; and we saw Ali Gomaa[23] allowing criminals to
spill the blood of Muslims. The mighty, oppressing tyrants in any period use
the leaders of corruption to enslave the people to their whims and to move
them away from God's true religion.

[Commentary from Al-Sahab:]

> *Sayed Qutb, RIP, says: "Statues do not speak, hear or see, only the priest or leader who*
> *stands behind them and who mumbles chants and speaks in their name with whatever*
> *he wishes in order to enslave and tame the people. If you see slogans raised anywhere on*
> *Earth where the leaders or priests decide, using those slogans, on matters that God*
> *disapproves of, such as matters of religious practices, rules, values, attitudes and actions,*
> *then these are the idols in nature, reality and function. If nationalism, the state, the*
> *people or class were raised as a slogan, and people were asked to worship those slogans*
> *rather than God, and to give up their lives, money, ethics and traditions, we will find*
> *that every time God's laws and Sharia, instructions and directions come into conflict*
> *with those slogans and their requirements, we will find that God's laws, Sharia,*
> *instructions and directions are put aside and those slogans are followed. To be more*
> *accurate, the will of the men behind those slogans [is followed]. This is like worshipping*
> *idols rather than God. An idol does not necessarily need to be a piece of wood or stone;*
> *it may be a slogan or creed. Islam did not arise just to break down wooden or stone*
> *idols; all the effort spent for its sake, starting from the prophets, and all the huge sacri-*
> *fices made for it and the pain suffered for it, was not merely to break stone and wooden*
> *idols. Islam arose so that it would separate the path of worshipping God alone from*
> *worshipping those other than God, in every nuance possible. We must follow images*
> *wherever they occur, so that we can realise the nature of the regimes and systems that*
> *exist and decide whether they are atheism or monotheism; is it worship of God alone,*
> *or worship of tyrants, lords and idols."*

[Ayman al-Zawahiri continues:]

This is why it was not unusual that the corrupt judiciary defended the corrupt
Mufti [Gomaa], and they ruled that anyone who shouted in the face of this

corrupt Mufti the words "In God we trust and rely" should be imprisoned for seventeen years.

As for the Christians of Egypt, especially the Orthodox among them whose leaders were lined up behind Sisi, I would like to tell them honestly and briefly: "I start by assuring you that we do not want a war with you, and we do not seek that, but Tawadros [Pope Theodoros II] is following in the footsteps of [Pope] Shenouda in placing you in the political battleground against a large section of the Egyptian people. And even though Tawadros has said that he believes in rendering to Caesar that which is Caesar's and rendering to God that which is God's, nevertheless he has shown, as did Shenouda before him, that they are allies of the tyrannical and oppressing Caesars. Who could forget how Shenouda supported Hosni Mubarak in his presidential campaign and called for people to stop the uprising of 25 January?

"Who could also forget how Tawadros stood in the first row behind Sisi and to his left, supporting his military coup? With those threatening positions they have gone back to the history of their predecessors: the leaders of the Church who used to say 'Render unto Caesar that which is Caesar's and render unto God that which is God's', and yet they conspire with the Caesars, leaders and tyrants in oppressing people; this is why people and nations have risen against them, just as we saw in the French Revolution when their slogan was 'Hang the last king, using the entrails of the last priest'.

"This is why reasonable Christians must put a stop to those driving them to the edge of the cliff. I reiterate to reasonable Christians that we have been your neighbours in this country for thousands of years now; Arab tribes moved to Egypt many centuries before Islam came; most of the Egyptian Copts accepted Islam without going through the Inquisition, unlike what happened in Andalucía, or through genocide, unlike in Bosnia; they entered Islam when they saw how just Islam is."

[Commentary from Al-Sahab:]

> Most Egyptians adopted Islam gradually over many centuries, and adopted Arabic as their language; these changes were partially due to the migration of some Arab tribes and the marriage between Egyptians and Arabs. Some Egyptians converted to Islam based on deep faith, while others converted in order to benefit politically and socially.

[Ayman al-Zawahiri continues:]

If the Muslims in Egypt wanted to get rid of the Christians, they would have done so just as the Christians did to them in Andalucía; and the Christians would have disappeared from Egypt, just as the Muslims did in Andalucía.

Many of the Muslims in this country are Copts, or have Coptic blood running through their veins due to marriage of Copts with Arabs and other Muslims. This is why what some of the Church leaders claim, that the Arabs invaded Egypt with the Islamic conquests and must therefore be thrown out of it, is erroneous in historical fact. If they wished to expel the invading Arabs, then what will they do with the millions of Coptic Muslim converts? Will they subject them to the Inquisition courts that the Muslims were exposed to in Andalucía? Or to genocide as their Orthodox brothers subjected the Muslims in Srebrenica and its sister towns? Or will they bury them in the dungeons of their abbeys and get them to join Wafaa Constantine[24] and her sisters?

I remind the sensible Christians that God almighty ordered the Muslims in His glorious Book to be merciful and compassionate with those who make peace with them; God said: *"It may be that God establishes friendship between you and those of them who were your enemies. God is all powerful and God is all forgiving, all merciful. God does not forbid you, regarding those who did not fight you and did not drive you out of your homes, to be generous to them and deal with them justly. God surely loves the just. God only forbids you, regarding those who fought you in religion and drove you out of your homes and assisted in driving you out, to take them for friends. Those who take them for friends are indeed the wrong-doers."* {Sura 60 (The Woman Tried), 7–9}

The Prophet Mohammed himself asked us to treat the Egyptian Copts well: *"You shall conquer a land known as al-Qirat, treat its people well as they have mercy and compassion."* He also said, *"If Egypt is conquered, treat the Copts well as they have mercy and compassion."* If this rule is a general one to all Muslims, it is more specific to the Muslims of Egypt who have strong links to the Copts due to being neighbours and sharing their country; indeed, many of the Muslims in Egypt today are converts from Copts.

This is why I ask the Egyptian Christians in general, and the sensible ones among them specifically: Why do your leaders stand against the rule of Sharia and align with its enemies? Are you angry with it because it differentiates between Muslims and others in posts such as presidencies or prime ministerial posts and the judiciary, because those are posts that can only be held by Muslims?

Glory to God! Many regimes live that way across the world, where they differentiate between those who live under their power and within their points of reference. If a Copt lived in America for a hundred years without obtaining US citizenship, he would not be allowed to participate in any politics, even if he had paid them millions of dollars in taxes, because the principles on which they build their state are secular and nationalist; they even have the right to withdraw his citizenship if they wish to, and if they have created a law to allow that.

And you, despite the claims you make that you are nationalistic, still do not permit the Sudanese who live in Egypt any political say. In fact, they are not allowed to enter Egypt without a visa, despite the close links they have and the close relations they have through marriage and religion, culture, civilisation, trade, mutual benefit and neighbourly links. Many Sudanese are closer to the Egyptian Muslims in southern Egypt than they are to the Christians in the north, and until recently the Sudanese were Egyptian citizens, before the British occupied the land and divided them. Do not complain or get annoyed and compromise the Sudanese who lived in Egypt all their lives, as did their fathers and those who have Egyptian mothers. How can you exclude them from any political action, when they know only Egypt as their country; while you give all those political rights to the Christian Copt, who was born in America and has never seen Egypt but who holds an Egyptian passport? And yet you say no injustice befalls those Sudanese in Egypt as a consequence, and you are not aware of the inequalities that afflict them as a minority?

You also have no problem in preventing the Palestinians from Rafah or the Libyans from Burqa from having any political say; you excuse that by saying that our principle is the secular national state that has borders drawn by the Western occupation, and that is our basis for differentiating between the people that live in Egypt. I mean the basis of the Sykes–Picot agreement and Lord Kitchener who broke up the united Ottoman Empire.

Why do you allow for yourselves what you forbid others to do? You permit yourselves to divide Egyptians based on the secular national state, and forbid Muslims to differentiate based on Islam.

Let us be frank, when you talk about divisions, do you mean by that that you hope to see a Christian become a President of Egypt one day? I think you know that this is an impossibility; if it was impossible in the past, it is now doubly impossible after your leaders supported Sisi's coup. If you say that you hope one day a Christian will rule Egypt because minorities have the right not to be prevented from holding any post based on the principle of citizenship, then why could not the Sudanese, Palestinian and Libyan minorities also not be forbidden any post based on the principle of the Muslim Brotherhood? Why do you exclude those Muslim minorities who are living in Egypt from any governmental posts and any political rights? Why can one of them not be a ruler of Egypt? This has happened before in the history of Egypt.

Your reference is citizenship, while ours is brotherhood in Islam; and in our faith this is more important than citizenship. I remind you that when the national secular judiciary in Egypt that you call others to obey, based on the principle of the national secular state, forced the church to allow divorce, Shenouda stood up and announced that no one should force you to disobey the Bible; and he challenged publicly the judiciary of this secular national state, the state of citizenship that you call for. We say that there is no power on this Earth that can force us to disobey the Quran, and the Quran created equality between all Muslims when God said: "*Believers are brothers.*"

I ask you again: Why are you angry at this Sharia? Is it because it prohibits theft, adultery, alcohol, gambling, adornments and corruption? Do you hate it for its rulings on apostasy? What have you to do with apostasy? This is for Muslims only, so why do you interfere with it? Sharia permits you to adjudicate amongst yourselves in matters related to you alone; it does not allow a judge to adjudicate for you unless you ask him to; and he cannot force you to divorce if it is against your religion, unlike the current judiciary that you seem to want to hold on to.

I repeat that we do not want, or seek, or hope to have a war with you; we want to live with you in peace and harmony, so do not allow those who are unreasonable to ruin that. We do not seek a war with you because you are our neighbours in the land where we wish to live harmoniously with you; we also do not seek a war with you because we are engaged with someone stronger than you: that is the Western–American alliance and its agents in the Arab world. This is why I call my Muslim brothers in Egypt not to be seen to be starting a war with the Christians unless they attack you first, where the attacks must be rebuffed; this is stressed in our document "General Guidelines the Work of Jihad".

What I see, and only God knows what is right, is that it is not beneficial to engage in fighting the Christians, and this is for many reasons:

We are engaged against the Western–Christian–Zionist–American alliance and we must become engaged in Egypt against the Americanised Sisi *coup d'état* in order to remove him and to establish a Muslim government in his place. The first step in that challenge is for us to gather the Muslim forces and unite them in monotheism. We must not seek a war with the Christians in Egypt, because there is a powerful movement of guidance within the Church which will shake it from its roots; its leaders will tremble with fear; we must allow that to take its course. It is to the benefit of the Church leaders to start a war with the Muslims and to align themselves with the corrupt tyrannical leaders who wish to cause corruption, so they use that as a cover to control that movement in the ugliest way possible.

We have not, and will not, forget those who are oppressed, such as Wafaa Constantine, Camilla Shehadeh[25] and their sisters, and in order to give them back their rights we must establish Islamic rule and fair justice, and then we will be able to get each oppressed person their rights.

Let us focus our efforts on that. We must not seek a war with the Christians, or we would present the West with an excuse similar to what happened in the past. We must be seen not to, although we reserve our right to defend ourselves. People who are assaulted and oppressed have the right to defend themselves, and no one should be permitted to take that right away from them.

I do not ask the Muslims simply to avoid trouble with the Christians, I ask them to treat those of them who are peaceful with mercy and compassion, just as we were ordered to do by our Lord in His Holy Book. I also urge them to help those who seek their help, and to cooperate with reasonable people in resolving disputes peacefully, so that they can be free to engage in their bigger battle.

I call on my Muslim brothers everywhere to read carefully the lovely tales of their Prophet, may God grant him peace, and to extract from them lessons and morals in reducing the numbers of their enemies and increasing the numbers of their allies and supporters: *"God will be the All Powerful but most people do not know."*

Before I end my talk regarding Egypt, I would like to address two small matters: the first is to our families in Sinai, and the second to Dr Mohammed Morsi.

For my message to our people in Sinai, I say:

Dearest steadfast, noble and honourable people; people of bravery, protection, loyalty and pride; people of Sinai, the gate to conquests; children of conquerors, soldiers of Islam, protectors of the faith and tribes of goodness; uncles and family members: I ask God to provide you with patience, and to reward you for your endurance against the armies of the Americanised Sisi who is collaborating with Israel against you, and for God to accept your martyrs and heal your wounds and release your prisoners soon. I urge you to give shelter to your brothers who have fled to your areas to escape the tyranny of Sisi, the collaborator. You are the people of pride who will not rebuff those who seek your help. I urge you in the name of Islam and family ties to support our people in Gaza and to try everything to break the siege around them enforced by Sisi, the agent for the crusaders and Zionism.

Now for my message to Mohammed Morsi, I say:

To begin with, I ask God to end your trouble and to guide your heart and to correct your life here and your faith. I ask God to strengthen your heart, and to fill you with confidence, faith and steadfastness so that you can support His religion and

Sharia law, fearing nothing and refusing to compromise or surrender. I pray that He will allow you to follow the words of the Chosen One: *"The best jihad is a word of truth [uttered] in front of a tyrannical ruler"* and *"the best martyrs are Hamza ibn Abdul-Muttalib and a man who came to a tyrannical ruler and enjoined good and forbade evil, so he was killed."* I advise you full of sincerity, wishing you guidance, success and steadfastness. I say to you: You have dealt with secularists and agreed with them and with crusaders; you have agreed compromises with them and with the Americans, and you gave them assurances. You also agreed with the Israelis and gave them acceptance of the peace treaties, and with Mubarak's soldiers who have been reared on America's aid; you kept the agreements with the hangmen of the Ministry of the Interior and made peace with them, but what was the outcome?

You are today undergoing a great test: you must hold on to what is right, without moving an inch or giving away anything, and you must demand the legitimacy of the rule of Sharia clearly, and reject the corrupt judiciary and secular laws and constitution, and insist on freeing every inch of occupied Muslim lands, and refuse to condone any agreement or pact, and pledge to God that you will declare the words of truth publicly, as determined by your faith, without stepping down an inch; if that happens, I can tell you that you will become a hero of our nation and a great symbol and leader, you will be able to gather the armies of the Arab and Muslim worlds behind you in the battle against the enemy. If you die with this in your heart, then rejoice for the great ending and the great reward that awaits you. Fear God within yourself and within your group and the groups in Egypt and the rest of the Muslim world, which is looking at you, watching your every move. Do not hesitate in supporting the faith and proclaiming it as the highest ruler. Remember the stance of the Imam of the Sunnis Ahmad ibn Hanbal (RIP) when he refused to retreat and God strengthened the nation after that.

[Commentary from Al-Sahab:]

> *Imam Thahabi narrated from Abu Jafaar al-Anbari: "I was notified when Ahmad was carried to al-Mamoon, so I crossed the Euphrates, and found him sitting in a Khan, so I greeted him and he said: Abu Jafaar I have suffered. I said: Today you are a leader and people follow you; if you replied regarding the creation of the Quran, they would too. Equally, if you do not [reply] then many people would not either. Despite this, even if the man did not kill you, eventually you are to die, death is inevitable, so fear God and do not answer. Ahmad began to cry and said: Praise the Lord! Abu Jafaar, prepare for me. So I did [prepare] and he repeated: Praise the Lord."*

[Ayman al-Zawahiri continues:]

If you carry on with what you are doing, God will know what you plan. I ask God for me, you and the rest of the Muslim world that we remain in his faith so that when we meet Him, He will be pleased with us.

This is what I wanted to say regarding the crimes that are repeatedly occurring in Egypt. I started by talking about the Chechens to show that endurance is the key to victory. Before finishing, I would like to deliver two more messages, one to our people in Syria and the other to our people in Libya.

To our people in Syria, I say to them in general and the *mujahidin* and scholars and propagators [specifically]: America has now got its assurances of safety for Israel from Assad's chemical weapons; God only knows what other secret deals have been struck in return for it, turning a blind eye to his crimes. The only way to survive the sedition that we see all around you is to unite around monotheism and the establishment of a Muslim government that will spread consultation and justice and that would free Muslim lands from invaders and tyrants. Unite and agree, and God will help and support you and grant you victory, and He will stop the enemy's attacks, and God will make your word as one.

For our people in Libya, I say that you have shed your own blood and sacrificed the dearest thing you have, which was your victory over Qaddafi. But you have fallen for the American Christian humiliation; have you been freed, or have you just exchanged one humiliation and oppression for another?

You have moved from Qaddafi's oppressive government to an American humiliating one, a puppet government that is controlled by the CIA. The arrest of Sheikh Abu Anas al-Libi (May he be released soon) has removed the mask of the collaborative feature of that government and its treachery and lack of pride. Will the free, honourable Libyans and those who pride themselves in its Islam accept that?

It pains me to tell you frankly that your revolution has been aborted and stolen by the collaborators. You need to finish it.

Our final prayers include our gratitude to God, the Lord of the Universe. May God pray for His Messenger and his kin and companions. May peace and God's mercy be upon you.[26]

PART 2

AL-QAEDA AND THE SYRIAN FITNA

THE SEVENTH INTERVIEW WITH SHEIKH AYMAN AL-ZAWAHIRI

REALITY BETWEEN PAIN AND HOPE

MAY 2014

Ayman al-Zawahiri and *Al-Sahab*

This is the seventh "interview" between Al-Sahab, Al-Qaeda's media production depart-ment, and Zawahiri, a tradition which started in 2005. This format gives Zawahiri the opportunity to discuss a wide variety of matters in great detail, whilst giving the impres-sion that critical issues have been addressed and approached from different viewpoints. This is the first significant statement about infighting among jihadis in Syria, and whilst Zawahiri seems keen to blame the turmoil on "external" factors such as criminality or alleged infiltration by the Assad regime, two key historical analogies that subsequently became prominent in his denunciation of this fitna [sedition/strife] emerge. These are comparisons with the fate of the Groupe Islamique Armé (GIA) that fought in the civil war in Algeria and became widely condemned as a jihadi outcast, and the infighting that spread throughout Afghanistan after Soviet withdrawal in 1989.

Zawahiri argues that the key to success for the militant movement is respecting popular support, marrying the objectives of the movements with the central grievances of the wider population and recognising the importance of communicating the message of the militant movements to the public. In this sense, Al-Qaeda, he argued, was a mission or a message before it was an organisation. This of course is a convenient position for a leader of a crumbling organisational structure to embrace, but nonetheless highlights the importance of public messaging.

Zawahiri discusses legal reform too, concentrating on constitutional developments in Egypt. This is a theme he has addressed on many previous occasions. Zawahiri's principal grievances are that Egypt's constitution only pays homage to Sharia through its second article, but does not implement it. Any subsequent attempts to articulate the importance of Sharia in more detail, he argues, have been meaningless.

The seventh Al-Sahab interview with Sheikh *mujahid* Ayman al-Zawahiri, may God protect him, the Amir of the Al-Qaeda organisation.

Part One, May 2014

[Al-Sahab introduction]

In the Name of God, the Most Beneficent, the Most Merciful

All the Muslim brothers, wherever they are, God's peace, compassion and blessings be upon you.

Al-Sahab Media Productions has the pleasure to host today Sheikh Ayman al-Zawahiri, may God protect him, for his seventh interview; we ask God, the mighty, to make it useful for us and the Muslims.

[Interview begins]

First, we say to Sheikh Ayman: God's peace, compassion and blessings be upon you, we welcome you as a guest of Al-Sahab Media Productions.

Sheikh Ayman al-Zawahiri: God's peace, compassion and blessings be upon you!

Interviewer: More than thirteen years have passed in the struggle between the mujahidin and the crusader—Zionist alliance and their cronies, and still the flame of this war burns; but in whose favour has the balance of the war tipped?

Al-Zawahiri: The balance of war has tipped towards the one who doesn't retreat from his land. Who retreated from Iraq and who didn't? Who retreated from Afghanistan and who didn't?

Interviewer: But Obama always reiterates that he crushed Al-Qaeda and it is on its way to defeat; he stressed this in his last State of the Union speech.

Al-Zawahiri: Obama reminds me of al-Mutanabbi's saying:

Life clears for an ignorant man or an idiot
For what has passed and what is expected

And for whoever falsifies the truths themselves
And overburdened with demanding the impossible will be greedy

He doesn't respect his audiences, as in the same speech he says that Al-Qaeda is spreading in Iraq, Syria, Yemen, Somalia, Algeria and Mali, and the members of Congress gave him applause, because their whole concern is to withdraw from Afghanistan with the least damage. I will add a line to the poem and say: Obama knows absolutely that Al-Qaeda is expanding in other places, praise be to God, and there will be a talk for every event, God permitting. And more important and serious than this, praise be to God, is that Al-Qaeda is a mission before it is an organisation or group and, in this sense, it is expanding more, praise be to God, and is widespread in all the Islamic world and amongst the powerless people in the world. My generous brother, there is an important historical fact which is that America is an empire that is disintegrating. It has been defeated in two major wars and it has been swept by a choking financial crisis that constantly bleeds its security budget. This descent was made possible by the glorious attacks on New York, Washington and Pennsylvania, and here the genius of the renewer, Imam Sheikh Osama bin Laden, may God have mercy upon him, becomes evident when he said: *"Today we are redrawing the map of the Islamic world to become a single state under the auspices of the caliphate."*

Interviewer: But they killed Sheikh Osama, may God have mercy upon him, and many of the mujahidin *leaders, so how can you say they didn't achieve their aims?*

Al-Zawahiri: Osama bin Laden sacrificed himself for his religion from his twenties [onwards] and he achieved the highest jihadi rank, the rank of martyrdom in the path of God. Whoever follows the path of jihad will not expect martyrdom, but also wishes for it. The killing of Osama bin Laden makes him a symbol to encourage the *ummah* [nation or community] to give more. The planes which bombard from the sky will not be able to gain victory on earth, for victory can only be achieved by those forces which can control the land and America is distant from this. Killing is psychologically painful as our dear ones depart from us, but it doesn't defeat the nations committed to jihad. The Americans were excessive in their acts of killing in Vietnam, Somalia, Iraq and Afghanistan, and they were defeated in all these places.

Interviewer: The bombing operations by drones are continuing: they have spread to Somalia and Yemen, and have come back again to Iraq, and they might spread to Sham [Syria]; don't you see that this way of confronting the mujahidin is constant and effective?

Al-Zawahiri: The bombing by drones will continue, and I expect it will increase, but whether it is effective, absolutely not! America bombards Afghanistan and Pakistan, and it is being defeated; it bombarded Iraq, and it was defeated; it bombarded Vietnam and completely destroyed it, and it was defeated. If America did not bomb with spy planes, it would bomb with heavy rockets. In the liberation wars, the retreating occupier will be harsher when they are defeated and in retreat. We have informed this criminal occupier for a period of thirteen years, and the *mujahidin* paid the price of victory with their lives and their families' lives and the steadfastness of [the jihadi] prisoners. Today, victory is achieved by them, praise be to God, in spite of all the bombs which will not save the Americans from defeat. So how can these planes be effective while Obama admits that Al-Qaeda is expanding and spreading?

Interviewer: There is a spying operation and recruitment of spies behind the strategy of drone bombings; how do you deal with this nasty war?

Al-Zawahiri: It is indeed a nasty war. We ask God for help, and we confront it at several levels, such as security, invocation and judicial. God almighty says: *"If you are suffering (hardships) then surely they (too) are suffering (hardships) as you are suffering, but you have hope from God (for the reward, i.e. Paradise) that for which they hope not."* {Sura 4 (The Women), 104} We hit them and they hit us, and who would forget what the hero Abu Djanah al-Khurasani, may God have mercy upon him, did to them? All the facts will be revealed one day, God willing! And the level of official Pakistani treason will be revealed for stabbing the *ummah* and its *mujahidin* in the back and their actual participation in a war against them. I sincerely call upon all those involved in this nastiness to repent before it is too late, and I confirm to Him that we, with God's help and success, will not shirk in our revenge of our martyrs, and we will be after the traitors as long as we have a pulse. They hear me very well, and they know very well the seriousness of the *mujahidin* and their determination. And those oppressed fugitive people whom God has granted to attack America in the heart of its homeland and its economic and military centres will plead to God to enable them to get the neck of every spy and traitor who doesn't declare his repentance and confirm the truth by revealing his role and the role of those who directed him and cooperated with him. I call upon every *mujahid* and Muslim who has dignity for Islam not shirk in their revenge of the martyred *mujahidin* against every spy and traitor, and to continue with this and to pass it on to their brothers' generation after generation. Has my message been received? O God, I passed the message; O God, I testify! Al-Mutanabbi says:

An ignorant extended in his ignorance and laughed
Until a hand came
If the lion's tusks appeared to be out
Don't think that the lion is smiling

Interviewer: I wanted to concentrate on the case of Sham [Syria], considering that is the most important struggle happening in our Islamic world today; but during the preparation of questions, the statements of Mahmoud Abbas came on the news when he said: We are not trying to drown Israel with refugees. He also said: We supported the survival of a unified Jerusalem. What are your comments on these statements?

Al-Zawahiri: In truth, I am not much surprised by the gaffes of Mahmoud Abbas, for he is a treacherous man who is selling out Palestine. However, I am surprised at the two factions: the first faction is the movements associated with Al-Amal Al-Islami, in spite of the fact that this traitor is their legal leader and their brother; the second faction is Al-Fatah, which claims that it is the movement which frees "the homeland", yet it has become the movement which is selling out its homeland and its citizens. And as for its homeland, in the region of 12 per cent of the citizens of Palestine, which was occupied in 1948, are content to be considered Israeli citizens. And I say to them: indeed, you have relinquished Islamic sovereignty and have satisfied yourselves with the fanaticism of nationalism and citizenship. And thus you have brought yourself low and you have separated yourselves from most of the homeland and most of its citizens. Your leader has surrendered the rights of refugees, thus pleasing Israel and America. Does there remain within you any remnant of religion or passion or zeal or honour? Do you sell out everything for the sake of the crumbs of this temporal existence?

Interviewer: Let us turn now to Sham/Syria. Perhaps you agree with me that the most important battle is taking place in Syria. Nowadays we hear about infighting between the ranks of the various jihadi groups. How did the situation develop that it got to the point where fighting developed between companions in jihad?

Al-Zawahiri: The infighting came about due to the victory of religious whims/ heresies, and ignorance and injustice against some. It is necessary for us to realise that the *mujahid* is not irreproachable [in his behaviour]; for the *mujahid* commits venial [minor] sins, and capital crimes. He commits that which corrupts his jihad and alters it from jihad for the sake of God to fighting for the sake of this temporal existence [*al-dunya*] and [human] desire. The noble Quran has resolved these issues:

God, the most praised, says: *(What is the matter with you?) When a single disaster smites you, although you smote (your enemies) with one twice as great, you say: "From where does this come to us?" Say (to them), "It is from yourselves (because of your evil deeds)." And God has power over all things.* {Sura 3 (The Family of Imran), 165} And He says: *And God did indeed fulfil His Promise to you when you were killing them (your enemy) with His Permission; until (the moment) you lost your courage and fell to disputing about the order, and disobeyed after He showed you (of the booty) which you love. Among you are some that desire this world and some that desire the hereafter.* {Sura 3 (The Family of Imran), 152} And He says: *Then after the distress, He sent down security for you. Slumber overtook a party of you, while another party was thinking about themselves and thought wrongly of God—the thought of ignorance. They said, "Have we any part in the affair?" Say: "Indeed, the affair belongs wholly to God."* {Sura 3 (The Family of Imran), 154} And He, the most praised, says: *Those of you who turned back on the day the two hosts met (i.e. the battle of Uhud), it was Satan who caused them to fail in their duty because of sins they had committed. But God, indeed, has forgiven them. For God is Oft Forgiving, Most Forbearing.* {Sura 3 (The Family of Imran), 155}

I do not rule out the presence of hostile penetration of the jihad amongst the *mujahidin*, and that penetration need not be intelligence gathering/spying. It may simply be criminal, or provocation between the *mujahidin*, or financial support conducted along a mistaken line/route.

Interviewer: What is your position on this fighting, and what efforts are you making to arrest it?

Al-Zawahiri: Our position on this fighting is that we issue the strictest warnings about it and we consider it to be a warning of potential calamity for the jihad in Syria. I do not rule out penetration by the regime in order to take control of the *mujahidin* in order to exterminate one another, and to bring about for the regime by their own hands (the *mujahidin*) that which cannot be realised [by the regime].

A statement was issued on my behalf inviting all to stop the fighting and for prosecution by a legal agency. We call for all *mujahidin* to refer the conflict to a Sharia committee for arbitration. It constitutes a mechanism for compelling all with its judgements, and this committee must be independent. All *mujahidin* and supporters of the jihad in Syria and elsewhere must take a position with regard to the situation, with the appropriate courtesy and good grace, and give prohibition against and disavow everyone who obstructs this organisation or fails to comply/feigns ignorance of this call/edict, or who does not abide by its decisions. And he who abides by this must not support, materially or spiritually, or be linked to him [who fails to comply], or assist [him] against his brothers. Rather, it is necessary that Islamic public opinion form a position against him and absolve him of his deeds. And let it be known that all who support him materially and spiritually thereby assist in the killing of the *mujahidin* and destruction of the jihad and can expect [to face] the consequences of their actions in this temporal existence and in the afterlife.

The removal of legitimacy is a very serious matter. In Algeria, when legitimacy was withdrawn from the armed Al-Jamaat Al-Islamiyya[1] it ceased [to operate]. In Afghanistan, when legitimacy was withdrawn from the warring factions after the withdrawal of the Russians they ceased [to operate]. On the other hand, when the legal community bestowed it [legitimacy] on the Taliban, they were victorious. I do not direct these remarks of mine to one organisation and not another, nor to one group and not another. Rather, I direct my remarks to all, without differentiation between Muslim and Muslim, and without differentiation between *mujahid* and *mujahid*.

At this juncture I must direct a message to every *mujahid* who is participating in the killing of his brothers, or who has committed an aggression against their wealth or things which they hold sacred [*hurumaat*] or possessions. I say this: the order of your Amir does not absolve you of responsibility; and no al-Zawahiri and no al-Golani[2] and no Hamawi[3] and no al-Baghdadi[4] will protect you against the punishment of God if you have committed aggression against your brother *mujahidin*. All those on Judgement Day will have no one who can rescue them from the reckoning [of their sins]. And if the orders of your Amir are to commit aggression against your brother *mujahidin*, do not obey him and demand of him that he send you to the front lines and the trenches [of the action] where you may face the criminal Baathist enemy and his Safavid [Iranian] allies. And to those of you who blow yourselves up amongst your brothers, or in their bases, know that you will die alone and you will be buried alone and you will be resurrected alone, and you will find yourself in the hands of your God alone; and you will answer for your deeds alone, nor will your Amir be with you in any of these situations, so prepare your response for that [your behaviour] on the grave day [the day of reckoning].

O *mujahid*, I know that you hastened to Syria because the word of God is supreme, and the words of those who disbelieve are lowest. So do not lose your way nor your direction. I warn you that some of the leadership will use you in their designs on the authority and titles and position and profit. And I say to you: If I ordered you to commit aggression against your fellow *mujahidin* and you did not obey me, and if I ordered you to blow yourself up amongst your fellow *mujahidin* and you did not obey me, I would not be able to do a thing against you on the Day of Judgement.

I demand from my brother *mujahidin* in Syria that they do not allow the secular [elements] to incite *fitna* [sedition/strife] between the supporters [*ansar*] and the emigrants [*muhajiroun*]. Nor must they tolerate enmity towards the emigrants on the pretext that they are not Syrians and we are Syrians, for that is blind fanaticism which is proscribed in Islam. We are all Muslims and thus not one of you may commit aggression towards an emigrant [*muhajir*] nor a supporter [*ansari*],[5] nor against his family nor his wealth nor his honour nor his dignity. And remember what the noble Quran says, it be praised: *And those who, before them, had homes (in Al-Madinah) and had adopted the faith love those who emigrate to them, and have no jealousy in their breasts for that which they have been given (from the booty of Bani Al-Nadir), and give the emigrants preference over themselves, even though they were in need of that. And whosoever is saved from his own covetousness, such are they who will be the successful.* {Sura 59 (Confrontation), 9}

Interviewer: Recently a declaration has been issued by the general leadership [of Al-Qaeda] confirming that there is no link with the Islamic State of Iraq and Syria. What are the circumstances behind this declaration?

Al-Zawahiri: The circumstances behind this resolution can be divided into two issues:

The first: it is the difference between two methods/approaches. Our approach is to focus on the false god of the age, America and its allies, the crusaders and the Zionists and their agents of treachery. They and their provocations against the jihad mobilised the *ummah* and so the peripheral battles were abandoned. Our approach is the preservation of blood [life], and operations are avoided in which blood is shed without justification in the markets and residential areas, but rather [they are restricted to] between the *mujahid* groups. Numerous statements have been issued on this by Sheikh Osama, and Sheikh Mustafa Abu al-Zaid, and Sheikh Attiya, and Sheikh Abu Yahya[6]—may God grant them mercy—just as I have discussed this subject on occasions as well. Therefore, we issued a document ("General Guidelines for the Work of Jihad") which we sent to all the brothers for consultation. And it was due to a fear of what is happening now that we issued this document. It may be that all realise now, after getting burned by the fire of this discord, just what the perils are that this document sought to avoid.

Our approach is also a desire to bring together the *ummah* and to unify it around the message of One-ness, and work towards the return of the rightly guided caliphate which is founded upon the consultation and agreement of Muslims, and to that end we published a document "Support for Islam" in order to bring together the two components of Islam and join them in a message of equality. Thus, we could not join the *ummah* together if our vision was a vision of absolute power over it, the usurper of its rights, committing aggression towards it, or the overpowering of it.

As for the second issue, it is the failure to meet obligations according to the principles of scholarly consensus.

Interviewer: Such as?

Al-Zawahiri: Such as the declaration of [the formation] of states without seeking authority, and without [prior] notification. When the direction came from the general leadership that we would not publicly announce any presence of Al-Qaeda in Syria, this issue was a point of agreement, even with the brothers in Iraq. So we were surprised by the announcement[7] that provided an opportunity to the Syrian regime and to America that they had hoped for. Also, it caused the general public in Syria to ask "Why does al-Qaeda bring disasters upon us? Is Bashar [al-Assad] not sufficient? Do they wish to bring America upon us also?"

And also, for example, the lack of adherence to decisions of Al-Qaeda in the division of authority or with regard to agreement on fighting in the *fitna* [sedition/strife]. Our dread was that amongst the most important reasons for the appearance of the well-known division in the Syria problem would be that bloody *fitna* which causes such unrest within the spirits of thousands of *mujahidin* today. It may be that all realise that if all had taken responsibility for [/ addressed] this division, then the blood of thousands would have been spared. This would have allowed them to dedicate their efforts exclusively to fighting the enemies of the Muslims rather than busying themselves with fighting Muslims. The last issue, which is of the utmost importance...

Interviewer: And what is that?

Al-Zawahiri: It is that Al-Qaeda, by the grace of God, is a message before it is an organisation. This is what Sheikh Osama bin Laden—may God grant him mercy—was so keen on, alongside his brothers in the Al-Qaeda group: that jihad is the keenest desire. If only you in the Al-Sahab Foundation would find the time to extract some of the written legacy of the sheikh, and his written correspondence with his brothers. The important thing is that Al-Qaeda, by the grace of God, is a mission before it is an organisation. If we distort this message, then we would lose/be damaged as if we had spread out as an organisation and in a physical fashion. We will fail in our Islamic mission, which is to incite the *ummah* to jihad against its enemies in order that Sharia will govern and that the caliphate shall return. Truly we are a mutual relationship; we provide a sound model for the *ummah*, and a message which matches words with deeds. Better for us this than that we be tens of thousands [in number] who the *ummah* are alienated from and also from their deeds and their conduct. And what if the *ummah* found us fighting one another over the spoils of war before reinforcing; and if we were trying to appropriate the right of the *ummah* and its most eminent and its best into the consultation [*shura*] and the government; and if the *ummah* found us participating in the combat of a *fitna* in which was shed the blood of our brother *mujahidin* and in which their sacred things [*hurumaat*] and wealth were violated; and if the *ummah* saw that we had lost the fruits of jihad before it had ripened with ill-considered behaviour, and hasty personal decisions, then how would the *ummah* believe in us? And how would it reconcile itself to us? Yet we offer our enemies the greatest opportunity to distort our reputation and to divert the community away from us. And the secular ones and the Americanised ones will say to the people: Look what the *mujahidin* are doing with some, what will they do with you?

And it may be that you heard the recent words of Hassan Nasrallah[8] in which he devotes his fighting [capability] to the criminal regime in Syria, which has violated the things held sacred [*hurumaat*] by Muslims for the last forty years, saying: He is trying to defend the people in Syria from the crimes of the *takfiris*.[9]

Interviewer: But why did you praise the Islamic State of Iraq previously?

Al-Zawahiri: My brothers and I were praising the good which was in it, and we were trying to improve that which was not thus [good] with advice and direction and orders, but we could not.

Interviewer: Were you not previously accused of being extremists, and the hawks of Al-Qaeda, whilst now you are accused of changing your approach? Yet some accuse you of deferment; is it true that there has been a change in your approach?

Al-Zawahiri: The approval of the people is of the utmost importance; do you not know? The crucial decisions are taken, by the grace of God, after consultation and agreement. And I do not imagine that I have changed my approach.

Interviewer: You are always calling for the mujahidin to broaden their engagement with the ummah *and that there has been no change of goal except that the* ummah *be within the ranks of the* mujahidin. *Yet how is this practical—for some describe what you call for as merely theoretical words?*

Al-Zawahiri: [Consider] the experience/example of the Taliban in Afghanistan and the support of the people for that against the militias of the warlords; and the experience/example of most of the *mujahidin* in Syria in their successful models of engagement of the *mujahidin* with the *ummah*.

Interviewer: You often call for the ummah *to participate in the consultation [shura], especially in choosing who should govern it. However, some respond to you that the* ummah *is not competent for this role and that this is the jurisdiction of specialists. So how do you respond?*

Al-Zawahiri: The *ummah* chooses from amongst its legally competent persons to represent it or for its governance, and does not choose any immoral person, or any deviant or anyone who is infected in terms of his religion. Thus the *ummah* chooses from amongst those who meet the conditions to take on those responsibilities, whether it be [in the form of] a deputyship [*niyaba*], an Emirate or an Imamate. Al-Sadiq [Abu Bakr, the first Caliph]—may God be pleased with him—when he remonstrated against the supporters [*ansar*]—may God be pleased with them—he said, in the account of al-Bukhari: *"This matter will only be known to this tribe of the Quraysh"*; and in the compilation of Ibn Abi Shayba: *"But you knew that this tribe of the Quraysh, within the rank of the Arabs, there was none but them [they had no equal], and they would not unify other than around one of their own."* And in his pledge of allegiance to Uthman Abd al-Rahman bin Awf—may God be pleased with him—said: *"And so, Ali, I reviewed the matter of the people and I found amongst them no equal to Uthman, so do not create your own path."* And he said: *"Pledge your allegiance to the Sunna [tradition] of God and his Prophet and the two Caliphs who succeed him."* Thus Abd al-Rahman pledged allegiance to him, and the people pledged allegiance to him, as did the emigrants [*muhajiroun*] and the supporters [*ansar*] and the commanders of the soldiers, and the Muslims.

Interviewer: Let's turn to Egypt and the situation there. The swift consecutive developments and the victims are well known. Dead and injured fell in their scores at every protest and the numbers arrested exceed 20,000. What is your position on what is happening in Egypt?

Al-Zawahiri: What happened in Egypt is a crime committed by the Americanised army and the secularists and the crusaders and the separatists and the party of the liar, Sisi, in order to enable the Americanised secular army to rule Egypt. This is a crime which must be resisted and defended against by every legal means possible.

Interviewer: We seldom look in detail at the situation in Egypt. I would ask you to evaluate the popular movements which have come out against the army and their secular allies. Do you think this approach is likely to lead to a result or not?

Al-Zawahiri: In order for the people and their vanguard to change the corrupt rule, they must first recognise why they should change and how they should change. As to the why, it is necessary for the leadership of the loyal and noble *ummah* to pay attention to the angry populace, for they must resist in order to strengthen the rule of Sharia, and to liberate the country from external control, and purge it of corruption within. They [the *ummah*] must be faithful to their Lord, and to themselves, and to their people. They must not try to consume the energy of angered people in labyrinths and unfruitful paths as happened with the revolution of 25 January [2011]. It continued on its way with the leading elements in situ not directing popular energy towards real change. They attempted to reach accommodation and to bargain with the army, the secularists and crusaders and agents of America, and caused the revolution to disappear. I would like every noble freeman in Egypt to compare the slogans and emblems of the *intifada* [uprising] in Syria with those in Egypt. In the early stages in Syria the slogan of the people was "Our leader forever is Sayyidna [our master] Mohammed." May God pray for him and grant him peace (peace be upon him). In Egypt, the slogans were mixed: many of the associates tried the Islamic movement, despite the fact that the clear majority were for the secular, and in the main its greatest role was the over-throw of Hosni Mubarak. So mutual accord was reached on the slogans, such as "Long live freedom, social justice and human dignity". But they had not the courage to say "Islamic law". They did not say it at the height of the revolution, but they said it after that, and after the military council had established itself in government and had seized control of matters. Most of the Islamic move-ments reached an agreement with it [the council] and it slowly moved them towards the quagmire of secular democracy. Time was lost, and this require-ment [for democracy] in the vortex of haggling and bargaining and alliances and desire had the effect of giving satisfaction to the West. Therefore, we call on the people to correct their revolution and to rejuvenate its progress by making its slogan "Islamic law is the way of freedom and social justice and human dignity".

Interviewer: Right, so all this was about why to change. I would like from you now a response on how to change; as I said, I would like an answer from you on what I asked: The popular movements which came out against the army and its allies, do you think that this approach will lead to a result?

Al-Zawahiri: You see, I would remind you of a general principle: the oppressed person is entitled to defend himself against an attack on his religion and his honour and his soul and his wealth with whatever he can. He may resist through words or protest or combat or demonstration or by occupation/sit-in. This is the basic principle, and the criminal oppressor has no right to curtail the way in which the oppressed resists him, so he must face it. However, every legal means is possible and available to the oppressed. Nor may anyone else forbid the legal means of resistance against oppression and defence against attack. America and the West wish to limit the opposition towards them by the *ummah* and their agents to peaceful methods only. All the while they use the most atrocious means against us. So the people of Islam and the zeal of the free in Egypt must choose those means which are suitable to lead them to victory, be that through demonstration or sit-in or combat or through communiqué or defending against the obscure and the lies. It is for them to choose [from amongst those options] which they wish [to pursue] in terms of a method or methods.

Interviewer: But there are also armed opposition and jihadi operations. What is your position on those?

Al-Zawahiri: We bless every jihadi operation against the Zionists and against the Americanised army to defend their borders, and against internal criminals and against the US agencies committing aggression towards Muslims; as long as such an operation is committed through legal precepts, to avoid the spilling of the inviolable blood of Muslims and others, or aggression against their most sacred beliefs and possessions.

We would like to advise our brothers that in order to succeed, any armed opposition must mobilise public support. Experience has shown that without this support combat does not turn into victory or success. Thus they must avoid any action, even though it may be legal they should abandon it, if it should alienate the *ummah* from them, or if the enemy media could distort it. We would advise them [also] to base their actions on advice from the best of people [people of good character] and experience and their agreement on a party line for their movement. Nor should they independently make crucial decisions. As I see it, the most important action they can take, which will mobilise popular

111

support around them, is action against the Zionists. Then come operations which link to the Muslim *ummah*, by defending them against aggression from the Americanised army and internal criminals. In sum, they must be very careful in selecting their operations, and also very assiduous in conveying their *dawa* [call/benediction] to the Muslim community, and be sure to make them aware about who their enemies are and to explain the extent of the vileness of their crimes. They should also be very eager to explain to the Muslim *ummah* repeatedly about the reason for each operation and its goals.

Interviewer: You have had experience of armed opposition with the regime. In light of this experience, what is your advice to the mujahidin in Egypt?

Al-Zawahiri: My advice to the *mujahidin* is that you must be intent on two basic issues in order to succeed in any armed conflict with a despotic, oppressive criminal power.

The first issue: they must have a base of popular support, and associated with this there must be between them and the people of the *ummah* a common cause, such as attacking Zionism or defence of the *ummah* against those who would commit aggression against them. It is necessary also that they avoid any operation which will alienate the *ummah* from them, or where the *ummah* does not understand its motives.

The second issue: the war of *dawa* and messaging is no less important, and rather sometimes it is more important than the military combat battle.

Interviewer: Many in the leadership of the Nour party have said that the amended constitution is better than the constitution that preceded it, as they stood in imposing form as a rank of military and secular. How do you assess their position?

Al-Zawahiri: The Hizb al-Nour al-Salafi, or as I call it "Hizb al-Zour [Party of the Fakes of] al-Sisi",[10] practises a campaign of deceit and deception on behalf of the Sisi coup. The key elements of this campaign are seeking to demonstrate that the current constitution is the best constitution, in clear contradiction of its previous position and in contradiction of any sound logic. In so doing it debases itself in the view of Muslims and accords no respect to its audience.

I say first: this constitution and the one which preceded it were both void. For both were secular, rooted in secularism and the popular nation state, which legislates for the will of the majority. Some of the disadvantages of the previous constitution were demonstrated in "Unifying the Word Toward the Word of Monotheism".[11] As for this constitution, there are many aspects to its falsehood.

Interviewer: How can there be many aspects to its falsehood when supporters of the constitution say that it guarantees the second article, which in their view will lead to the application of Sharia?

Al-Zawahiri: This article is not expected to lead to the application of Sharia. For there are two serious defects associated with it: the first is that it is unable to apply Sharia, and the second is that it is governed, not governing.

Interviewer: Why do you describe it as "unable to apply Sharia"?

Al-Zawahiri: I describe it thus for two reasons. The first reason is that it [the second article of the constitution] specifies the "principles of Sharia" but not the "statutes of Sharia". The "principles of Sharia" is a generic term that is of no benefit for government. The author of the constitution from the constitution of 1971 to the current one—whom [Yasser] Al-Barhami and the Nour Party praise effusively—deliberately laid it down and committed it so that it would evade the statutes of Sharia. And yet Yasser Barhami himself attacked this term [principles of Sharia] because it would lead to avoidance of the statutes of Sharia. But the article of which he was so proud, Article 219, which interpreted the principles of Sharia, stipulates: " *'The principles of Sharia' include the evidence of fundamental jurisprudential precepts [textual proof] and also its esteemed sources in the doctrine of the Sunni community [as understood by the legal schools].*" This article abrogated the constitution, as well as Article 4, which stipulates: *"The view of the senior religious scholars of al-Azhar are taken in matters related to Sharia."*[12]

Interviewer: What is the second reason?

Al-Zawahiri: The second reason is that it specifies that the principles of Sharia are the main source for legislation. Being the main source for legislation, this means that it permits for the existence of sources other than the main ones. If we suppose that all the laws and regulations of the state are in conformity and agreement with Sharia, but if it [the state] drew up one law and enacted it, it would be incompatible with Sharia, so it would become a non-Islamic state. It would be necessary to do battle over it with the consensus of scholars in order to come back from that [i.e. non-Islamic status].

Interviewer: It has been argued that the main source does not allow for secondary sources to oppose it.

Al-Zawahiri: These words don't require a response; for they lack evidence, and because the structure of the article [2 of the constitution] does not indicate that. Let me give you an example: if the Imam said to the worshippers: I will read 90 per cent of my prayers for you from the Quran, but only 10 per cent of them from the Torah or from the Bible, or from verses of poetry—in order to explain what I want—is his appointment to the Imamate void, and is the conduct of prayer behind him [i.e. with him in front leading] void?

If a judge were to say to you: I make 99 per cent of my judgements according to Sharia, but in 1 per cent of cases I judge in contradiction to it: is this judge acting legally? Is his appointment [as a judge] void? Is an appeal to him void?

Would one accept, if it were said "You are the main husband to your wife"? Or "you are the main father to your son"? Or "you are the main owner of your wealth"? Would the president of the republic be satisfied if it were said to him "You are the main president of the republic"? Would the judges of the constitutional court accept it if it were said "The constitutional court is the main court in disputes over the legal constitution"?

Would Sisi accept it if he were told "You are the main Defence Minister"?

Would Barhami accept it if he were told "You are the main secretary for your group"?

If they would not accept it in their temporal existence, then why accept it in their religion?

Interviewer: But Yasser al-Barhami argues that the preamble to the new constitution stipulates that the principles of Sharia interpret the rulings of the constitutional court, including a ruling in 1985 requiring the legislature to refer to Sharia.[13]

Al-Zawahiri: The response to that is that the constitutional court has made rulings which clash violently and clearly with Islam. It rejected the argumentation in Article 2 of the constitution to invalidate some of the laws which were divergent from Sharia. A number of rulings were issued by the constitutional court rejecting the challenge of unconstitutionality against Articles 274 and 277, which permit adultery and link punishment to the wish of the husband. This ruling was based on the refutation provided by the two articles which diverged from Sharia, which were mentioned in Article 2 of the constitution. That was in 1990, 2000 and 2004, that is to say, after the judgment that al-Barhami applied. There was also a previous judgement of the supreme constitutional court in 1993, that is to say after the judgement which al-Barhami and the Hizb al-Zour clung to, that Article 2 of the constitution does not apply retrospectively. Thus, all laws which precede it [1985], and this comprises most of the laws, are legally enforceable. However, many of them, if not most of them, are divergent from and sometimes counter to Sharia. And since the vast majority of laws were issued before Article 2, and before the appearance of the current constitution, this means that this constitution accepted the continuation of the vast majority of laws that diverge—for the greater part—and even clash with Sharia.

Interviewer: One might infer from what you say that the issue of a group of rulings from the constitutional court is a serious [matter] and should result in the rejection of rulings which clash with Sharia.

Al-Zawahiri: Of course. I wonder what al-Barhami and the Nour Party will do with these judgements which very clearly and evidently call for blatant unbelief [*kufr*]. Will they cancel them or will they stay silent? It's a serious situation.

Interviewer: What is?

Al-Zawahiri: This court rules in favour of the constitution whose judgements diverge considerably from Sharia—as will be explained—and which takes its legitimacy from the wishes of the majority and not from Sharia. It can chop and change on the basis of the inclinations of the people. Thus, tomorrow the council of deputies could repeal Article 2 completely, and put that to a referendum—and then who is the real ruler, Sharia or the wishes of the people? And who has sovereignty in this constitution, Sharia or the wishes of the people?

Interviewer: Do there not exist in the constitution and the laws good measures for choosing a judge?

Al-Zawahiri: The selection of judges is not conditional on the constitution, nor the laws, nor legal justice. There is something more serious than that. Neither the constitution nor Islamic laws may lay down any conditions on any office of state. The equality of all citizens is underlined in this regard, and this situation was one of the reasons why Judge Abd al-Ghafaar Mohammed stipulated on the matter of the Great Jihad [as the court case that indicted over 300 Islamists for Sadat's assassination is known] that Sharia is not applied in Egypt, despite the existence of Article 2 in the constitution with the same current stipulation.

Interviewer: Would you say that the secular judiciary accepts that other articles contradictory to Islam hinder Article 2?

Al-Zawahiri: Yes. This judgement became final according to the understanding of the jurisprudents, and even Hosni Mubarak approved it himself.

Interviewer: Did Hosni Mubarak approve it himself despite the fact that Sharia was not being applied in Egypt?

Al-Zawahiri: Yes.

Interviewer: And is this legal situation still in force today?

Al-Zawahiri: Yes, as acknowledged by the Egyptian judiciary and approved by the state in the form of the president on the matter of this law. The judiciary and the state accepted that Article 2 of the constitution did not lead to rule by Sharia, because there are other articles in the constitution which contradict it.

Interviewer: Judge Abd al-Ghafaar Mohammed, by his own description a secular judge, who presided over the greatest legal cases within the Egyptian judiciary, did not say what Yasser Barhami and his party said to him; except to say that the articles contradictory to Islam in the constitution restrict Article 2 of the constitution.

Al-Zawahiri: No, no, he said the opposite. He said that with the existence of Article 2 in the constitution [the following had been] established firmly in the conscience of the court: Sharia could not be applied in Egypt due to the existence of articles in the constitution and laws which contradict Sharia.

There is also another matter: the constitution must rule over the judges of the constitutional court, and not the other way around. Thus it is necessary for expressions of the constitution to be very clear and definitive, in order that even the judges of the constitutional court are bound by their full content.

Furthermore, this court demonstrates the extent of corruption that has taken root in it; how it tried to thwart all efforts of the groups affiliated with Islamic activity in every way through the abolition of the people's council and the abolition of the foundation committee for the drafting of the constitution; and through its decision, as expected, to dissolve the Shura [consultative] council, as well as other matters not on record.

Interviewer: Indeed, so this relates to the fact that Article 2 is not able to apply Sharia. What about the second drawback that you mentioned, namely that it is governed, not governing?

Al-Zawahiri: It is governed, not governing; because there are numerous other articles in the constitution which restrict it, and in some cases clash with it. Let us suppose as an example that Article 2 stipulated that Sharia was the source for legislation. This is not the case, but we are hypothesising—and there was one of the articles which was contrary to it and restricted it, and could even modify or nullify it, for example: the article which stipulates that sovereignty belongs to the people, and that referendum is the highest source for legislation; and that the Council of Deputies have the right to propose amendments to the constitution and put them forward for referendum; or that the majority of the council has the right to repeal Article 2 of the constitution, or stand in opposition to Sharia if that were accepted in a referendum and it became a legal requirement, demanding its implementation and making it obligatory by constitutional contract and ratifying it and making it compulsory to submit to it. An example of that would be if a court had a judge who judged according to Sharia, and above this judge was another council of judges amongst whom there were a Muslim and a non-Muslim, one who was content with Sharia and one who was not content with it; and they ruled according to inclination and fancy with no obligation upon them; and they ratify that which they wish from the judgement of the first judge, or reject or amend it. Is this an Islamic court ruling by Sharia, or is the judge who ruled by Sharia ruled by the council above him, ruling by inclination and whim and fancy?

[Examples include] Article 11, which stipulates that there should be equality between men and women with regard to all rights. Or Article 93, which specifies the obligation of the state to comply with all treaties and conventions on human rights. Similarly the rescinded Article 44,[14] which forbade insulting messengers and prophets. Or Article 65, which guaranteed freedom of thought and opinion without restriction, whose wording stated that freedom of belief [worship] is absolute. Also Article 67, which restricted the questioning of perpetrators of creative excesses for the sake of social and cultural stability, except where there is incitement to violence or discrimination.

Interviewer: But Yasser al-Barhami claims that all these articles are limited by Article 2 of the constitution, which is interpreted according to the collective rulings of the constitutional court, as stated in the preamble to the constitution. This would be consistent with those collective rulings issued in 1985, requiring the legislature to resort to Sharia.

Al-Zawahiri: Firstly, I explained earlier that Article 2 was impotent and would not lead to Sharia on the basis of the wording of rulings by the constitutional court about constitutionality. Rulings concerning adultery run contrary to Sharia, and according to the wording of a ruling of that constitutional court on constitutionality, most of the laws on the pretext of precedence [sit above] Article 2. [Likewise other laws have precedence], according to a ruling of the Supreme Court of State Security in the matter of jihad, which was ratified by the head of state and president of the republic. Furthermore, this ruling was issued in 1985, 29 years ago. Was Sharia applied? On the contrary, after that, rulings from the same court were in conflict with Sharia. If we were to say that Article 2 stipulates the jurisdiction of Sharia, then a secular or anti-Islamic or crusader objection could be raised, [wherein though] Article 2 is a supreme article [there are] numerous articles in clear contradiction of Islam and clashing with it that restrict Article 2. Thus, al-Barhami uses the same argument and we enter into a fruitless debate. [Who knows] which is the supreme article and which is the restricted article?

Interviewer: If this is a fruitless debate, what is the cause of it?

Al-Zawahiri: The cause of it is collusion between al-Barhami and the Al-Zour Party, using smoke and mirrors and twisting and turning around the constitution. It bestows upon the Americanised secular Sisi coup a fake Islamic veneer.

Interviewer: But Yasser al-Barhami and his party claim that they defended the articles [that enshrine Islam] in the constitution, and that they did not sell out the faith, nor did they change their positions.

Al-Zawahiri: Unfortunately, al-Barhami has no respect for the intelligence of his audience. Throughout the drafting of the previous constitution, the al-Barhami group insisted on the inclusion of the term "rule of Sharia" and not "Sharia principles" and threatened to withdraw from the constitution drafting committee—the ruling was in 1985—which al-Barhami was talking about and is invoking now. This judgement from that constitutional court had been there for one day when al-Barhami objected and said it must be "rule of Sharia" and not "principles of Sharia". So what has changed? Yet the al-Barhami group did not accept the interpretation of the Muslim Brotherhood that the rule of the constitutional court is equal to the rule of Sharia. So what has changed? Al-Barhami himself said that insistence on adherence to the expression "principle of Sharia" is to evade the "rule of Sharia" and that was the judgement of the existing constitutional court, so what has changed? More than that, Yasser al-Barhami could see the falsity of the methods of the parliamentary work.

Interviewer: In your opinion, what has changed?

Al-Zawahiri: What has changed is the position of al-Barhami and his party. They were far away from the tank [i.e. their closeness to the military], but today they are now at the top of the tank. And so they feasted upon democracy with the commander of the tank, then turned against one another.

Interviewer: Would you say that there was an intention to produce the constitution in this way?

Al-Zawahiri: Of course. There is a serious question hanging over al-Barhami and the Al-Zour Party and all those who prevented the implementation of Sharia. Why is there an insistence on obscurity and twisting and turning and ambiguous expressions, as if the constitution has turned into a game of mysteries? This article can only be understood through this article, and they claim that this article restricts that article. They try to convince you, after your mind has been confused, that another article is not anti-Islamic. Why is there this insistence on not giving a clear and unequivocal statement, and evidence that Sharia is the source for legislation and invalidates anything which stands against it; nor that this text [Sharia] supersedes the constitution and that no referendum nor vote has any effect upon it; nor any decisions, nor article, nor law, nor ruling of the constitutional secular court, nor any of the scattered remnants of the Mubarak camp? Why this insistence on avoiding clarity and plain speaking, and interfering with the belief of the *ummah* and its fate and with serious matters? This question will continue to hang over al-Barhami and the Al-Zour Sisi Party[15] and all those who cooperate over this "smoke and mirrors" and twisting and turning.

Interviewer: They may claim that this is all that circumstances permit, and that nothing more is feasible.

Al-Zawahiri: Why is nothing more feasible? Can their tongues not speak, nor their hands write, nor their eyes see, nor their minds discern? Why can they not demand that Sharia be the source of legislation? Why can they not abide by that? What is preventing them? What drives them away from that [course]?

Interviewer: They claim that they are seeking for the country to settle down and for the situation to become calm.

Al-Zawahiri: They are seeking for Sisi and his gang to settle in and for matters to calm down, thus paving the way for them. Unfortunately, we have to recognise that al-Barhami and the Al-Zour Party were one of the US—Saudi instruments in the plot to seize control of power in Egypt by the Americanised army and the secularists and the crusaders and the Mubarak criminals.

Interviewer: But they would claim that they are trying to extinguish civil strife and prevent bloodshed.

Al-Zawahiri: But they were the cause of the shedding of sacred blood of thousands. The Americanised secular army took advantage of al-Barhami to frighten and threaten the (Muslim) Brotherhood: if they touched any of the pillars of the rule of Hosni Mubarak, they would resist them in the street, despite the fact that the al-Barhami and Sisi camps had banned demonstrations in the 25 January revolution. And yet they threatened that the pillars [of the "deep state"] and men of Mubarak would remove the [Muslim] Brotherhood from power through street protest. However, when the military shed the blood of the Brotherhood in the street, the al-Barhami and Sisi camps did not protest in the streets. And there is a point I want to alert all thinking and sensible people to, and that is the conformity in approach and behaviour between the Sisi Al-Nour Party and the government of the House of Saud.

Interviewer: What do you mean by that?

Al-Zawahiri: Abd al-Aziz al-Saud,[16] since meeting with Roosevelt on board the cruiser *Quincy* in the Great Bitter Lake towards the end of the Second World War—a meeting of which the Saudis were proud—transferred his allegiance from Britain to America, which (now) presides as leader of the West. During this meeting the mutual understanding between Abd al-Aziz al-Saud and Roosevelt was sealed, such that America would protect the Al Saud kings in exchange for their complete cooperation with America. Thus was formed the Saudi–Western accord. It pretended to uphold the faith and to fight heresy and polytheism, but there are two serious issues [to consider]: the first is the service of American interests both within and outside the Saudi kingdom; and the second is the immorality and corruption and oppression that is rife amongst the Al Saud and their entourage and their supporters. This antithetical [to Islam] Saudi pact is consistent with the behaviour of the Salafi Al-Nour Party or, rather, the al-Sisi Al-Zour party. They pretend to uphold the belief in *tawheed* [the oneness of God], yet all the while not endangering the interests of Sisi and the Americanised military, and working faithfully for the success of the US plan in Egypt and across the region.

Interviewer: How so?

Al-Zawahiri: They imbued the Americanised military regime in Egypt with an Islamic hue—albeit false—so that it can claim that it has the support of the Islamic movement.

Interviewer: But are not all Salafis in Egypt like that?

Al-Zawahiri: Let me be clear: there are many who claim to be Salafi who are not. Because it is unimaginable that a Salafi would come to power with secularists embracing Sharia. Al-Barhami and the Al-Zour Party are not Salafis, they are "Sisi-ists". As for Egypt, she is full of the best of people, who have righteousness and knowledge and piety, and many of them stood up against al-Barhami and the al-Sisi Al-Zour Party.

Interviewer: We'll leave it there for now and continue our discussion in the second part of this interview, God willing. Thank you, Noble Sheikh, and thank you to our brothers who are watching. Until part two.

Al-Zawahiri: May God reward you, peace be with you, and the mercy of God and his blessings.

Part Two

[Al-Sahab introduction]

> In the name of God, the Merciful and Compassionate. O Muslims everywhere, peace be upon you and the mercy of God and his blessings. Al-Sahab Media Productions is pleased to complete the second part of its seventh interview with Sheikh Ayman al-Zawahiri—may God protect him—and we ask God that we and all Muslims may profit by it.

> Sheikh Ayman al-Zawahiri, peace be upon you and the mercy of God, and his blessings. You are a welcome guest at the Al-Sahab Foundation again in the second part of our discussion with you.

Al-Zawahiri: And upon you be peace and the mercy of God and his blessings.

Interviewer: We stopped in the first part of the interview when we were discussing the position of the Al-Nour Party. However, I would make one observation and that is: Noble Sheikh, don't forget that the Muslim Brotherhood entered into a mutual agreement with the military before the Al-Barhami group. They promoted him [Sisi] twice in the space of nearly a year from Major General to Lieutenant General then to General. And Morsi went to the Interior Ministry on the day of his victory to reassure them that he would do them no harm.

Al-Zawahiri: Correct, and unfortunately this is the bitter truth. Many raced to appease the military and the secularists and the criminals, but all this haste did no good. This is a very important point, and in truth it is two points. The first is that we want to learn from the mistakes which were committed and initiate a new beginning to unite all the workers for Islam, and unify them around the single word *"tawheed"* [oneness of God]. Second, the Muslim public should know that there are personalities who are not at the appropriate level to be in conflict with the Americanised military, nor with the secularists or those who back them from the crusader Zionist alliance. These personalities do not comply when they are asked to refrain from repeating the same cycles of futility and failure.

Interviewer: The Muslim Brotherhood continues its condemnation of violence and its resistance to the current regime in spite of the fact that dozens of their youth have died and thousands of their leaders and members are shackled in prisons. What is the value [secret] of pursuing this method of [political] change, given that they have been accused of terrorism (like so many other Islamists)?

Al-Zawahiri: As I said previously, it is the right of the oppressed and the victim of aggression that the attacker of his religion and his honour and his property and his soul should fight him through every Sharia means. There are those who are trying to portray the confrontation (with the attacker to gain recompense) as a crime, but this is talk that is not supported by reason or law. However, the leaders of the world's criminals welcome this kind of talk. One must fight the attacker who violates the religion and honour and property and soul through all Sharia means, amongst which are: *dawa* [benediction], *Bayan* [rhetoric], and protest, and sit-in, and combat, and boycott, and all forms of passive resistance and active resistance, and peaceful resistance and violent resistance; taking the decision to start fighting revolves around [self] interest; and the victim of aggression has the right to choose appropriate means to confront this aggression. Let me give you by way of example what happened in Syria and Libya. The demonstrations began peacefully, but then in the face of the violence of the regime, the people were unable to find a means of resisting the oppression other than through combat.

Interviewer: But some accuse you of inciting violence and civil strife and conflict whilst not thinking about providing a decent existence for the downtrodden Egyptian people.

Al-Zawahiri: We only resorted to fighting after all avenues of change were blocked off. I myself participated in demonstrations against Gamal Abd al-Nasser and Anwar Sadat. However, how can you provide a decent existence for the citizens if the rulers and the leadership and the heads and leadership of the army and those responsible for security are thieves and robbers and looters and embezzlers and the disreputable and dancers and homosexuals? The system of corruption in Egypt spread and became a cancer comprising all sorts of moral, financial and social corruption. See how the 25 January revolution was stolen—it was stolen by the Americanised army and the secularists, and the Al-Nour Party which banned participation in it [the revolution] and returned the remnants of the Mubarak regime [to power] again.

Interviewer: And what was the main cause of this theft?

Al-Zawahiri: The fundamental reason is the retreat of many of the movements associated with Islam in the face of secularists and agents of international powers. They retreated in both their principles and their methods and they agreed to open up to the arbitration of Islam via non-Islamic arbitration. Is it reasonable that the Islamic-affiliated movements should accept entrance into political activity based on a law which forbids the parties from participating on a religious basis? Why this self-defeat and behavioural withdrawal when they [Islamic movements] represent the majority? They retreated in the face of secular forces and the leadership of the international criminals in numerous fields, starting with the pledge not to apply Sharia; then the acceptance of treaties of surrender; then participation in the siege of Gaza; then support for corruption in the name of tourism; then submission to the structure of the corrupt judiciary; then the pledge not to exterminate the pillars of the former regime. Then when the secularists, and the Americanised ones and the crusaders bared their canine teeth and began their killing and the destruction, they behaved towards them as if they were lambs, and those who did not show the courage of lions were devoured by the wolves.

Interviewer: What is behind this campaign of getting Egypt to return to military rule again and the appointment of Sisi as the successor to rule in Egypt?

Al-Zawahiri: What is behind this campaign is that the law of strength governs the world, and the strongest devours the weakest. The goal of all the political deception that took place from the time that Mubarak stood down until the election of Sisi was to dissipate completely the energy of the volcano that was the anger of the people, just as a roaring torrent would lose its power if it spread out into the middle of a quagmire or jungle. Egypt is the heart of the Arab and Muslim worlds, and it is the gateway which opens on to Jerusalem, God willing. Therefore the Islamic forces must brush aside/ remove the government there, whatever the level of affiliation of those forces to Islam; and they wish to bring in another force from abroad to rule Egypt, and resist any movements affiliated with Islam. What helped them in that was the retreat and the hesitance and the great weakness of the movements affiliated with Islam, which claimed for a long time that they informed people about politics; and then it became clear that even the political fundamentals of the world eluded them. What also helped them in that is that there are movements affiliated with Islamic activity which are driven by money and direction from the Gulf.

Interviewer: This leads us on to discussion about the revolutions in the Arab world in general and the escalating struggle between the secular parties and the movements affiliated with Islamic activity. This is in spite of the fact that at the beginning of these revolutions it appeared that there was coordination between the secularists and the Islamists, especially in Egypt and Tunisia. What has been the cause of the change?

Al-Zawahiri: The secularists only remained silent until the absorption of the energy of popular anger, which mainly assisted in crushing the Islamic movements. Then when many of the movements associated with Islamic activity got lost in the vortex of political bargaining, the secularists and the military attacked them with Gulf money, and US planning, and Israeli provocation and crusader imperiousness.

Interviewer: But why did the relationship between the two sides turn to a bloody struggle in Egypt, whereas in Tunisia they achieved cooperation and agreement?

Al-Zawahiri: They did not achieve cooperation and agreement in Tunisia, but one side got to dictate the weakness and subservience of the other. Unfortunately, the side which was subservient was the one that had the support of the majority. Which goes to show that strength is strength of the heart and soul and not strength of numbers.

Interviewer: But some say that the Islamists of Al-Nahda [Party in Tunisia] avoided civil strife by surrendering power to the secularists in the expectation of returning it [to power] again, and stronger.

Al-Zawahiri: The surrender by the leadership of the Awakening [Al-Nahda] is not the first instance; rather it is an established and consistent policy. Al-Ghannouchi[17] portrayed himself to the West as a moderate alternative who could look after their interests and who could deliver them from the extremists. The primary reason that permitted the Awakening to come to power was the presence of the *mujahidin* in the Islamic Maghreb. They [al-Ghannouchi et al.] thoroughly used them [the *mujahidin*] for their own ends in terms of passing a secular constitution and dissipating popular anger, though they had had the sympathies of the great majority in the Islamic movements. After all this, orders were issued from Paris and Washington and carried out by al-Ghannouchi, who needs only a telephone call to offer a new surrender. One is surprised at what is happening in Tunisia. When Ali Abd al-Razeq released his book in Egypt in the 1930s, *Islam and the principles of governance*, a Tunisian Imam confronted him: Sheikh Mohammed al-Khadar Hussein, the Sheikh of al-Azhar, and Sheikh Mohammed al-Taher bin Aashour, Sheikh of the al-Zaytouna Mosque—may God grant him mercy—wrote a book entitled *Refutation of the book "Islam and the principles of governance"* and a second book entitled *Scientific refutation of the book "Islam and the principles of governance"*. After the judicial error of Ali Abd al-Razeq was defeated in Egypt, it returned and nurtured a new generation of adherents and their descendants to its thinking in Tunisia on knowledge and jihad and *Ribat* [defence of your religion]. But they went to extremes and even exceeded [the judicial error]. If Ali Abd al-Razeq had said "There is no governance in Islam", they would have said "There is no Islam in governance". I would urge everyone in the Awakening Movement who possesses Islamic zeal to resist these surrenders and slips and to raise his allegiance to Islam over his allegiance to the group and the party.

Interviewer: Why does the West, and at its head the US, not accept the results of the elections in Egypt and Tunisia? And why is it trying to remove the Muslim Brotherhood and the Awakening Movement from government, in spite of their victories in the elections? The Brotherhood has even won in Egypt five times in succession.

Al-Zawahiri: Democracy is a Western game, and it is not possible to practise it when it is not in accordance with the will of America, nor to practise it in a fashion whereby it presents the merest suspicion of a threat to the West, the US and Israel. The West considers all who subscribe to Islam as an enemy, no matter what they concede to it [the West]. Even if they had regarded the elections to have the appearance of the very highest form of democracy, the fact that democracy is associated with the movements linked to Islam means that it is not more [important] than the elections. It means the renunciation of the link to Islam, no matter whether this link is tenuous, and acceptance of Western values and beliefs. And there is a serious point that I would like to draw attention to...

Interviewer: And what is that?

Al-Zawahiri: The West does not wish to ally itself with Islamic movements, no matter how much it has achieved their breakdown and collapse. However, it wants to use them to deceive the *ummah* for the furtherance of its interests, precisely as we discussed concerning the unholy Saudi-US pact. It claims to defend the faith through devoted service to the American plan. Thus, after it had allowed the Brotherhood and the Awakening [Al-Nahda] to take power for a temporary period, thereby easing and releasing popular pressure and appeasing popular sentiment, they then moved to a transitional stage after which they removed these parties from power. The Awakening, as is its custom, was malleable and tame and they appeared under a submissive Islamic cover, crouched in the left-hand corner behind the "bishops of evil" and the crusader campaign, standing in formation behind Sisi.

Interviewer: Everyone was speaking in favour of the Turkish model, and saying that the Islamic world should follow this model. This is what many of the leaders in the West declared, but we note that they have now reversed that position to the extent that they are now seeking the overthrow of Erdoğan—at least so he claims. Perhaps a preferred model exists, namely the Tunisian model, in which Al-Nahda attained a majority then conceded power to the secularists. A secular constitution was allowed to be written, from which anything that mentioned Islam was removed. In fact, there are clauses which criminalise he who adheres to his religion.

Al-Zawahiri: There is no doubt that the al-Ghannouchi model is the preferred model in the view of the West. Erdoğan, in spite of all his failings and his considerable collaboration with Israel, has a firm grip on power. As for al-Ghannouchi, he surrendered power after he renounced Sharia and offered Muslims as sacrifices to attain Western approval. However, they [the West] did not bestow upon him their approval and were distant towards him and thus he lost [both] his religion and [in] this temporal existence.

Interviewer: We now turn to Yemen and the significant events there: the seizure and control by the Shia of many districts, while the Yemeni government and army are busy fighting against the mujahidin *and spying on them for the benefit of the Americans. Why this weakness in spite of the fact that almost half of the Yemeni government is linked to Islamic movements?*

Al-Zawahiri: Unfortunately, many linked to the Islamic movements have submitted to the US—Gulf plan in Yemen and have grabbed the wages of their participation in it, namely shares in [high] office and booty. They have colluded with their participation or their silence at the US military presence and its repeated aggression against the Yemeni people. Today they are reaping the bitter fruits of the Yemeni government's policy of exploitation in the service of American interests. It will not fight to defend against US and Iranian aggression towards Yemen and the Yemenis, but only against the *mujahidin* and the pious people of Yemen, and its religious scholars, and its free people, and its leaders and its chieftains. The great responsibility today on the free people of Yemen and its noble characters is to incite the Yemenis to jihad and support for the *mujahidin* to prevent Yemen from falling into the precipice of US or Iranian occupation or both.

Interviewer: Have you been following the recent developments in US—Iranian relations? Is there anything new in this relationship?

Al-Zawahiri: As regards anything new in that relationship, you will be better informed than me about that. However, I should like to make it clear that US—Iranian relations have not been suspended for a long time. The Iranians and the Americans cooperated in the Iraq and Afghanistan conflicts, and evidence of this cooperation was shown in my tape "A reading of the events and the facts of jihad, and the falsehoods of hypocrisy". This cooperation is a continuation of the same methods as their predecessors, who colluded with the Tatars over the sacking of Baghdad[18] and the fall of the Abbasid caliphate; and who allied themselves with the Portuguese against the Ottomans; and the approach of Al-Qaeda and Sheikh Osama bin Laden—may God grant him mercy—was to concentrate on the biggest enemy and to avoid any peripheral conflicts. However, the Iranians, with their violent ideological fanaticism, chose to cooperate with America in their wars in Afghanistan and Iraq. [Former president Mohammad] Khatami summed up that policy when he said that the Taliban are our enemies and America sees that the Taliban are their enemies, and if they toppled the Taliban then that would serve the interests of Iran to a considerable degree. The Americans began to appear convinced that the Iranians could cooperate with them in the realisation of their interests in the Middle East and Central Asia. And do not rule out the fact that a US—Iranian agreement might comprise undeclared aspects relating to matters of shared interest, such as Egypt and Syria and the oil wells and resistance to the spread of jihad in Afghanistan and Central Asia.

Interviewer: In the past, Iran would not shy from chanting Death to America and Israel. It is now in open agreement with America, yet the Iranian leadership describes the agreement as a diplomatic victory.

Al-Zawahiri: The explanation for that—and God knows—is that the Iranian regime is in crisis because of the economic sanctions, and in a bigger crisis because of its loss of credibility before its people. No longer are the slogans that used to circulate accepted by the general public, who are complaining about the deteriorating economic conditions. For the people see that the corruption which has spread into the ruling class has affected its stock, and no longer do the people accept the exorbitant expenditure on projects of the religious leaders outside Iran.

Interviewer: I don't understand why Iran did not refrain from spreading, and who helped her in this, the notion that the attacks on Tuesday Al-Mubarak [the blessed Tuesday, i.e. 9/11 attacks] were a US Zionist plot and not attacks by the mujahidin.

Al-Zawahiri: Concerning the system of *Wilayat e Faqih* [Rule of the Jurisprudent] in Iran, Sunnis would not wish to accord it any virtue. For it assists in the perpetration of lies and falsehoods. Recent years, since the beginning of the US war in Afghanistan, have revealed the extent of their [Iranian rulers'] hatred for Sunnis, and their willingness to cooperate with the crusader West against them. And even the bereaved would laugh at the myth spread by the system of *Wilayat e Faqih*, that America arranged the events of 11 September as an excuse to strike Iran. Yet after 13 years of attacking Afghanistan and then Iraq, they have not yet attacked Iran on the basis of the mendacious Iranian theory, because the Iranian regime is in an ongoing exchange deal of mutual interest with America. The Iranian regime, in any dispute, curses its adversary as an agent of Israel, with even [former president Mahmoud] Ahmadinejad arguing with [former prime minister Mir-Hossein] Mousavi in the elections, describing him as an agent of Israel. I ask anyone of intelligence and understanding: Why this insistence from Iran and its followers on describing anyone who disagrees with it as a traitor and a Zionist agent, to add to the list of other insults? Can they not see that it reveals their way of thinking and their motives and methods?

Interviewer: What is the story behind the alliance between Iran and its assistants in Iraq and Lebanon, and the Nusayiri[19] regime in Syria, against the jihadi intifada there?

Al-Zawahiri: Read the history of the people and the history of their predecessors in order to understand the present. The people [in these areas, i.e. the Shia] do not accept that the true people of Islam have a state, and consider the attempt to restore the caliphate as an attempt to commit a crime. For the caliphate in their view is a crime, and the fall of the Assad regime would take more than half of the strength of the Iranian alliance which is trying to establish a Shia state from Afghanistan to southern Lebanon. And they [Iranians] know that the jihadi movements in Syria are a greater threat to Israel, and that they have desperately defended the Assad regime up to the borders of Israel for over forty years. They describe it [the Assad regime], according to their custom of lying, as a regime of resistance and opposition. We need to understand the facts which are: there is an Iranian Safavid[20] plan aimed at spreading to southern Lebanon and vehemently opposed to any attempt at forming an Islamic jihadi state in the region.

Interviewer: What is the way to repel this regime and criminality from our people in Syria?

Al-Zawahiri: The way is jihad to bring down the criminal Assad regime, and the *ummah* must support this jihad in every way it can. The *mujahidin* must unite around the word *tawheed* [oneness of God], for unity is their protection against the deluge of plots that have been hatched against them. It makes no sense for the Shia to unite and the Sunnis to fight each other. Thus, each must place the interests of Islam over his partisan and organisational interests, even if he concedes to his brothers what he believes to be right. Also, we call on the good people of the *ummah*, its rich and its merchants, to supply the people of Syria with what they need, and not to leave them prey to being starved by the regime, nor to the oppressor's siege, nor leave them to suffer the hardship of life in the camps for displaced persons. The images which are carried by the media make the heart bleed, and I call on all who can help to donate towards the assistance of our people in Syria with everything that they can—and all who have a specialisation, especially in the medical field. As God is my witness, if I could I would hasten to them so I might relieve the suffering of my people in Syria. So all who have experience, help our people in Syria, for they are in need in their jihad and in their lives and the education of their children. Thus, it is the duty of everyone to take up arms until victory is near, God willing.

Interviewer: Is it necessary to open up a front with the Party of God [Hizbollah] in Lebanon? What is your direction on this point?

Al-Zawahiri: My view—God knows—is that the so-called Hizbollah is an enemy which attacks the souls of Muslims and their honour and the things which they hold most sacred. It is an ally of one of the most violent criminal regimes [Assad's] and it is necessary to repel the attacking enemy through every Sharia means. One of the benefits of the jihad in Syria is that it shows the true picture of the so-called Hizbollah and its leader, Hassan Nasrallah.

Interviewer: Saudi Arabia stood against the Brotherhood in Egypt, and yet they are helping them in Yemen, and are giving some support to them in Syria and Iraq. How do you explain these contradictions?

Al-Zawahiri: Saudi Arabia is one of the most important tools of American policy and it is carried out wherever she [Saudi Arabia] is. US policy in Egypt is the installation of a military regime or a military backdrop to protect Israel's borders, and to suppress any Islamic movement. Its policy in Syria and Iraq is to exhaust Iran, and at the same time to prevent any Islamic movement from coming to power in Syria. Thus, there is no contradiction in Saudi policies in this regard.

Interviewer: Yet at the same time while it claims to support the Sunnis in Iraq and Syria, King Abdullah issued a recent decree sentencing anyone who joined jihad to twenty years.

Al-Zawahiri: As I said to you, the key to understanding Saudi policy is that she is an American tool, and [the state's founder] Abd al-Aziz established this policy when he transferred his allegiance from Great Britain to America during his meeting with Roosevelt in the Second World War.

Interviewer: After this decree, what is the role of the Ulema [religious scholars] and the loyal preachers in the Arabian Peninsula?

Al-Zawahiri: The role of the loyal preachers and the Ulema is explained in the Noble Quran and demonstrated in the Sunna, so says the Truth [God], may he be praised and exalted: *"(And remember) when God took a covenant from those who were given the Scripture (Jews and Christians) to make it (the news of the coming of Prophet Mohammed SAW and the religious knowledge) known and clear to mankind."* {Sura 3 (The Family of Imran), 187} And the Prophet said, may God pray for him and grant him peace: *"The master of martyrs Hamza bin Abdul-Muttalib stood against the oppressive Imam and so the Imam ordered his killing and got rid of him."* Therefore, according to this explanation, there should be emigration to the places of jihad so that they can continue the call against the external and internal enemies of Islam and challenge this decree by their deeds and their behaviour.

Interviewer: A number of years ago you wrote about martyrdom operations in your book Remedy for the hearts of the faithful; *then you dedicated a book to the subject with the title* Scent of Paradise. *Finally, you issued a second edition. Why this emphasis upon martyrdom operations?*

Al-Zawahiri: These operations are an effective weapon of the oppressed against the arrogant, and they break the blockade which the arrogant have created with their monopoly of advanced weapons of destruction which the oppressed do not possess.

Interviewer: But do you not see that there has been such an expansion in martyrdom operations that we have now begun to hear that martyrdom operations are not a necessity/have become excessive? By your support for this method, do you not bear part of the responsibility?

Al-Zawahiri: There is no doubt there has been deviation and excess in some of these operations, and he who makes a mistake bears sole responsibility for his mistake. God, the Truth, says: *"He who commits a sin, commits it on his own, and God is knowing and wise."* {Sura 4 (The Women), 111} Jihad is like any human activity, mistakes happen, but it came from the Companions of the Prophet—may God be pleased with them—in the time of the Prophet, may God pray for him and grant him peace, that it is inconceivable that it be said that he who incites a subordinate to jihad bears the mistakes of the *mujahidin* who contravene the law. Martyrdom operations, like any other method, can be abused, and I and my brothers, such as Sheikh Osama and Sheikh Mustapha Abu al-Zaid and Sheikh Attiya and Sheikh Abu Yahya [Al-Libi]— may God grant them mercy—we repeatedly condemned and repudiated the abuse of this method, and failure of officers to comply with Sharia and obligations in the endeavours with regard to sacred matters and blood, which Sharia safeguards; in addition to the need to weigh up the pros and cons in the planning of these operations in order that the enemy media cannot exploit the *ummah* and set them against the *mujahidin*. This deviation must be resisted through the enjoining of good deeds and denial of bad deeds [*hisbah*] to create trust between the *mujahidin* and the *ummah* and to negate these deviations. If these errors happen, then it is necessary to condemn them; and those who committed them must apologise for them and accept the legal consequences. You will notice that in the introduction to the second edition of the book *Scent of Paradise* I pointed out the misuse of this practice, and the corruption of it, and the need to address that corruption.

Interviewer: Perhaps those who follow French policy have noticed that it has begun to take the place of America in resistance to the mujahidin in the Islamic countries in Africa? What is the reason for this neo-colonial approach from France?

Al-Zawahiri: This is a new-but-old approach, and it may be that the reason for it is the exhaustion of America after its defeat in Iraq and Afghanistan. And it may be that this jihadi activity is taking place in regions of French influence.

Interviewer: What is your commentary on what is happening in Central Africa?²¹

Al-Zawahiri: What is happening in Central Africa is a new tragedy amongst the tragedies of the Muslims. It is incumbent upon all Muslims everywhere to take the initiative to assist their persecuted brothers, and upon the Muslims of Central Africa to unite and to adhere to their religion and Sharia in order to resist this aggression which France and its followers have pursued against them. It may be that through these events what will be revealed to them is the lies and mythology of what is called the secular nation state; and that the West's defence of human rights is in reality a defence of human rights of criminals against oppressed peoples.

Interviewer: How do you see the conflict with France in the future?
The conflict with France is part of the wars of the crusades against the Muslims since time immemorial.

Interviewer: We have heard of the candidature of [president Abdelaziz] Bouteflika in the presidential elections in Algeria, despite his failing health. What is the secret behind this clinging to power?

Al-Zawahiri: The secret is France's commitment to him, because he is their preferred man.

Interviewer: We return now to America and its handling of Muslim prisoners in Guantanamo and the continued abuse of them, from sexual abuse to solitary confinement and force-feeding them through barbaric methods, and other violations. What is the reason for this escalation [of abuse] against Muslims?

Al-Zawahiri: A study of the history of the West and its beliefs explains all of this conduct. The West is a system which believes only in power and the realisation of advantage and pleasure. Thus, that which they call morals and values and principles are a sort of moral hypocrisy. They are morals and values and principles which work to their benefit, and they see it as their right to debar who they want if they threaten their interests. How can we forget that America wiped out an entire nation, namely the Red Indian [Native American] nation? And how can we forget that the West brought nearly five million slaves from Africa to work in its fields and factories, and to populate its countries and to fight in its wars without any rights? Then when it no longer had need of human energy and turned to other forms of energy, it began to talk about the emancipation of slaves. How can we forget that it was the West that occupied our country and perpetrated countless crimes and atrocities and plundered our wealth, and continues to plunder it in order to enjoy luxury? How can we forget that the secular West established a religious [Jewish] state in the heart of our Islamic world? It is secular and it established a religious Zionist state, and continues to support it in all causes. So, treaties about the treatment of prisoners and prevention of torture and human rights, all of them were written by the West for themselves, in order that they could be applied to Westerners in their wars between themselves and others. But the West abrogated them and denied them completely when they fought the Muslims. Just as with democracy, which they consider to be a belief and practice special to them. It is not necessary for others to enjoy their advantages, and Algeria and Egypt and Gaza can testify to that.

Interviewer: What would you advise Muslims and the mujahidin *about their obligations with regard to their prisoners in America's prisons, and elsewhere those of their allies from amongst the Arabs and non-Arabs?*

Al-Zawahiri: I would advise them to take Westerners and especially Americans as prisoners, which they can exchange for their own prisoners.

Interviewer: We have discussed Muslim prisoners and we must mention the scholar Mujahid Doctor Umar Abd al-Rahman and his suffering in captivity in the prisons of the crusaders.

Al-Zawahiri: I ask that God, praise him, help us to free Doctor Umar Abd al-Rahman from captivity along with the remaining Muslim prisoners. And I ask God to help us to capture Americans and Westerners in order that we can exchange them for our prisoners.

Interviewer: Noble brothers, that was our interview with Sheikh Ayman al-Zawahiri—may God protect him—and we offer him and you and all Muslims our thanks.

Al-Zawahiri: May God reward you richly.

Interviewer: Finally, praise be to God, Lord of the Worlds, peace be upon you, and God's mercy and his blessings.

Al-Zawahiri: And upon you be peace, and the mercy of God, and his blessings.

TESTIMONY TO PRESERVE THE BLOOD
OF THE *MUJAHIDIN* IN AL-SHAM[22]

MAY 2014

By Ayman al-Zawahiri

Here Zawahiri addresses the turmoil and infighting in Syria more directly, emphasising that ISIS is subordinate to his organisation. He traces the origin of the Islamic State of Iraq, highlighting the fact that whilst that group also operated in objectionable ways, it still pledged allegiance to bin Laden. Zawahiri claims to have inherited this fealty. He details correspondence between the two organisations at the outbreak of civil war in Syria, which he seeks to use to demonstrate his overall control. He accuses Abu Bakr al-Baghdadi of being driven predominantly by power, thus preparing the ground for more direct public denunciation of the ISIS leadership.

In the name of God, and praise be to God, and prayers for and peace upon the Prophet of God, and his family and his companions and his clan.

O Muslim brethren in every land, peace upon you and the mercy of God and his blessings.

I had decided that I was content with my pronouncement with regard to the *fitna* [sedition/strife] between the *mujahidin* in Syria until I listened to the urgent appeal from the beloved and eminent brother emigrant and professor of the truth, who has remained steadfastly in the trench of *dawa* [benediction] and communication and counsel on behalf of his *ummah* [nation or community], his eminence, Sheikh al-Aziz al-Mukarram [the great and revered] Doctor Abu Karim Hani al-Sabaaee,[23] may God protect him from all evil, and grant him success in upholding the truth and support him in the restoration [of good relations] between the Muslims and the *mujahidin*.

I therefore decided, after consultation and having sought guidance, that I would revisit the discussion concerning this matter in general, and what he had put to me regarding it [this matter] in particular, in his statement dated 25 Jumada al-Uwla 1435 [26 March 2014] broadcast on Channel Maqrizi.[24]

I am determined to return to the discussion to address two issues:

The first issue: what the beloved brother, His Eminence Sheikh Doctor Hani al-Sabaaee, said to me: namely that my response to his questions may be a cause for the extinguishing of [bringing an end to] the *fitna* amongst the *mujahidin*. And I said: "I have no compunction speaking words which God uses to put a stop to the bloodletting of the Muslim warriors."

And the second issue: to comply with a request from a compassionate and generous brother adviser, who has the truth [*al haqq*] of the brothers.

I shall divide my discussion—God willing—into a testimony, an order and an earnest appeal.

As regards the testimony, it concerns the relationship between the Islamic State of Iraq and Syria and its Amir, the noble Sheikh Abu Bakr al-Baghdadi—may God protect him—and the Jamaat Qaeda Al-Jihad [the Qaeda Al-Jihad group].

Thus I say, seeking the help of God: concerning this testimony from me, I swear to God that:

The Islamic State of Iraq and Syria is a branch subordinate to Jamaat Qaeda Al-Jihad, and I would like at this stage to expand on some details:

1. When the Islamic State in Iraq set itself up, it did so without consultation with the leadership of Jamaat Qaeda Al-Jihad, and at its head, the *mujaddid* [renewer] Imam Osama bin Laden, may God grant him mercy. In fact, things did not deteriorate until the State was issued a warning. The Martyred Sheikh, whom we hold in great esteem—Abu Hamza al-Muhajir—may God have mercy upon him, sent a letter to the general leadership [of Al-Qaeda], in which he sanctioned the establishment of the State, and confirmed the allegiance of the State to Jamaat Qaeda Al-Jihad. The brothers in the Shura [advisory council] took a pledge to the Martyred Sheikh—whom they hold in great esteem—Abu Umar al-Baghdadi,[25] that

their Amir was Sheikh Osama bin Laden, may God grant him mercy; and that the State was subordinate to Jamaat Qaeda Al-Jihad. However, although the brothers had been informed of this, they did not disseminate the information due to some policy considerations which they had identified in Iraq at that time.

2. The brothers in the general leadership of Jamaat Qaeda Al-Jihad and in the Islamic State of Iraq cooperated with one another over the establishment of the principle: that the Islamic State of Iraq is part of Jamaat Qaeda Al-Jihad. And as an example of that [there is]:

A. The letter which the Americans disseminated from amongst the documents which they found in the house of Osama bin Laden—may God grant him mercy—number: SOCOM-2012–0000011 Orig.

It is a letter from Sheikh Attiya to Sheikh Mustafa Abu Yazid,[26] may God grant him mercy. In it, Sheikh Attiya confirms to Sheikh Mustapha Abu Zaid the obligations to write letters of firm direction to al-Karoumi [by which he means Abu Hamza al-Muhajor] and to Abu Umar and their people, for fear that they may make some errors of policy.

B. When Sheikh Abu Bakr al-Husseini al-Baghdadi (may God grant him success) took over the Emirate without the sanction of the general leadership, Sheikh Attiya—may God grant him mercy—sent a letter to the leadership of the Islamic State of Iraq on 7 Jumada al-Uwla 1431 [10 May 2010] which said:

"We suggest to the noble brethren of the leadership that they appoint a temporary leadership to administer matters until consultation is complete. We think it best that they be patient—unless there is any objection or strong likelihood thereof, to the proposal of a permanent official appointment—until such time as they send us suggested names and a statement about each [candidate] (name, a description, qualifications, etc.). We will then seek for Sheikh Osama to advise you."

C. Sheikh Osama sent a letter to Sheikh Attiya—may God grant them both mercy—on 24 Rajab 1431 [26 June 2010] which said:

"It would be much appreciated if you were to provide us with comprehensive information about our brother Abu Bakr al-Baghdadi, whose appointment has been effected as successor to Abu Umar al-Baghdadi, may God grant him mercy, and the first deputy to him, Abu Suleiman al-Nasser al-Deen Ullah. And it would be best if you were to ask a number of our brothers whom you trust about them, in order that the situation [regarding them] is made explicitly clear to us."

This was the letter which the Americans took from the home of Sheikh Osama—may God grant him mercy—and disseminated it with the number: SOCOM-2012–0000019 Orig.

D. Sheikh Attiya responded to him [bin Laden]—may God have mercy upon him—in a letter dated 5 Sha'baan 1431 [17 July 2010] in which he stated:

> "God willing, we will seek information about Abu Bakr al-Baghdadi and his deputy, Abu Suleiman al-Nasser al-Deen, and we will gain a more detailed picture."

E. Sheikh Attiya sent a letter to the Ministry of Information/Media in the Islamic State of Iraq on 20 Shawwal 1431 [29 September 2010] which said:

> "O Sheikhs, we seek an overview of the Sheikhs of your new leadership, may God grant them success and support you: Abu Bakr al-Baghdadi, commander of the faithful in the Islamic State of Iraq, and his deputy, and his minister for war, and if it pleases you, others in positions of responsibility. You may tell the Sheikhs about this, and so perhaps they might write the introduction/pen picture themselves, or record it on audio [media]."

F. A Shura representative of the Islamic State of Iraq [member of consultative body] responded at the beginning of Thu Al-Qida 1431 [October 2010] replying thus:

> "My eminent brother, we received your esteemed letter dated Rajab Al-Harram 1431 [July 2010] and likewise your last letter in which you gave some directions from the noble Sheikhs—may God protect them—concerning the position of the State here and the need for patience in the appointment of a new Amir. However, they arrived after the announcement of the new Emirate, and in any case, the resolution of the brothers here since the beginning has been with a view to keeping the Sheikhs over there [who are with you] fully informed as to the reality of the situation, such as it is.
>
> We inform you our Sheikhs and **our noble rulers** that **your Islamic State** in the land of the dissenters [Shia] is in good health and is calm and collected.[27]

Our esteemed Sheikhs, after the killing of the two Sheikhs, the Majlis Al-Shura [advisory council] tried to delay the announcement of the new Amir until **instruction had come to us from you** in the wake of clear communication. However, we were unable to extend the delay any longer due to a number of reasons, most important of which was the membership both at home and abroad, who were waiting [for a decision].

The brothers here concurred, and before them, Sheikh Abu Bakr [al-Baghdadi]—may God protect him—and the Shura [advisory] council had no objection that this was to be a **temporary** Emirate.

If anyone were to be sent on behalf of the Sheikhs over there [with you], then they would see that things had been fully carried out to best effect, in order to hand over the Emirate, and with no objection from us. And all here will be **soldiers** for him, and they have a duty to listen and obey. And this obligation is agreed on by the Majlis Al-Shura and Abu Bakr, may God protect him."

G. After the martyrdom of Sheikh Osama, may God grant him mercy, the noble Sheikh Abu Bakr Husseini al-Baghdadi issued a statement saying:

"I am indeed confident that the martyrdom of the Sheikh will only increase the cohesiveness and steadfastness of his brother *mujahidin*. Indeed, I say to our brothers in the Al-Qaeda organisation and before their head, Sheikh Ayman al-Zawahiri—may God protect him—and his brothers in the leadership of the organisation: May God make great your reward, and may God make good your mourning in this tragedy, and continue upon the path in the blessing of God and respond to what you see before you. And you in the Islamic State of Iraq have **faithful men** keen to seek the truth in their path; and blood is blood, and destruction is destruction [Arab proverbs]."

H. Following this statement a communications representative in the Islamic State of Iraq sent a letter to Sheikh Attiya—may God grant him mercy—on 20 Jumada al-Akhira 1432 [23 May 2011], which said:

"The Sheikh advises—may God protect him—that we reassure you concerning the situation here: with regard to improvement, and progress and cohesiveness, praise be to God. He also asks about the suitability, from your point of view, of the announcement of the new Amir for the organisation. **Should the State renew its oath of**

allegiance publicly or in secret, as was done previously? This is so that you know that the brothers here are **arrows in your quiver**, and their relationship with you is as the Sheikh said in his public statement (blood is blood and destruction is destruction)."

I. After I took charge of the Emirate in succession to Sheikh Osama—may God have mercy upon him—Sheikh Abu Bakr al-Baghdadi al-Husseini communicated with me in my capacity as his Amir. Even the last letter from him to me—on 29 Jumada al-Uwla 1434 [10 April 2013] began with the words:

"To **Our Amir** the pre-eminent Sheikh"

And he ended it with the words:

"Word has reached me that [Nusra Front leader] al-Golani has issued a speech in which he has announced his immediate vow of allegiance to Your Eminence. This is what he had planned in order to protect him, and those who support him, from the consequences of the mistakes and misfortunes for which he was responsible. And the humble servant and his brothers who support him here in Syria [Al-Sham] believe this. It is necessary that our Sheikhs in Khorasan [referring to the Al-Qaeda leadership in Afghanistan/Pakistan] issue a clear position, without ambiguity, in order to bury this conspiracy before blood starts to flow and we become the cause of a new misfortune for the *ummah*.

We believe that any support for what this traitor does, even indirect, will lead to enormous internal strife, and thereby the enterprise in the name of which [so much] Muslim blood has been shed would be lost. And any delay in issuing a statement about the true position would lead to the situation taking root and a split in the ranks of the Muslims and the descent of fear upon the **Jamaa** [Group]. The only effective cure would be yet more bloodletting."

J. Also, [ISIS spokesperson] Sheikh Abu Mohammed al-Adnani sent me a testimony which he ended with these words:

"The humble servant Abu Mohammed al-Adnani wrote this on 19 Jumada al-Uwla 1434 [31 March 2013], seeking the forgiveness of God, the exalted, and then the *ummah* and then his Amirs, Sheikh Doctor Ayman al-Zawahiri, then Sheikh Doctor Abu Bakr al-Baghdadi, may God protect them."

K. Sheikh Abu Bakr al-Husseini al-Baghdadi—may God protect him—sent a letter dated 21 Ramadan 1434 [29 July 2013] to one of the officials of the Jamaa [group] which said:

"Our studies of the last letter of Sheikh al-Zawahiri went through three phases:

1. The phase of consultation with the leadership of the Islamic State located in Syria.
2. The phase of consultation with the Amirs of the states of Al-Sham who are members of our Shura [advisory] council.
3. Study of the letter from a legal perspective before the Sharia council in the Islamic State.

We only decided to remain as we are after it was explained that our obedience to our **Amir** [al-Zawahiri] is disobedience to our Lord and is a perilous situation for those *mujahidin* who are aligned with us—and especially the emigrants [*muhajiroun*]. And so we obey our Lord and we prefer his approval over the approval of **the Amir**......... and is it not said of him who disobeys the orders of the Amir [in which] he sees a perilous situation for the *mujahidin* and disobedience to our Lord, may he be exalted, for he has committed no offence."

And I am content with these examples.

3. As regards the question surrounding the nature of the judgement about the problem, is it an order from an Amir to his soldiers? Or is it a judgement about a private dispute between two parties, which had been taken before a *qadi* [religious judge]? In fact, I explained this case in detail in my comprehensive letter to the brothers in the [Islamic] State, dated 28 Shawwal 1434 [4 September 2013], in which I confirmed that this judgement was a judgement issued by an Amir concerning a problem that had emerged amongst his soldiers. It was not a judgement of a *qadi* [judge] between two adversaries which they had brought before him as part of a private dispute between them.

4. And now to the question which is sometimes posed: namely, why did the group and its leadership praise the Islamic State of Iraq, and why were they pleased with them, yet they were not pleased with the Islamic State in Iraq and Syria?

The response: Despite the fact that the general leadership of Jamaat Qaeda Al-Jihad [the Qaeda Al-Jihad group] and its Amir, Osama bin Laden—may God have mercy upon him—were not consulted, and were not notified before the announcement of the establishment of the Islamic State in Iraq, they think that they can see many differences between it and the Islamic State in Iraq and Syria.

a. The Islamic State of Iraq was not set up on a foundation of *fitna* amongst the brothers in which they made threats to provoke the fear of bloodshed in the event of support [from Al-Qaeda] for Jabhat [Al-Nusra].

b. The Islamic State of Iraq was formed after consultation between the Shura [advisory] Council of the *mujahidin* and Sunni tribes, as reported to us by Sheikh Abu Hamza al-Muhajir—may God have mercy upon him. Indeed, he is someone whom we trust and believe due to our long association with him. Moreover, he endeavoured to communicate with all the jihadi groups to invite them to join the State. On the other hand, the Islamic State in Iraq and Syria consulted on the matter [of its formation] with a limited circle within the group. Indeed, Jabhat Al-Nusra state that they did not consult them at all.

c. The announcement of the Islamic State in Iraq and Syria was in clear contravention of the orders of the leadership of Jamaat Qaeda Al-Jihad to its soldiers in Iraq and Syria not to announce any official presence of Al-Qaeda in Syria. On the contrary, the general direction of the leadership of Jamaat Qaeda Al-Jihad was not to declare any Emirate at this stage. Indeed, this order was confirmed in detail by Sheikh Osama bin Laden—may God grant him mercy—in his letter to Sheikh Attiya, may God grant him mercy, which is the letter that the Americans published under the reference: SOCOM-2012–0000019 Orig.

Sheikh Abu Yahya—may God grant him mercy—reminded the brothers of the State of Iraq, and then I reiterated it to Sheikh Abu Bakr al-Baghdadi in my letter, dated 25 Jumada al-Akhira 1435 [25 April 2014], in which I wrote:

> "If you had asked us our opinion before the announcement of that State, then we would not have consented. For, we [the] brothers here believe that this announcement causes more harm than it does good, and the basic components of a state are still not available in Syria even now."

d. The announcement of the Islamic State in Iraq and Syria caused a political disaster for the people of Syria. The Syrian people came out to participate in demonstrations in support of Jabhat Al-Nusra, when the US government classified it at the top [of the list] of terrorist organisations, and yet they began to criticise this announcement; the State [in effect] offering [Al-Nusra] to Assad on a gold plate. Moreover, the announcement provoked the rest of the jihadi groups, who thought that the State was trying to impose itself upon them without consultation or approval.

e. The announcement of the Islamic State in Iraq and Syria caused a deep rift within the single grouping, and infighting broke out. Sheikh Abu Bakr al-Husseini al-Baghdadi himself threatened that any support for Jabhat Al-Nusra, or delay in adopting what he perceived to be the correct position, would lead to bloodshed. And so it came to pass.

f. The bloodshed continues unabated in Syria. And yet if the State had accepted the decision to bring an end to the problem, which sought to stop the bloodletting of the *mujahidin*, and to avoid the anticipated *fitna*, and to focus efforts on Iraq, which demands much more of their efforts; if they had accepted that and acted according to the principles of consultation [*shura*], listening [*sam*], and obedience [*taa*] to their Amir, and had not rebelled against their Amir and their leadership, then I believe they would have avoided that bloodshed; and they would have harmed the renegade Safavid [Persian/Shia] government and they would have supported the Sunnis many times more. But praise be to God, in any case.

This was the testimony and I now follow it up with this order and earnest appeal:

Concerning the order, which is for Sheikh al-Fatih Abu Mohammed al-Golani—may God protect him—and for every noble soldier of Jabhat Al-Nusra; and the urgent appeal, which is for all the parties and groupings of the *mujahidin* in Syria. They are to cease immediately all fighting against one another, and [any fighting over] the sacred property of their brother *mujahidin*, and all remaining Muslims, and are to focus on fighting the enemies of Islam from amongst the Baathists, and the Nusayiris and the other Rawafid [renegades, Shia].

As I have demanded repeatedly on many occasions before, all must appeal to the independent Sharia council to pass judgement where differences occur between them. I also demand that everyone desist from mutual accusations and condemnations of one another, and the provocation of *fitna* amongst the *mujahidin*, in the media and via other means of communication. For they are the keys to harmony and the lockers up of evil.

It only remains in conclusion to provide a reminder and some advice.

The reminder and general advice are for the rest of the *mujahidin* in the territory of Syria. Enough of this shedding of sacred Muslim blood. Enough of this killing of the leadership of jihad and its sheikhs. Enough, for the blood of all of you is dear and beloved to us. We had hoped that you would offer it as a sacrifice for the victory of Islam over its enemies. And a reminder and special advice for the noble Sheikh Abu Bakr al-Husseini al-Baghdadi and his supporters. Return to the fold of listening and obedience to your Amir. Return to the endeavours being undertaken by your Sheikhs and Amirs, who preceded you in the path of jihad and emigration [*hijra*].

Focus on the wounded land of Iraq, which needs the multiplicity of your efforts. Focus on it even if you believe yourselves to be oppressed and deprived of your rights in order to stop this bloody massacre, in order to focus on the enemies of Islam and of the Sunni people in the land of Iraq, which is shackled and in a state of jihad. Respond to my reminder in order to spare the blood of the Muslims and to give them unity and for their victory over their enemies. Do that even if you consider it to be oppression, and injustice and suffering.

And I give a reminder and special advice to the esteemed Sheikh Abu Bakr al-Baghdadi: emulate your ancestor al-Hassan, may God be pleased with him, who surrendered the caliphate and spared the blood of the Muslims.[28] Thereby the good tidings of his grandfather and your ancestor, our master the Prophet, peace be upon him, came to pass: "My son is a master [*sayyid*], by whom God may bring harmony to reign between two great factions of the Muslims. Thereby kinship and love and brotherhood may be restored to them."

Are these good tidings not sufficient? Does this dominion not please you? Are you not happy that you are making a decision which causes God to raise up your stock [with him] in this life and the hereafter, through his permission and *tawfiq* [success granted by the grace of God]? And thereby you will resist the enemies of Islam in Iraq, which needs so much of your help. And thereby you will extinguish the *fitna* between the Muslims, and return to them kinship and love and brotherhood.

Trust in God, and take this decision, and you will find that all your brother *mujahidin* and all of their supporters will be an aid to you, and a support and a reinforcement. O noble Sheikh, emulate your ancestor and be the best successor to the best *Salaf* [ancestor]. Make ready a great feat from amongst the great feats of the house of the prophets. You shall be victorious in this life and the hereafter, by the grace of God.

Those who are of the community love faith and hate unbelief [*kufr*], and security and refuge are close for them.

Finally, praise be to God, Lord of the Two Worlds, and may God pray for and grant peace to Sayyidna [our master] Mohammed and his family and his companions. Peace be upon you, and the mercy of God and his blessings.

PART 3

AL-QAEDA AND THE "ISLAMIC STATE"

FRIDAY PRAYERS AND SERMON
IN THE GRAND MOSQUE OF MOSUL

JULY 2014

The "Islamic State", featuring Abu Bakr al-Baghdadi, presented as "Caliph Ibrahim"

In this part we take a brief break from our focus on Zawahiri's output to look at two key communiqués from the Islamic State organisation, which was declared as a new Islamic caliphate following the consolidation of territory captured by the Islamic State of Iraq and Syria.

On 4 July 2014 "Al-Furqan", one of the media outlets used by ISIS, published "exclusive coverage" of a Friday sermon delivered by the organisation's leader Abu Bakr al-Baghdadi at the Grand Mosque in Mosul.

ISIS had taken control of the city in northern Iraq in early June after a dramatic surge against local Iraqi forces who quickly capitulated and fled south to Baghdad. ISIS was quick to establish its ruthless theocratic order in the city, merging it with territories under its control in Iraq and across the border in Syria. The capture of Mosul was a major strategic milestone for the group that to many now seemed unstoppable. With a vast arsenal of weaponry, mostly captured from local armoires and fleeing soldiers, and huge sums of looted cash and other resources, coupled with a relentless thirst for expansion and warfare, ISIS had become one of the most powerful forces in the region.

It was with this confidence and sense of purpose that the leadership of ISIS declared at the beginning of the holy month of Ramadan that it was establishing a worldwide caliphate which would be called the Islamic State. Al-Baghdadi, the group announced, was to become Caliph Ibrahim, commander of the faithful.

As he greeted worshippers at the Grand Mosque, he presented the caliphate's creation as a divine mission which all believers would be obliged to support.

The split from Al-Qaeda could not be clearer or more public, the rejection of al-Zawahiri's authority could not be more stark. The two separate jihadi entities were no longer just competitors locally, embroiled in the turmoil in Syria, but engaged in a global confrontation, vying for the hearts and minds of the same constituency.

Special coverage of the Friday speech and prayers at the Grand Mosque in the city of Mosul
6 Ramadan 1435 [4 July 2014]
Caliph Ibrahim, the Amir of the believers in the Islamic State, May God preserve him.

All praise to God, we seek His help and forgiveness. We seek refuge in God from the evil in our hearts and the sins of our deeds. Whoever God grants guidance will never be led astray; whoever He leads astray will never find guidance. I bear witness that there is no God but God, the one who has no partners, and I bear witness that Mohammed, peace and prayers be upon him [PPBUH] and his household and companions, is His slave and messenger.

O who you who believe, fear God as He should be feared and do not die except as Muslims. {Sura 3 (The Family of Imran), 102} O you who believe, fear God and speak words of appropriate justice. He will amend for you your deeds and forgive you your sins. And whoever obeys God and His Messenger has certainly attained a great attainment. {Sura 33 (The Allied Troops), 70–71}

The most truthful speech is that of the Book of God [Quran], and the best guidance is that of Mohammed, PBUH; the worst of evils are the newly invented matters, every invented matter is a heresy, every heresy is misguidance and every misguidance leads to the hellfire.

O you who believe, decreed upon you is fasting as it was decreed upon those before you that you may become righteous. [Fasting for] a number of days {Sura 2 (The Cow), 183}. God, almighty said: *The month of Ramadan in which was revealed the Quran, a guidance for mankind and clear proofs for the guidance and the criterion. So whoever of you, who sights [the new moon of] the month, let him fast. {Sura 2 (The Cow), 185}*

O Muslims! Witnessing Ramadan is a great blessing from God the almighty. Its beginning is mercy, its middle days are blessing and forgiveness, and its end brings rescue from hellfire. He who fasts this month out of sincere faith and belief will have all his past sins forgiven, and he who spends the night in prayer during Ramadan will have all his past sins forgiven. Narrated on Abu Huraira, may God be pleased with him, he said: "God's Messenger, PBUH, said: 'He who fasts during Ramadan out of sincere faith and belief is purified and will have all his earlier sins forgiven; and he who performs night prayers during Ramadan out of faith and belief will have all his past sins forgiven.'"

At the beginning of Ramadan, the gates of heaven are opened and the gates of hell are locked; the devils are chained down. It is a month that has a night, where rewards from worshipping are higher than a thousand months; whoever is excluded from its blessing will be deprived of all its rewards, and its loss is irreplaceable.

The night of Decree [Laylat al-Qadr] is better than a thousand months. The angels and the Spirit descend therein by the permission of their Lord for every matter. Peace it is until the emergence of dawn. {Sura 97 (Determination), 3–5}

It is a month devoted entirely to worshipping God, where a person is freed from hell every single night. It is a month where jihad is planned. The Messenger of God, PBUH, used to organise brigades and mobilise the armies during Ramadan in order to fight the enemies of God and wage jihad against the infidels. O believers! Make the most of this holy month, worship and obey God, He will double your rewards; and the believers will duly compete between them so God can be pleased with them.

O believers! God, the exalted, has created us to worship Him and to establish His religion. God said: *"And I did not create the jinn and mankind except to worship me."* {Sura 51 (Qāf), 56} God has ordered us to fight His enemies and to carry out jihad for His sake in order to spread His religion. He says: *"Fighting has been enjoined upon you, even while it is hateful to you."* {Sura 2 (The Cow), 216} God also said: *"Fight them until there is no more sedition and worship is for God alone."* {Sura 8 (Spoils of War), 39}

O people, the religion of God will not be implemented and the aim for which God created us will not be attained unless we implement His ruling, revert to His Sharia for arbitration and abide by His laws and boundaries; this can only be achieved through power and force. God, the exalted, said: *"We have already sent our messengers with clear evidence and sent down with them the Scripture and the balance that people may maintain [their affairs] in justice. And we sent down iron wherein is great military might and benefits for the people, and so that God may make evident those who support Him and His messengers unseen." Indeed, God is Powerful and exalted in Might.* {Sura 57 (Iron), 25}

The basis of the faith is a book which guides the believers and a sword that brings them victory. God, the exalted, has granted your *mujahidin* brothers victory and success; He has empowered them after long years of jihad, patience and fighting against the enemies of God; He has granted them success and enabled them to achieve their goal. Hence, they rushed to announce the caliphate and appoint an Imam. This is a duty incumbent on each believer, a duty that has been lost for centuries and omitted by many believers, most of whom ended up ignoring it. Indeed, Muslims committed a sin by neglecting this obligation; they should continuously carry out their responsibilities and endeavour to reinstate the caliphate. With the grace of God, and all praise to Him, they have succeeded in doing so.

You have been entrusted with this mission and I have been entrusted with this heavy task; I was chosen to become your leader. I am by no means the greatest amongst you nor am I better than you. Help me if you see me acting in the right way, but if you see me doing wrong, then advise me and lead me to the right path. Obey me as long as I obey God; if I disobey Him, you should not obey me.

I do not promise you the security, prosperity and wellbeing that kings and rulers usually promise their subjects and followers. I promise you what God, the exalted, has promised His true believers: *God has promised those among you who have believed and done righteous deeds that He will surely grant them succession [to authority] upon the earth, as He granted it to those before them, and that He will surely establish for them [therein] their religion which He has preferred for them and that He will surely substitute for them, after their fear, security, [for] they worship Me and do not associate anything with Me. But whoever disbelieves after that, those are the defiantly disobedient.* {Sura 24 (The Light), 55}

God says: *"So do not weaken and do not grieve, and you will be superior if you are (true) believers."* {Sura 3 (The Family of Imran), 139} He also says: *"if God grants you victory, then you will have no superior".* {Sura 3 (The Family of Imran), 160} He also says: *"and incumbent upon us was support of the believers".* {Sura 30 (The Romans), 47} He also says: *"And to God belongs [all] honour, and to His Messenger, and to the believers, but the hypocrites do not know."* {Sura 63 (The Hypocrites), 8} This is God's promise to you. If you want His promise, then fear Him and obey Him. Fear God, the almighty, in every matter and in every situation. Seek the truth in everything you like and dislike and adhere to it. If you want what God has promised to you, wage jihad for His sake, incite the believers and face up to hardships and misfortunes; if you knew the benefits of jihad and the rewards, honour, dignity and pride it brings in this world and the hereafter, none of you would have neglected this noble duty.

God has revealed a trade that will spare you humiliation and grant you dignity in this world and the hereafter. *You believe in God and His Messenger and you strive in the cause of God with your wealth and your lives. That will be best for you, if you should know. He will forgive you your sins, and admit you to gardens beneath which rivers flow, and pleasant dwelling in gardens of perpetual residence. That is the great attainment. And [you will obtain] another [favour] that you love—victory from God and an imminent conquest. And give good tidings to the believers.* {Sura 9 (Repentance), 88–89}

I say this and I ask for God's forgiveness for you and for myself, so pray to God and be sure that He will answer your prayers.

All praises to God, as He should be praised, and prayers and peace be upon the last of His Prophets, and upon the Prophet's family, household, companions, party and soldiers, and all who followed him until the Day of Judgement. There is no God but God who fulfilled His promise, granted victory to His soldiers, and defeated the parties alone. There is no God but God, who has no partners, to whom we are sincere in faith, even if the disbelievers dislike it.

O slaves of God! Hold on to your faith and fear God as He should be feared; He will grant you glory in this world and the hereafter. If you want security, fear God; if you want livelihood, fear God; and if you want a decent and honourable life, fear God and wage jihad for His sake. We pray God the almighty, the Lord of the exalted throne, to unite and bring you together, make peace between you and put an end to your hostilities.

O God, grant victory and glory to Islam and the Muslims, and degrade polytheism and the polytheists [the audience cheering Amen]!

O God, support your monotheist *mujahidin* in the East and the West!

O God, make them steadfast, strengthen their souls and support them; make them achieve their targets, and guide them to the right path!

O God, bestow your guidance and provide them with ample supply!

O God, make our souls steadfast on our faith and eager on your obedience!

O God, purify our hearts from hypocrisy, our deeds from deceit, our speech from lies and our mind from treachery!

O God, we ask you true faith, obedient souls and accepted deeds!

O God, we ask you for forgiveness, good health and continuous strength in our religion and our life!

O God, bestow your forgiveness and blessing upon this gathering and prevent us from misdeeds and wrongdoing when we leave!

O God, don't leave anyone among us in pain or in need!

And our last prayer is all praise be to God the Lord of the universe, and peace and prayers be upon His messenger Mohammed.

Let us perform the prayers.

[Followed by the call to prayer by a different male voice]

God is great [twice]

I bear witness that there is no God but God [twice]

I bear witness that Mohammed is the Messenger of God [twice]

Hasten to prayer [twice]

Hasten to success [twice]

God is great [twice]

There is no God but God

[Al-Baghdadi leads the prayers]

INDEED, YOUR LORD IS EVER WATCHFUL

SEPTEMBER 2014

Sheikh Abu Mohamed Al-Adnani Ash-Shami, spokesman
for the Islamic State

In this second example of key texts from the Islamic State group, the IS spokesperson Abu Mohamed al-Adnani presents his group as a force that emerged in defence of believers, which will ultimately spread to conquer the world. He promises to defeat Rome, representing Christian-dominated hegemony, enslaving the infidel women and defeating its Arab "guard dogs", such as the Saudi military. He speaks directly to Muslims in Iraq, Syria, Egypt, Libya, Tunisia, Yemen and elsewhere, in direct competition with Zawahiri. Contrasting his stance, he welcomes the slaughter of non-believers and calls for IS loyalists to carry out attacks wherever they can. The disbeliever can be killed like a dog. This is sanctioned by God, Adnani insists. The contrast with Zawahiri's message at this time, therefore is stark.

Praise be to God the powerful, the utmost firm; peace and blessings be on he who was sent with the sword as mercy for the worlds; God almighty says, *"The people of Noah and the confederates after them denied (their Messengers) before these, and every (disbelieving) nation plotted against their Messenger to seize him, and disputed by means of falsehood to refute therewith the truth. So I seized them (with punishment), and how (terrible) was My punishment!"* {Sura 40 (The Believer), 5} And He says, *"And (remember) when the disbelievers plotted against you to imprison you, or to kill you, or to get you out; they were plotting and God too was planning, and God is the best of the planners.”* {Sura 8 (The Spoils of War), 30} *“Those (i.e. believers) unto whom the people (hypocrites) said, ‘verily, the people (pagans) have gathered against you (a great army), therefore, fear them’. But it (only) increased them in faith, and they said: ‘God is sufficient for us, and He is the best disposer (of affairs).’ So they returned with grace and bounty from God. No harm touched them; and they followed the good pleasure of God. And God is the owner of great bounty. It is only Satan that suggests to you the fear of his supporters and friends (polytheists, disbelievers in the oneness of God and in His Messenger), so fear them not, but fear Me, if you are (true) believers.”* {Sura 3 (The Family of Imran), 173–175}

Rejection and mockery of the truth and belying its people, plotting, mobilisation, intimidation, enmity and war; this has been the position of the disbelievers towards what is right and the followers of the Prophets since ancient times. The characteristics of the battle have been similar throughout the ages. Theirs is an arrogant encampment of falsehood that attempts to appear powerful and invincible, yet in reality they are fearful and terrified, weak and humiliated, defeated and insecure. And despite their presence in countries, their satellite channels and sorcerers are in a state of alert day and night. They argue in their favour, falsify the events and realities, fool people and endeavour to mobilise them against the rightful while portraying the people of falsehood with every aspect of rightfulness and power in desperate attempts to falsify at all times the truth and to scare and defeat its followers.

This is the case in every age and time. In the opposite encampment, we see the followers of the Prophets are smaller in numbers, less equipped and less heard. However, their willpower is indestructible and their strength is unbreakable, they remain steadfast in every battle, courageous in every fight and ever victorious from the battle of Noah, peace be upon Him, to the day God inherits the Earth and those upon it due to their faith in God, the mighty, the compeller from whom they draw their strength; He is sufficient for them; they trust Him and blindly rely upon His support for victory, and with His generosity and kindness they make changes and fear no one but Him.

O soldiers of the Islamic State, what greatness you have achieved! Your rewards will be granted by God; by God, He healed the hearts of the faithful through the killing of the Nusayiris[1] [Syrian regime] and the Rafida [the Shia] by your hand and He filled the hearts of the disbelievers and the hypocrites with rage through you. What great men! Who are you? Who are you, O soldiers of the Islamic State? Where did you come from? What is your secret?

Why do the hearts of people in the East and the beat in terror before you? Why do America and her allies shiver in fear of you? Where are your aircraft? Where are your fleets? Where are your missiles? Where are your weapons of mass destruction? Why has the world allied against you, and why are the nations of disbelief gathered in the same trench against you? What kind of threat do you pose to faraway Australia who is sending her legions to you? What about you provokes Canada? O soldiers and children of the Islamic State everywhere, listen up! While people do not believe you, refuse your state, reject your call and mock your caliphate; the Prophet (PBUH) was not believed and his call was rejected and he was mocked. Your own people fight you, accuse you of the worst things and attribute the most horrible descriptions to you. He (PBUH) was fought by his own people who forced him into exile and accused him of much worse than you have been accused of.

If all the parties gather against you, then know that they gathered against him (PBUH) too. This is the rule of God, or did you expect people to welcome you with joy and shouts of "God is the greatest"? *Without such (trials) as came to those who passed away before you, whereby you taste what they have tasted?* {Sura 2 (The Cow), 214} No, you will be shaken! *And we indeed tested those who were before them. And God will certainly make (it) known (the truth of) those who are true, and will certainly make (it) known (the falsehood of) those who are liars.* {Sura 29 (The Spider), 3}

God has given you glory after humiliation and made you rich after poverty, and has helped you despite your weakness and small numbers; He has shown you that victory is from Him, the almighty, and will grant it to whoever He wills whenever He wills. So know that, by God, we do not fear the swarms of planes, nor ballistic missiles, nor drones, nor satellites, nor battleships, nor weapons of mass destruction. How could we fear them while God almighty says, *If God helps you, none can overcome you; and if He forsakes you, who is there after Him that can help you? And in God (alone) let believers put their trust.* {Sura 3 (The Family of Imran), 160} How, while He the almighty also says, *so do not become weak (against your enemy), nor be sad, and you will be superior (in victory) if you are indeed (true) believers.* {Sura 3 (The Family of Imran), 139} How, while you have proven to be the knights and men of war?

When you defend, you are like the most solid mountains; and when you assault, you are like fierce predators. You face death with bare chests while the worn-out world is under your feet. By God, I have not known any of you but to be the first to run to the battle cries, keen to find the place of death in every battle. I see the Quran walking alive amongst you. What great men you are!

The weakest among you is brave; the most merciful among you is ruthless in battle. We have not known you but ardent and angry. Your ardency is not but for the religion of God, and your anger is not but for the violation of the sanctities of God; you tell the truth and implement justice according to it; you love God and His Messenger (PBUH) and you are the most fervent in following his tradition (PBUH), hard on the disbelievers, merciful with one another, and you do not fear, in the cause of God, the criticism of any critic. Therefore, God will grant you victory. Indeed, God will grant you victory! By God, God will grant you victory.

So, guarantee for us two things, and we will guarantee for you, with the permission of God, constant victory and empowerment. Firstly, do not oppress anyone or accept oppression by keeping silent about it and not raising it [with those in authority] in order to keep yourselves safe. Secondly, do not be vain or arrogant. This is what we fear from you and fear for you. So, if you are victorious, attribute victory to God alone and move on with modesty and humbleness thanking God; yet, if you fail, blame it on yourselves and your sins and attack again [your enemy] asking God for forgiveness and repenting to Him with remorse. We declare our innocence before God of any injustice that is carried out by one of you and that we are not aware of, and we declare our innocence before God of any injustice that one of you covers up or turns a blind eye to. Know that from time to time a trial, purification and selection are necessary since some people, who are not of you, as well as pretenders have entered your ranks and disorder has taken place. A trial is therefore necessary to drive out the dirt and to purify the ranks. We ask God for forgiveness and wellbeing. Vanity and arrogance have entered the hearts of some of us, and some have transgressed and oppressed. A purification of the sins is therefore necessary, so you may return [to the Lord]. God has [always] loved the *mujahidin* and has therefore chosen to take some martyrs; we ask God to make us of them, not from the disgraced or afflicted [by *fitna*, sedition/strife].

O soldiers of the Islamic State, be prepared for the final crusade. Yes, it will, God willing, be the final one. Thereafter, we will raid them, with God's permission, and they will not raid us. Be ready, as you are, with God's permission up to it. The crusaders have come back with a new campaign. They have come to you so that the dust clears, the fog dissipates and the masks fall, so that the deception of falsehood is exposed and the truth becomes visible, and *so that those who were to perish (for their rejecting the faith) might perish upon clear evidence, and those who were to live (i.e. believers) might live upon clear evidence.* {Sura 8 (Spoils of War), 42}

O America and allies of America, know, O crusaders, that the matter is far more serious than you think and greater than you can imagine; we have warned you that today we are in a new era, in a state where its soldiers and children are masters not slaves; people who through the ages have not known defeat, and the outcome of their battles is known before they begin. They have not prepared for a battle since the time of Noah except with the conviction of victory. Getting killed, for them, is victory. This is where the secret lies; you are fighting people who can never be defeated. They either gain victory or are killed.

O crusaders, you are defeated in both situations, because you do not know that any of us who is killed resurrects with his blood the dead; and that any of us who is killed leaves behind him a story that—when told—awakens the Muslims from their slumber. The weak among us and the one who has no experience in fighting and no strength, and he who thinks that he is unable to offer anything practical on the ground, has no aim but to be killed in order to enlighten the path with his blood so that hearts will live with his story, generation after generation, making his body and remains a bridge for those who awaken after him to cross over. He has realised that the life and glory of his *ummah* [nation or community] are through blood, so he goes with bare chest and bare head towards death seeking life and glory. If he survives, he will live victorious, free, powerful and as a master; and if he gets killed, he lights up the way for those who come after him, and goes to his Lord as a happy martyr, as he has taught those after him that pride, dignity and life are through jihad and fighting, and that humiliation, disgrace and death are through submission and subservience.

O crusaders, you have realised the threat of the Islamic State, but you have not discovered the cure, and you will not discover the cure because there is no cure. When you fight it, it becomes stronger and tougher; and if you leave it, it flourishes and expands. If Obama has promised you to defeat the Islamic State, then Bush lied before him; our Lord almighty and exalted has promised us victory, and here we are now victorious. Our Lord will grant us victory at every test. The almighty never breaks a promise. We promise you, with the permission of God, that this will be your last crusade, and that it will be defeated as were all your previous ones. Except that this time we will raid you and you will be unable to counterattack; we will conquer your Rome and break your crosses, enslave your women, with the permission of God almighty.

That is His promise to us, the almighty; He does not break a promise. If we do not achieve it ourselves, then our children or our grandchildren will, and they will sell your children as slaves in the slave market. It has been reported that Abdullah ibn Amr ibn Al-As (may God almighty be pleased with him and his father) said, "We were with the Messenger of God (PBUH) writing down what he was saying when he was asked, 'Which of the two cities will be conquered first, Constantinople or Rome?' So God's Messenger (PBUH) said, 'The city of Heraclius will be first to be conquered', meaning the city of Constantinople." So mobilise your forces, O crusaders, mobilise your forces, terrify [like thunder], fume with fury, threaten, plot and arm your troops, prepare yourselves, strike, kill and destroy. This will not avail you; you will be defeated! This will not avail you for God almighty has promised us victory and your defeat. Send arms and equipment to your agents and dogs, and equip them with the most modern equipment; send many of them, as they will end up, with the permission of God, as war booty in our hands. You will deploy them only for them to become a source of regret for you as you are defeated. Here are your armoured vehicles, machinery, weaponry and equipment in our hands. God granted them to us; we fight you with them, so die in your rage!

Verily, those who disbelieve spend their wealth to hinder (men) from the path of God, and so will they continue to spend it; but in the end it will become an anguish for them. Then they will be overcome. And those who disbelieve will be gathered unto hell. {Sura 8 (Spoils of War), 36}

O Obama, O mule of the Jews, go to hell! Go to hell! Go to hell! You will be disappointed, Obama. Is this all you could do in this crusade of yours? Has America reached this level of incapacity and weakness? Are America and all her allies amongst the crusaders and the atheists incapable of fighting on the ground? Have you, O crusaders, not realised yet that proxy war has not availed you and will never avail you? Have you not realised, O mule of the Jews, that the battle can never be decided from the air? Or do you consider yourself to be more intelligent than Bush, your fool of a leader, when he brought the crusaders' armies and placed them under the fire of the *mujahidin* on the ground? No, you are more stupid than him. You claimed to have withdrawn from Iraq, O Obama, four years ago. We told you then that you were lying, that you would not withdraw and that even if you did you would return after a while. Here you are: you have not withdrawn, rather you hid some of your forces behind the lackeys and withdrew with the rest. Your forces will come back greater than before; they will come back, but your lackeys will not avail you as we will come to your homeland with God's permission.

You claimed, O mule of the Jews, that America will not be drawn to a war on the ground. No, it will be drawn and dragged indeed; it will come on the ground and it will be led to its death, to its grave and to its destruction. You claimed, O Obama, that America's hand was long and that it could reach as far as it wished. Know then that our knife is sharp and stiff; it cuts off the hands and strikes the necks and that our Lord, almighty and exalted, is ever watchful over you!

Did you (O Mohammed) not see how your Lord dealt with 'Ad (people)? Who were very tall like lofty pillars, the like of which were not created in the land? And (with) Thamud (people), who cut (hewed) out rocks in the valley (to make dwellings)? And (with) Pharaoh, who had pegs (who used to torture men by binding them to pegs)? Who did transgress beyond bounds in the lands (in the disobedience of God), and made therein much mischief. So your Lord poured on them different kinds of severe torment. Verily, your Lord is ever watchful. {Sura 89 (The Dawn), 6–14}

As for 'Ad, they were arrogant in the land without right, and they said: "Who is mightier than us in strength?" See they not that God, who created them, was mightier in strength than them. And they used to deny our proof, so we sent upon them furious wind in days of evil omen (for them) that we might give them a taste of disgracing torment in this present worldly life, but surely the torment of the hereafter will be more disgracing, and they will never be helped. {Sura 41 (Adoration), 15–16}

O Americans, O Europeans, the Islamic State has not initiated war against you as your governments and media try to make you believe. It is you who started the aggression against us; he who initiates [wrong] is more at fault. You will pay a dear price; you will pay the price when your economy collapses; you will pay the price when they send your children to fight us and they return to you disabled or in coffins or mentally ill. You will pay the price when you are afraid to travel to any country. Even more so, you will pay the price when you walk on your own streets, looking over your shoulders in fear of the Muslims and not even feeling safe in your own bedrooms. You will pay the price when this crusade of yours collapses and we invade you in your own homeland, so you will never ever be able to transgress against anyone else again. You will pay the price, for we have prepared for you, with the permission of God, what will harm you.

O Muslims, America claimed when it began this crusade that it was defending her interests in Erbil and Baghdad and protecting its citizens. Then, its stumble became clear and its false claims became obvious. So, it claimed that, through its airstrikes, it would save those left homeless and displaced in Iraq, and defend the civilians. Then it realised that the matter was much more dangerous and greater than it thought it was. So, it shed crocodile tears over the

Muslims in the Levant and promised to save them and support them, and vowed to save them from the terrorists. But instead, America and its allies continued to watch the misery inflicted on the Muslims by the Nusayiris, happy with the killing, abuse, expulsion and destruction, not concerned about the hundreds of thousands of dead people, the wounded and the imprisoned, and the millions of displaced Muslims including men, women and children everywhere at the hands of the Jews, the crusaders, the Rafida, Nusayiris, Hindus, atheists and apostates in Palestine, Yemen, Syria, Iraq, Egypt, Tunisia, Libya, Burma, Nigeria, Somalia, Afghanistan, Indonesia, India, China, the Caucasus and elsewhere.

Its [America's] feelings were not moved during all the years of starvation and blockade in Syria; it turned a blind eye to the barrels of killing and destruction; it did not have any fervour when watching horrific scenes of Muslim children and women taking the last breaths with their eyes wide open because of the chemical weapons used by the Nusayiris. Those scenes are repeated on a daily basis, revealing the truth about the show of the so-called destruction of the weapons of mass destruction belonging to its Nusayiri dogs, guardians of the Jews. America and its allies were not moved or outraged by any of this; they blocked their ears to the cries for help of the weak, and closed their eyes to the massacres carried out against the Muslims in all those countries for years and years. However, since those Muslims have had a state that defends them, avenges them and reciprocates, America and its allies shed crocodile tears for a few hundred of the criminal Rafidhite and Nusayiri soldiers who were imprisoned and killed by the Islamic State during the war. The hearts of America and its allies were broken for the rotten heads of some agents, spies and apostates that were cut off by the Islamic State.

America and its allies were also horrified by the lashing and stoning of the fornicators, the cutting of the thieves' hands and the striking of the sorcerers' and the apostates' necks. So, America and its allies rose allegedly to save the world from the terrorism and barbarity of the Islamic State. They mobilised the world's entire media and used them to argue in favour of falsehood, to deceive people and lead them to believe that the Islamic State is the source of evil and corruption and that it is the one that is displacing and killing people, arresting and murdering the peaceful ones among them, demolishing houses, destroying cities and terrorising women and children who were safe; they portray the crusaders as kind and merciful, noble and generous, the people of fervour who allegedly feared for Islam and the Muslims from the corruption and violence of the Kharijites in the Islamic State,[2] to the extent that the uncircumcised old man, [John] Kerry, became an Islamic jurist issuing fatwas to the people, claiming that the Islamic State was defaming Islam and that what it was doing was in contradiction with the teachings of Islam, and that the Islamic State was an enemy of Islam.

Obama, the mule of the Jews, became a jurisprudent scholar and an Islamic preacher advising people, preaching and defending Islam, claiming that the latter has nothing to do with the practices of the Islamic State in all of his six speeches in the same month, all of which were about the threat of the Islamic State. Those people turned into jurisprudents, muftis, scholars and preachers defending Islam and its people. It seems that they no longer trust the ability or loyalty of their sorcerers in the various councils of senior scholars of the sultans, supporters of the tyrants.

O Muslim people, America did not come with its crusade in order to defend the Muslims and spend its own money, despite the fact that its economy has collapsed, and take it on itself to train and arm the awakening councils (Sahawat)[3] in the Levant and Iraq out of compassion and fear for the *mujahidin* from the tyranny of the Kharijites, and to support them, as they claim; *"If only my people knew!"* {Sura 36 (Yā Sīn), 26} Would the crusaders rush to defend the *mujahidin* in the cause of God from the Kharijites?! "Live long enough and you will see strange things!" "Woe to my people!" When will they remember? God almighty says, *Neither those who disbelieve among the people of the Scripture nor the polytheists like that there should be sent down unto you any good from your Lord.* {Sura 2 (The Cow), 105} And He says, *And they will never cease fighting you until they turn you back from your religion if they can.* {Sura 2 (The Cow), 217}

America came for nothing but to fight Islam and the Muslims; it only gathered its allies and spent its money in order to break the *mujahidin*. So, these are the words of God on one hand, and those are the claims of the crusaders on the other hand; who are you going to believe, O Muslims? The crusaders' hearts did not break, their feelings were not moved, and their tears were not shed until they saw the Safavid army, their lackeys in the Iraq war, collapse under the strikes of the *mujahidin*, their soldiers fleeing like rats and being crushed like insects under the feet of the monotheists. Indeed, America went mad and its allies lost their senses when the Nusayiri forces, the guard dogs of the Jews, began collapsing in terror, fleeing in panic in the face of the *mujahidin's* advance. America and its allies were broken when they saw the herds of the Nusayiris being driven like animals and slaughtered like sheep in the greatest battle that the Nusayiris had lost in their dark history, allowing the advance of the Islamic State army towards Damascus.

Only then did the crusaders realise the real danger; only then were their feelings moved; only then were their hearts hurt and their tears shed; only then did they feel pain and suffering; only then did America and its allies rise in terror and call upon one another, "The Jews, the Jews! Save the Jews!" This is the reason why they came; this is the purpose of their mobilisation. "If only my people knew! If only my people knew!" Indeed, the truth behind their opposition and resistance has become very obvious: the Nusayiris and the Rafida could not contain themselves, so the former openly called upon America for support and welcomed their strikes on the Islamic State, forgetting their alleged sovereignty and their imaginary strength and abilities, as well as their fake animosity towards America. The same applies to Iran, since its coalition with its "greatest Satan" became clear, when the uncircumcised old man, Kerry, recently announced that Iran has a role to play in the war against the Islamic State. So it became clear that the opposition is for the sake of the Jews and the crusaders and that the resistance is against Islam and the *mujahidin*.

O Sunnis of Iraq, it is time for you to learn from the lessons of the past, and that nothing works with the Rafida but the slicing of their throats and the striking of their necks; they pretend to be helpless until they get strong; they hide their hatred, anger and enmity towards the people of the Sunnah, they plot and conspire against them; they show false affection towards them and flatter them as long as the Sunnis are strong, while they try to keep in step with them, compete with them and try their hardest to weaken them when they are equal in power. If they manage to overcome them, they reveal their sharp teeth and their claws and start biting them, tearing them apart, killing and humiliating them.

History is right here between your hands, O people of the Sunnah! Read it and find out how many times the Rafida conspired and what they did whenever they had more power. Read their history and look at their present. Nouri [al-Maliki], the loser, showed you their true faces. So, don't be fooled by the soft touch and the sweet tongue of their new snake. You have previously been betrayed by the so-called reconciliation with Nouri, the loser. So beware! Beware! Our people in the Levant, this is the truth; it is becoming clearer day after day. Draw a lesson from our people in Iraq, for history is repeating itself. In fact, the crusaders began building the Safavid Iraqi army by training its core in Jordan with a few thousand soldiers, in the same way it has now been decided for the Levant. The Sunnis gained nothing from that army, except that they allowed the Rafida to have complete power over them. They experienced humiliation, disgrace and suffering by that army over a period of ten years. Moreover, what did the children of the Sunnis gain from joining that army, other than apostasy from the religion of God, the demolition of their homes and having their heads cut off? Those of them who survived lived in ongoing terror, not knowing when a bullet would hit them or their guts would be ripped by an adhesive IED, or when they would be lacerated by a booby-trapped vehicle or an IED, or when their breath would be stopped by a silencer or their throats cut by a bayonet, or when they would go back to their homes to find them demolished, turned into rubble after being whole.

What would all this have been done for? So, learn your lesson O people of wisdom! *And how many a generation we have destroyed before them, who were stronger in power than them, and they ran for a refuge in the land! Could they find any place of refuge? Verily, therein is indeed a reminder for him who has a heart or gives ear while he is heedful.* {Sura 50 (Qāf), 36–37} Be careful, O Sunnis. For the army they have planned to form today by the Saudis is nothing but a new set of guard dogs for the Jews and a stick in the hands of the crusaders [to use] against Islam and the *mujahidin*.

For this very reason, we advise the *mujahidin* in the Levant to target anyone who belongs to that army or intends to join it. Forewarned is forearmed! As for the awakening councils (Sahawat) and their political godfathers, they will be unable to hide their truth which will be so obvious that, from now on, they are the shoes of the crusaders. So, rally around the *mujahidin*, O people of the Sunnah in the Levant; forbid your sons to join the army and the awakening Sahawat. What kind of good can come from an army that is formed by the crusaders and trained in the arms of the tyrants? Forbid your sons! Whoever refuses can blame no one but himself if a day comes for him when he will have to dig his own grave, [before] his head is cut off and his house demolished.

Blessed is he who learns from other people's mistakes. To God belongs honour, to His Messenger and to the faithful, and the final outcome will be in favour of the pious. Let me not forget before ending to praise our brothers, the *mujahidin* in the brave Sinai, for hope has shone on the land of Kinana [Egypt] and joy has appeared in Egypt with their blessed operations against the protectors of the Jews, soldiers of [president] Sisi, the new Pharaoh. Continue on this path as it is the correct one. Bless you! Disperse those behind them wherever you may find them; booby-trap the roads, attack the headquarters, attack them in their homes and cut off their heads. Do not allow them to feel safe, and hunt them wherever they may be; turn their lives into horror and hell. Remove their children from their homes and blow [their homes] up; do not say it is *fitna*! The *fitna* is that their people defend them and do not disavow them.

He [God] said: *O Noah! Surely, he is not of your family; verily, his work is unrighteous.* {Sura 11 (Hūd), 46} *If you do not do so (i.e. become allies, as one united block to make victorious God's religion of Islamic monotheism), there will be fitna (wars) and oppression on earth, and a great mischief and corruption.* {Sura 8 (Spoils of War), 73}

To our monotheist brothers in beloved Libya, for how long is this division and factionalism going to last? Bring your groups together, unite your words and your groups; strengthen your ranks and identify who is with you and who is against you. For your division is inspired by Satan. *Verily, God loves those who fight in His cause in rows (ranks) as if they were a solid structure.* {Sura 61 (Formations), 4}

We also call on the monotheists in occupied Tunisia to follow in the foot-steps of their brothers in the land of Kinana. O monotheist brothers, what are you waiting for, while the tyrants have forbidden you to practise *da'wa* [benediction], to migrate, and have opened for you the prison doors of their fake freedom? They are arresting and killing your brothers every day. What are you waiting for? Is it the life of humiliation, or have you come to love life and hate death? Rise, because a monotheist is an army by himself! Where are the descendants of Uqba, Musa and Tariq?[4] *Fight against them so that God will punish them by your hands and disgrace them and give you victory over them and heal the breasts of a believing people.* {Sura 9 (Repentance), 14}

As for Yemen, O alas, what has become of Yemen! Alas! Alas for Sanaa. The Rafidhite Houthis enter it, yet booby-traps do not grill their skin; explosive belts and IEDs do not rip their guts. Is there not in Yemen anyone who can bring us joy by taking revenge against the Houthis? *And if you turn away (from Islam and the obedience of God), He will exchange you for some other people, and they will not be your likes.* {Sura 47 (Mohammed), 38}

O monotheists [i.e. true Muslims] in Europe, America, Australia and Canada; O monotheists in Morocco and Algeria; O monotheists in Khorasan, the Caucasus and Iran; O monotheists everywhere on the face of Earth, O brothers in creed, O people of loyalty to the Muslims [*wala*] and disavowal of the disbelievers (*bara*), O supporters of the Islamic State, O you who have pledged allegiance to Caliph Ibrahim everywhere; you who love the Islamic State, you who support the caliphate, you who consider yourselves to be among its soldiers and its supporters, your state is facing a new crusade. O monotheist, wherever you may be, what are you going to do to support your brothers? What are you waiting for, as people have fallen into two encampments and the war is heating up day after day? O monotheists, we call upon you to defend the Islamic State at a time when tens of countries have gathered against it. They initiated war and enmity against us at all levels. So rise, O monotheist, rise and defend your state from wherever you are; get up and defend your Muslim brothers, because their homes, property and honour are threatened and have been made cheap [by the enemies] and because they are fighting one of the most decisive battles in the history of Islam. For if the Muslims were to be defeated, they would be humiliated in a manner that is second to none; and if they were to be victorious—and that will be the case, with the permission of God—they will live in glory that will make the Muslims become the masters of the world and kings of the earth.

Come on, O monotheist; do not miss out on this battle wherever you may be. Target the soldiers, the police of the tyrants and their supporters, their security forces and their allies. Destroy their dwellings and spoil their life for them. If you can, kill an American or a European disbeliever—especially the filthy hateful French—or an Australian or a Canadian or any other fighting disbelievers, including the citizens of the coalition of allies against the Islamic State.

Rely on God and kill in any means or way you can; do not take advice from or ask for a fatwa from anyone, whether the disbeliever is a civilian or a military, since the same ruling applies to both; they are both disbelievers and both fighters, and both their blood and property are permissible [to take]. Because blood does not become illegal or permissible based on clothing; a civilian outfit does not make blood illegal, and the military uniform does not make blood legal. The only things that make blood [i.e. killing] legal and illegal are Islam and a covenant and it becomes legal [to kill] in the case of disbelief.

Whoever is a Muslim means that their blood and property are sanctified; and whoever is a disbeliever, their property becomes legal for the Muslims to take and their blood legal to spill like that of a dog, there is no sin committed against them or blood money [owed].

God says, "*Then when the Sacred Months (the 1st, 7th, 11th, and 12th months of the Islamic calendar) have passed, then kill the polytheists wherever you find them, and capture them and besiege them, and prepare for them each and every ambush.*" {Sura 9 (Repentance), 5} He also says, "*So, when you meet (fighting Jihad in God's Cause) those who disbelieve, smite at their necks.*" {Sura 47 (Mohammed), 4} The Messenger of God (PBUH) also said, "*A disbeliever and his killer will never meet in hellfire*"; and he said, "*Whoever kills a disbeliever can have his loot.*"

O monotheist, you who believe in loyalty to the Muslims, disavowal of the disbelievers [*al wala wal bara*], will you let an American, French or any one of their allies walk safely on earth while the armies of the crusaders are bombarding the land of the Muslims with their aircraft, fighters not differentiating between a civilian and a fighter? Nine Muslim women were killed a few days ago when they struck the bus that was driving them from the Levant to Iraq. Will you let the disbeliever sleep safely in their homes while fighter aircraft are terrorising Muslim women and children with noises over their heads day and night? How can you enjoy your life and sleep when you have not supported your brothers and cast terror in the hearts of the worshippers of the cross and retaliated harder than they hit?

O monotheist, wherever you may be, defend your state in any manner you can, and the best that you can do is to devote your efforts to killing any French or American disbelievers or any of their allies. *O you who believe! Take your precautions, and either go forth (on an expedition) in parties, or go forth all together.* {Sura 4 (The Women), 71} If you are unable to use an IED or a bullet, then single out the French or the American disbeliever or any of their allies and smash their head with a rock or slaughter them with a knife, or run them over with your car or throw him down from a high place, or strangle them or poison them.

Do not fail or be contemptible, and let your slogan be "may I not be saved if the worshippers of the cross, supporters of the tyrants, survive". If you are unable to do so, then burn their house, car, business [premises] or destroy their crops. If you are unable to do so, then spit in their face. If you refuse to do that while your brothers are being bombarded and killed, and while their blood and property are being attacked everywhere, then review your religion! You are in a dangerous condition because religion cannot stand without loyalty and disavowal.

Let us not forget to send a message to our Muslim Kurdish brothers in Iraq, the Levant and elsewhere that our war with the Kurds is a religious war, not a nationalistic war, God forbid! We do not fight the Kurds because they are Kurds; we fight the disbelievers amongst them, allies of the crusaders and the Jews in the war against the Muslims. As for the Muslim Kurds, they are our people, brothers wherever they may be. We spill our blood to save theirs. The Muslim Kurds in the ranks of the Islamic State are many, and are amongst the toughest fighters against the disbelievers among their own people.

O God, America, France and their allies attacked us; they came with their legions to fight us out of animosity towards your religion. They prevent us from establishing your religion and implementing your punishment and from ruling with what you revealed. O God, you know our weakness; we have no solution against their aircraft. O God what You have said is the truth, *so do not become weak (against your enemy), nor be sad, and you will be superior (in victory) if you are indeed (true) believers.* {Sura 3 (The Family of Imran), 139}

O God, we have believed in you and relied on you; you are sufficient for us and the best disposer of affairs [for us]. O God, America and its allies disbelieve in you, as do their associate partners; O God, you placed them above us with their aircraft; O God, you know we have no strength or power against them except through you; O God, let them not be above us while you are above them. O God, let them not be above us while we are higher [than them]. There is no god but you, you are mighty and do not fail your promise; we seek forgiveness from you and repent to you; O God, you will prevent them from harming us with whatever and however you will; you are the mighty, the compeller!

O God, may you bring them down to the ground and place us above them; you are the king, you prevail! O God, make it their last crusade; we will then raid them, and they will not raid us. There is no god but you; you are the almighty, we have been among the wrongdoers, we ask for your forgiveness and repent to you, so do not hold us responsible for what the foolish among us have done; you are sufficient for us and the best disposer of affairs [for us]; we sought refuge in you and turn over our affairs to you. You are the almighty, the almighty! You are the best protector and the best helper.

Peace and blessings be upon our Prophet Mohammed, his family and all his companions. Our final prayer be to God, the Lord of the worlds!

SUPPORT YOUR PROPHET—PEACE AND BLESSINGS BE UPON HIM

MARCH 2015

By Ayman al-Zawahiri

In this video message, Zawahiri celebrates the attack on the headquarters of the French satirical magazine Charlie Hebdo and is quick to claim credit for it on behalf of Al-Qaeda in the Arabian Peninsula. This of course comes at a time when Al-Qaeda's central command is broadly seen as inactive and marginalised. He focuses on alleged double standards of the West regarding its support for democracy, tracing, as always, his grievances back to colonial times, whilst emphasising more normative components of this grievance, with an obvious focus on the prohibition of ridiculing the Prophet. He reiterates his criticism of the transgressors in Syria, noting that the route taken by IS contravenes the more inclusive plan for caliphate creation drafted by bin Laden.

Al-Sahab Media Productions, March 2015

The video footage begins with Osama bin Laden's voice saying: "If the freedom of your words has no boundaries, then open your hearts to the freedom of our acts."

[Ayman al-Zawahiri begins]
In the name of God; praise be to God, peace and blessings be upon the Messenger of God, His family and supporters.

169

O Muslim brothers around the world, peace and blessings be upon you! The world was recently shaken by the blessed battle of Paris[5] with which the heroic knights, may God bless their souls, healed the hearts of the faithful and caused sorrow and grief to the hearts of the criminal enemies of Islam, the materialistic secular ones whose hearts are dripping with crusaders' hatred; those who invaded the land of Islam, killed its people, appropriated their riches and mocked their beliefs before spreading their dissoluteness and indecency in Muslim countries.

Those fortunate knights also caused grief to the hearts of the followers of the enemies of the Prophet, the beggars who sell their religion in return for vanities of the world. However, before I talk about this lofty event [that took place] in contemporary history, it is important that I begin with prayers of mercy and forgiveness, and the highest and ample rewards for the heroes, lovers of the Prophet (PBUH), the proud and noble knights who fought under his banner in defence of his position and holiness, our noble and free brothers who carried out the Paris operation against the vile newspaper and against the Jews in Paris.[6] It is that newspaper which assailed the honour of our beloved Mohammed (PBUH). So, may God grant them the best rewards, for they have healed the hearts of the faithful and delighted them; they took their revenge and taught their enemies a lesson that they will never forget, with the permission of God.

May God also reward all those who helped in achieving that blessed deed. I specifically refer to our brothers in Al-Qaeda in the Arabian Peninsula, whom we have always known to be people of ardency, sacrifice and loyalty; may God grant them, on behalf of Islam and the Muslims, His best rewards and victory against their crusader enemies as well as their tail lackeys and their vain Rafidhite Houthi allies. May God bless their position in the Arabian Peninsula and in Yemen, the land of faith, wisdom, Jihad, *Ribat* [fortification] and assistance against the crusaders, the secular and the Rafida. May God bless their pursuit of the biggest criminals in the world in punishment for their attack against Islam and the Prophet of Islam, peace be upon him and the Muslims. It is no wonder, as the people of jihad in the Arabian Peninsula and in faithful and wise Yemen are of the same origin as the supporters [*ansar*], may God be pleased with them, who were praised by our master Abu Kaab ibn Zuhair, may God be pleased with him, as he said:

> He who has been pleased with the generosity of life is he who remains amongst the elite knights and cavalry (prior to a battle) of the *ansar*; they inherited virtues from one master to another, they are the best and children of the best, who sacrifice

themselves for their Prophet in days of turmoil and invasions by ruthless invaders; defenders of people's faith with the sword and the accurate spear, they have sold their souls to their Prophet for death in days of fierce confrontational battles; they purify themselves, and see it as sacrifice, with the blood of the disbelievers who get trapped; if you come to them and are faced with rejection, you find yourself at the edge of worthlessness; if the living had the knowledge I have about them [the *ansar*], truly even my detractors would believe me.

May God bless the *mujahidin* in the Arabian Peninsula, who are the people of loyalty, ardour and support for the Prophet (PBUH). If history knows about Al-Aws wal-Khazraj [two enemy tribes known for their fighting skills that were united by Islam], then the "supporters" are God's other Aws wal-Khazraj. I also ask God the almighty to bless with His mercy and acceptance the hard-working *mujahid* and scholar Sheikh Harith al-Nadhari, who was a role model for the knowledge seekers and active ones who die as martyrs in the battlefield, mixing the scholars' ink with the martyrs' blood, and left no room for arguments for anyone who has failed to wage individual jihad to push away the crusader, Rafidhite, or secular invaders of the Islamic land.

I therefore beseech God to give the Muslim nation and us a worthy replacement, to grant his family and his brothers patience and consolation and to unite us with him [in the hereafter] unchanged. I will, God willing, deliver a session from the series of "The Islamic Spring" about the Safavid, Rafidhite [Shia] danger, about the Arabian Peninsula and Yemen, land of faith and wisdom. It is the series that I have decided to postpone till after this address, and in which I will talk about the crusade against the Levant and Iraq; God is He who determines what is good. May God have mercy on our brothers, martyrs of the battle of Paris, grant them a place in the *Firdaus* [highest level in Paradise] and unite them with the beloved Prophet (PBUH) in a true gathering [in the afterlife as opposed to a false gathering in this world] before the powerful king [God]; O God, allow us to join them without shame, regret or division.

My Muslim brothers and children, who are ardent towards their religion and the sacredness of their Prophet (PBUH), O *mujahidin* in all the Jihadi groups and in Al-Qaeda, let those brothers be our role models and let us devote our efforts against our enemies, not against each other. My Muslim *mujahidin* brothers and children, this is a victory for all of us; it is a victory for the Islamic *ummah* [nation or community] against the dissolute Westerners who have abandoned their Christianity, and yet their hearts are still dripping with the hatred of crusaders for the Muslims. Those who are religiously agnostic and sentimentally crusaders are the same people who are launching against us today the biggest crusades in the history of Islam, from Indonesia to Western Africa. Let us then join our efforts and unite our ranks in order to harm the enemies of Islam in seeking the acceptance of God and in support of our Prophet (PBUH); let us compete in achieving this good, rather than competing in accusing each other of being disbelievers and attacking our brothers, excelling in their accusations to justify the shedding of their blood.

I pray God to unite the *mujahidin* and the Muslims around what He favours; it is He who has the power to make it happen. Congratulations, O Muslims, congratulations to all the *mujahidin* for this great victory and distinct conquest; I pray God by His mighty attributes and by His names to make this the beginning of good and unity of the ranks and the word, the end of rivalry amongst the Muslims and the *mujahidin*, and return to our previous state of unity, concord and mercy and to help us keep our promise to our leader, the great *mujaddid* [renewer of the Faith] Sheikh Osama bin Laden, may God have mercy on him, who said to the Western crusaders, "if the freedom of your words has no boundaries, then open your hearts to the freedom of our acts", and to show the enemies of Islam what they hate to see us do, not what makes them gloat; I ask every free and honest Muslim, ardent about their religion and the sacredness of their Prophet (PBUH), to pursue whoever dares to disrespect the Prophet and never to give up pursuing them, to deprive them of security and sleep, and to forget neither Salman Rushdie nor the Danish artist,[7] the American Coptic,[8] nor all those who have dared insult our master, the Messenger of God (PBUH).

Europe and the boastful West are uprising in defence of freedom, which in reality is their freedom to do whatever they like with us, to attack us in any way they wish and to commit sacrilege against us. If this is not the case, then where was that freedom when America committed genocide against the native Indians? Where was that freedom when Great Britain waged a war against China to guarantee the free trade of opium? Where was that freedom when they bombarded Japan with conventional weapons and then with atomic bombs? Where was that freedom when America reduced Vietnam to ashes and killed about five million people? Where was that freedom when they occupied our countries, stole and continued to steal our riches? Where was that freedom when they appointed a bunch of corrupt agents as our leaders? Where was that freedom when Napoleon occupied Egypt, destroyed its cities and occupied al-Azhar with his horses, which defiled copies of the Holy Quran and books on Islamic jurisprudence with their hooves on two occasions, before moving to Acre where he delivered his famous call for the Jews to occupy Palestine? Where was that freedom when France invaded Algeria and imposed a law that was other than the Islamic law, forbade the use of the Arabic language and killed more than one million martyrs? Where was that freedom when the soldiers of France [the Algerian government] carried out a coup against the Islamic Salvation Front, cancelled the elections and imprisoned its members?

Nonetheless, we admit that the Islamic Front was wrong to take part in secular elections. But I here wish to show the double standard of France and the crusader West regarding their sense of freedom which follows a one-way system. Where was that freedom when they bombarded Mali and forced its people to migrate? Where was that freedom when the West planted a Jewish state in Palestine with iron and fire? Where was that freedom when Gaza was set alight three times and when thousands of women, children, men and the elderly were killed? Where was that freedom when they killed about one million children [in Iraq] with the embargo? Where was that freedom when they burnt down mosques and villages in Afghanistan? Where was that freedom when they sullied the Holy Quran time and time again in Guantanamo, Afghanistan and elsewhere? Where was that freedom in Abu Ghraib? Where was that freedom when America practised torture, attacks and arrests without trial millions of times in her secret prisons and in Guantanamo? Where was that freedom when Obama, the CIA executioner, granted immunity regarding the trials? Where was that freedom when Blair stopped the investigation of the corruption scandal in Al-Yamama[9] in obedience to the corrupt Saudi government? Where was that freedom when France made the fact of standing up to the Jews a crime, claiming it was anti-Semitism and made it a crime to question the holocaust? Where was that freedom when France and other European countries banned Muslim women from wearing the veil, and Switzerland banned the construction of minarets? Where were their human rights when they supported Sisi in his coup against Mohammed Morsi, even though both of them were presidents of a secular state; a den of apostates?

Yet, I only wish to demonstrate their contradictions, because they consider democracy legitimate, while they turn against those who reach power through democracy, revealing their true view about it, as it is nothing but a means to achieve their interests! Other than that, it has no value whatsoever for them. On the other hand, it has become obvious for the Muslims that trying to reach power and rule according to Islam through democracy is a loss both for religion and in life [in this life and in the afterlife].

Where was that freedom and where were their human rights when thousands were killed in Rabia al-Adawiya and Nahdha and other squares in Egypt? Where was their freedom in the detention centres and slaughterhouses of the state security where men are killed and women are raped?

[A video footage features a female wearing a *niqab* testifying about her experience in a detention centre where her husband is imprisoned. A scrolling text on the screen reads, "Wife of prisoner Hassan Anwar" talking behind a microphone to an audience; her testimony is broadcast by Al-Shaab TV channel]

[The woman talks about her experiences in prison]

He said to me, "Look behind you," but because the strike was so hard I couldn't see anything, but he said again, "Look behind you," so I did. Then he asked me, "Who is this?" I replied, "He's my husband." He added, "See what he did to you?" I said, "No, it wasn't him, he didn't do anything to me, it's you who brought me here and hit me; it wasn't him. You're taking revenge on us!" He then said, "OK, let me take revenge on you then," and took me to the room where my husband was detained and he ... they tried to rape me. He then told him, "Stop, stop," that was of course when the other guy was telling someone to undress me etc., so he told him, "Just leave her alone, I will speak, but just take her out." He was told, "No, you speak first, then we will take her out." "I swear to God, I will speak, just take her out." I had the face cover on before I was brought into that room, but he had already started taking my veil and niqab off, so the face cover fell off. They took me inside the room and tried to do the thing, so I obviously screamed really loudly and shouted, "This is haram!*" He [the husband] then told them, "What do I have to say? I'll say it, but don't do that!" That is it really. I saw that my husband couldn't take it any more and kept saying, "Just take her out of here; just list the accusations and I'll admit to them." So they took me out and he told him [she pauses as she cries]. They laid him on the floor and one said, "See if he speaks, and if he doesn't, bring her back in." He argued, "OK, just tell me what I have to say and I'll say it, but leave her alone." At that point he shouted at him and ordered a guy to bring me in, which he did; when I was out, he blindfolded me and tied my hands behind my back, picked me up and dropped me on a chair close to a door and said they'd hang me too unless he speaks. At that point, he [the husband] started swearing to God that he would say anything they wanted, as he didn't even know what he was accused of. [She pauses and cries] I find what happened very strange and incomprehensible, and told the guy, "I heard my husband scream in a horrible way and I cannot imagine that he'll cope if you hang me." My husband was still asking them to tell him what he had to say. They hit him in revenge from 10 until 12 o'clock and I could hear him scream before the guy ordered for me to be brought back, which I was. At that point the blindfold moved as they were hitting me, so I managed to see around five men over my husband. Then they dragged me into the room.*

[Continuation of Ayman Al-Zawahiri's speech]

My Muslim brothers, theoretically democracy is the high-handedness of desires and the dictatorship of the majority over the minority based on no moral values whatsoever, but in practice it is the control of the West over the rest of the world. That is why only five of the biggest criminals of the Security Council have total control of the international order regardless of the existence of democratic systems [in the West]; and although the charter of their human rights claims that it does not segregate against people according to their gender, religion and race, yet it has kept a blind eye on two serious discriminative facts that the dictator West uses to segregate against people: the first one being with the use of force, which explains the control of the five biggest criminals of the Security Council of the international order; and the second one being the segregation of people based on the countries they belong to. They used force to invade our countries and then legitimised their invasion; they destroyed our caliphate and distributed our land using a quota system; they planted Israel in Palestine and justified that act. They divided the Muslim nation, which was united by one caliphate, into more than fifty states; this is the truth about the international order that they keep silent about. However, we will, with the permission of God, soon recover our caliphate from East Turkistan to the Atlantic coast according to the Prophet's way, based on the Shura [advisory system] and the choice of the *ummah* of its leader and holding him accountable for his leadership, based on justice and consent, and according to divine law and the principle of humbleness towards the faithful and force against the disbelievers.

My dear Muslim brothers, the enemies of Islam, including India, China, Europe, Russia and America, did not show any respect for us or any consideration for our religion. Therefore, we have the right to respond to their aggression and to punish them. In order to achieve that, we have to transfer the battle to the enemies' land, especially in Europe and America, because they are the leaders of the contemporary crusades; they have to be killed in the way they are killing, and to be injured in the way they are injuring, to be bombarded in the way they are bombarding, cry and become orphans and widows in the way they are making our people cry, become orphans and widows; *and fight them until there is no more fitna (disbelief and worshipping of others along with God) and (all and every kind of) worship is for God (Alone). But if they cease, let there be no transgression except against the wrongdoers. The sacred month is for the sacred month, and for the prohibited things, there is the law of equality. Then whoever transgresses the prohibition against you, you transgress likewise against him. And fear God, and know that God is with the pious.* {Sura 2 (The Cow), 193–194}

This blessed battle, like previous blessed battles, has unveiled the alliance, and vileness and the decline of the "turbans of the sultan" [lackeys], State

Security officials and servants of the secular armies, such as the hypocrite personnel of the sheikhdom of al-Azhar who have tarnished the history of that lofty establishment. It has also exposed their like, such as the marines' sheikhs [in favour of the US] and beggars for residence permits and citizenship, such as secret services' and embassies' preachers, who have mourned, with such obvious hypocrisy, the fools who mocked the Messenger of God (PBUH), and adulated them for the sake of some earthly leftovers they get donated by the crusaders.

O Muslim nation, O Muslim youth *mujahidin*, it may have become clear to you who are your honest scholars, who speak out the truth and fear no blame for the sake of God, and for whom time and events have shown their honesty and good deed in support of their religion and defence of their Prophet (PBUH). So honour them, respect them, and do not allow the fraudulent to assail them for the sake of political gain. We, at Al-Qaeda, put all our trust in both the leading fighters and the scholars of jihad, whose honesty, perseverance and care for the *mujahidin* have been proven by time, such as our dear Sheikh Abu Mohammed al-Maqdisi and Sheikh Abu Qatada al-Filistini—may God preserve them—and Sheikh Abu al-Waleed al-Filistini and Sheikh Mohamed al-Zawahiri, Sheikh Salem Morjan and Sheikh Ahmad Ashoush— May God release them from prison—and Sheikh Hani al-Sabaaee, Sheikh Tariq Abdul Halim and other honest preachers like them. We believe they are; yet God alone decides if they are. And finally, the leader of the jihadist sect, its teacher and educator, the chained lion Sheikh Omar Abdurrahman—may God release him from prison.

I call upon all those honest men and their like whenever possible to migrate to the liberated land of the *mujahidin* in order to be assets to them. I also invite the *mujahidin*, scholars and honest preacher brothers to revive the call of the *mujaddid* [renewer] Imam Osama bin Laden—may God bless his soul—that which he directed the elite *mujahidin*, the Muslims' leaders, scholars, businessmen and people of authority to do; that is to set up the foundation for an executive council with the consent of the *ummah* and which will be a first step to advise the *mujahidin* in their endeavour to revive the caliphate in the Prophet's way. Sheikh Osama—may God bless his soul—said in his paper "Inciting Jihad" in December 2003 that:

> it is the duty of honest people who may be concerned, such as scholars and those who have authority within their community, the elite and the businessmen, to call upon one another to hold a meeting in a safe place, away from the shadow of those tyrannical regimes, and set up an executive council that would fill in the gap caused

by those regimes which have become void from a religious point of view, hence unable to run the countries, and that only the people have the right to choose their leaders and to hold them accountable in case they deviate from the right path. They also have the right to depose them if they commit acts that justify that decision, such as apostasy and treason. This temporary council should comprise a very small number of members without excluding the rest of the people from decision-making except when necessary and as permitted by the Sharia in "force majeure" until circumstances improve and the full numbers are reached, with the permission of God, and that they should rule in the Prophet's way (PBUH).

Then he—may God bless his soul—explained the duties of such a council during its initial phase, when he said:

during this critical phase they should begin by making the Muslims focus on priorities and lead them to safety as long as their primary target is to unite them under the word of monotheism [repeated twice], and to defend Islam and its people, to incite the Muslims to prepare and undergo jihad and to facilitate the supply of weapons for the people, especially small arms, anti-armour such as RPG rockets and anti-tank mines, and make a general call for the *ummah* to be ready to push away the treachery of the Romans that has begun in Iraq, ending who knows where. God is sufficient for us.

So, Sheikh Osama—may God bless his soul—had determined the duties of this temporary council in the current situation, which he described as being critical. However, the designation of a caliph was not on the list of duties that he had mentioned; on the contrary, he frankly said that the designation of the Imam [leader] is the sole right of the people and that no one else, including this type of temporary council, could hijack such a right. Actually, this goes in line with what he repeatedly mentioned to his brothers in Al-Qaeda, as he insisted that the current situation is not favourable for the creation of emirates, but that the current situation should be the preparation phase for an Islamic state; he also said in his speech of support for the revolutions in Egypt and Tunisia, and which was published in May 2011 following his death as a martyr—May God bless his soul:

O children of the Islamic *ummah*, you stand at a dangerous crossroads: this is a great and rare historic opportunity for the *ummah* to rise, to free yourselves from slavery of the rulers' desires, man-made laws and Western domination; it is a great sin and an act of ignorance to miss out on this opportunity which the *ummah* has waited for decades to see take place. Seize this opportunity, destroy the idols and install justice and faith.

Following this, let me remind the honest men that the creation of a council that provides suggestions and advice in all important fields for Muslim peoples is a religious duty; I would like to insist as I address those ardent men, who quite prematurely called for the uprooting of the oppressing governments, that since they are highly trusted by the Muslim people, they should start up this project and announce it very soon, away from the domination of the dictator rulers, and set up an operation room that is up to date with events in order to carry out parallel work that would cover everything people need, while benefitting from the suggestions made by insightful people within this nation, and seeking the help of suitable research centres as well as the people of knowledge in order to save the peoples that are struggling to bring down their tyrants, and whose children are being killed; also, they should help those who have already brought down the rulers and some of their pillars to take the right steps and protect the revolution and its goals.

It is also important to help the countries that have not started their own revolution yet to determine the zero hour and what needs to be done prior to its announcement, because delay might lead to missing out on this opportunity; yet at the same time, doing it prematurely increases the numbers of victims. In any case, I believe that the currents of change will spread throughout the Muslim world—with the permission of God—which is why the youth have to prepare seriously for it. But they should not take any step into it before seeking advice from honest people with experience, who do not accept compromise and adulate the oppressors [repeated twice]; wisdom comes before courage!

That is why I call upon all the Muslims and the *mujahidin* to endeavour to revive this call and to facilitate the ways to make it happen. The first step towards this goal is for us to unite around our hard-working and honest *mujahidin* scholars, and protect them from anyone who would attack them for political purposes.

My Muslim *ummah*, the courageous heroes of the battle of Paris have shown that sullying Prophet Mohammed (PBUH) and the Jewish criminal attacks on Palestine are two crimes committed by the same criminal i.e. the Zionist—Western coalition. This is the reason why they attacked the Jews in Paris and the despicable newspaper, because in both cases the criminal was one and the same. [Benjamin] Netanyahu went to mourn the poor Jews, who had been helping Israel, and took their bodies to be buried in Jerusalem. That hypocrite mourned four Jews, while it was he who set the whole of Gaza alight in retaliation for the death of three Jewish individuals. This ungrateful man who chose to forget that the Muslims protected the Jews from the expulsions and tribunals [the Inquisition] in Andalusia; they [the Jews] rewarded the Muslims by allying with the crusader–secular West in order to occupy

Palestine in exactly the same way they are allying with them today in defending those who sullied the Prophet of Islam (PBUH).

Those who have sullied the Prophet (PBUH) are the same ones who campaigned for and contributed to the creation of Israel and continue to support it to this day. Neither we nor our future generations will forget that the secular Napoleon stood by the walls of Acre and made his famous invitation for the Jews to go back to Palestine, and that France strongly supported the creation of Israel and was a crucial sponsor of its nuclear programme. Today, France continues to defend the criminals, who carry on attacking the Prophet (PBUH). We will not forget nor will our future generations that on 2 November 1917 [Lord] Balfour, the British Prime Minister [then Foreign Secretary], made his declaration to support the Jews to set up a national state in Palestine, and that around a month after that, precisely on 9 December 1917, the fanatic protestant and leader of the coalition against Palestine, [Viscount] Allenby, said when he entered Jerusalem, "Now the crusades are complete."

[Black and white video footage that features British troops in Palestine is accompanied by a commentary]

[Video begins]: On 9 December 1917 the British troops entered Jerusalem led by General Allenby, head of the Egypt campaign forces; the Crusader Allenby insisted on entering Jerusalem in a military parade on foot to mark the greatness of the place. Another crusader also insisted on attending, and that is the secret services officer [T. E.] Lawrence, who was the mastermind of the Arab traitors among the children of Noble [Sharif] Hussein, who betrayed the Ottoman state and helped the crusaders to defeat it and drive it out of the Levant and then enter Jerusalem. When General Allenby entered Jerusalem, revealing his crusader's hatred, he made his famous statement that neither we nor our future generations should ever forget: "Now the Crusades are complete." This is how the "Judaisation" of Jerusalem began, since Britain handed Palestine over to the Jews in May 1948 [after which they] entered Jerusalem in 1967. [Video ends]

[Continuation of Ayman Al-Zawahiri's speech]

Britain handed Palestine over to the Jews in 1948; recently Queen Elizabeth awarded Salman Rushdie a knighthood; today the British Prime Minister is defending the criminals who insist on continuing to sully the Prophet (PBUH). The current President of America, which played a major role in the crime of setting up of the state of Israel, is also defending the same vile people, while his predecessor Bill Clinton received Salman Rushdie in the White House as a mark of honour. Sheikh Osama bin Laden—may God bless his soul—was aware of the creation of this criminal coalition that is guilty of both crimes; that is why he incited the Muslim nation to stand up for it and to defend itself against it.

Sheikh Osama said, "I swear by the Lord who raised heavens without pillars that America and the people who live in America will not even be able to dream to live in peace until the latter becomes reality in Palestine and until all the disbeliever armies leave each and every piece of the Prophet Mohammed's [Muslim] land." He also said:

> To our brothers in Palestine, we say that the blood of your children is the blood of our children, and your blood is our blood. So, it is blood for blood and destruction for destruction, and we bear God almighty our witness that we will not give up on you until victory is achieved [or we share] the same fate as Hamza ibn Abdul-Muttalib [the Prophet's uncle who died in battle]—may God be pleased with him; be aware that Islam's assistance is on its way, and that reinforcements from Yemen will continue with the permission of the almighty; praise be to God for the reinforcements that came from Yemen in support of the Messenger of God (PBUH).

Osama bin Laden is also the one who said, "May our mothers be bereaved of us if we fail to support the Messenger of God (PBUH)." I pray God to help all Muslims and *mujahidin* to take part in the revival of call of the renewer Imam—may God bless his soul.

However, before I conclude my speech on the blessed battle of Paris, I would like to deliver two messages; the first is for the Islamic *ummah*. It may have become clear to you that your jihadi children have proven that you are a nation that does not sleep on revenge and that the position of the Messenger of God is great in their hearts; it may have become clear to you too that your jihadi children have kept the promise they made to you through the brief message of revenge for the Prophet (PBUH) that Sheikh Osama bin Laden sent over six years ago and in which he said, "If the freedom of your words has no boundaries, then open your hearts to the freedom of our acts"; and also, "May our mothers be bereaved of us if we fail to support the Messenger (PBUH)".

During that period the *mujahidin* have carried out several operations to avenge the Messenger of God (PBUH); one of which was a martyrdom operation against the Danish Embassy in Islamabad, followed by another one in Afghanistan and then by the blessed battle of Paris against the premises of wrongdoing. Even though revenge took a long time to happen, the criminals have and will continue to pay the price of their attack against our Prophet—with the permission of God. We warn whoever dares to sully our religion that they will be punished sooner or later—with the permission of God—even if

God chooses some of us to be martyrs, so those who remain will continue on the same path and will keep the promises they have made to support Islam.

It may have become clear to you, O our Islamic nation, that the struggle is that between Islam and disbelief, and is not counter-terrorism. It is a struggle between the religion which was called up by Prophet Mohammed (PBUH), and the religion of the West, which derives from the idolism of the Greeks, eroticism of the Romans, corrupted Christianity and the ignoble material secularism. It is a struggle between monotheism and polytheism, belief and atheism, purity and fornication and between moral values, integrity and prostitution, loose morals and usury, sex trade and the robbery and genocide of peoples; it is a struggle between the worship of the one God and the worship of humans and desires and money; it is a struggle between Divine Law and the escape from moral values and the governments of the elite that lead the lay people in the hysterical pursuit of desire and self-interest.

O our Islamic nation, this is the religion they felt so angry about that three million people demonstrated against three *mujahidin*. They went in the street to defend their wrongdoing and their sullying of our Prophet (PBUH); they insisted on continuing to undermine our Prophet (PBUH) and to say to us, "we will continue to commit this crime and this kind of transgressing". Various magazines published those bad cartoons; in fact, the same low newspaper was even published with a nasty cartoon of our Prophet on its cover after the blessed battle. This is the anger of the materialistic West and the hateful crusaders in defence of their criminals.

So, where is your anger and where is your ardour, O Muslims, in defence of your Prophet and your religion? Where is your support for the position of the Messenger of God, and where is your defence for his sacredness? Would you have less ardour and zeal than those who worship desire, self-interest and charlatanism, while you are the people of monotheism and faith and the purified Sharia? How close are you to God's words, *"The Prophet is closer to the believers than their own selves"* {Sura 33 (The Allied Troops), 6}, and *"So those who believe in him (Mohammed), honour him, help him, and follow the light (the Quran) which has been sent down with him, it is they who will be successful"* {Sura 7 (Wall Between Heaven and Hell), 157}, and *"Verily, We have sent you as witness, and a bearer of glad tidings and warnings in order that you (O mankind) may believe in God and His Messenger and that you assist and honour him, and (that you) glorify (God's) praises morning and afternoon."* {Sura 8 (Spoils of War), 8–9}

How close are you to the Prophet's words, *you will not believe until I become dearer to you than your own sons, fathers and everyone else*? O Islamic nation, I implore you in the name of "there is no god but God" [Islam] and in the name of your love for the Messenger of God to take revenge for the repeated humiliation of our master and dear Prophet (PBUH). I make that request to every Muslim and every *mujahid*; especially my brothers in Al-Qaeda who have always lived up to our expectations regarding their sacrifice of both the person and of property to defend religion and the Prophet (PBUH). Let us keep our promise and the promise of our Sheikh and leader of the *mujahidin*, the renewer Imam Osama bin Laden—may God bless his soul. O nation of Prophet Mohammed (PBUH) and youth of Islam around the world, be prepared with honesty and in anticipation of God's rewards to pursue whoever dares to attack Prophet Mohammed (PBUH). Be aware that your brothers in Al-Qaeda will assist you in every way possible; they will not hold back from any form of help in terms of reinforcement, advice or prayers.

O Islamic *ummah*, this war is not a war between an organisation and a newspaper; it is a war between Islam and disbelief, the crusaders and their lackeys against Prophet Mohammed and his followers, who defended him with their blood. This is your war and the one who is being attacked is your Prophet (PBUH). It is a war between the vile oppressors who suck people's blood and dominate them, and the Sharia of Prophet Mohammed (PBUH), law of justice, mercy and purity, support for the weak and jihad in the way of God.

My second message however is for the French and the West. I say to them, it may have become clear to you how serious and extended is the war that you have involved yourselves in; you may have some wise people who should advise you to withdraw from it. If not, it is our jihad that will force you to withdraw and to deter you—with the help of God. You get help from your power and armies, and we get our help from God, *but Sufficient is your Lord as a Guide and Helper*. This is only the beginning of the war, so expect more grief as we will be nothing but loyal to our Prophet, ready to defend our Sharia and to wage jihad in the way of our Lord. Blame no one but yourselves, because your persistence in fighting Islam and tightening your security measures will only work in our interest, because your lives become more complicated, your economy gets affected, only to see God help us to hit you yet again; you will continue in a downward spiral that will end up by throwing you into the swamp of defeat, God willing. The 11 September operation and others that followed, including the most recent one, are the best testimony to what I have said.

In conclusion I say Praise be to God; peace and blessings upon Prophet Mohammed (PBUH).

[A screenshot of a video footage features Osama bin Laden pointing a machine gun in a shooting position and a spear stained with blood. The voice of Osama bin Laden is heard saying along with a script in Arabic that reads, "May our mothers be bereaved of us if we fail to support our Prophet, Peace be upon him." Another script in English reads, "The answer is what you see, not what you hear." The text reads, "Omar al-Farooq, may God be pleased with him, said, "We are a nation that God gave glory to with Islam; therefore, we will not seek glory with anyone else." Al-Sahab Media]

THE ISLAMIC SPRING, PART 1

SEPTEMBER 2015

By Ayman al-Zawahiri

Here we arrive at another multipart series, where Zawahiri seeks to make sense of ongoing events in Syria and beyond, focusing on the split with ISIL. The date on the initial Al-Sahab release was Jumada al-Akhira 1436, corresponding to March 2015, although the series became available from autumn that year. It had clearly been in preparation for some time and Zawahiri made reference to it in his previous statement, "Support your Prophet". I have included five parts of this series, focusing on those elements that cover a broad range of issues, rather than technical or geographic details.

Zawahiri begins the series by mourning the death of the leader of Al-Shabaab, whose fealty he had accepted in 2012, and reaches out to affiliates, allies and sympathisers in places like Somalia, Palestine, Yemen, North Africa, and the Caucasus, as well as Syria. He claims to have wanted to temper his criticism of ISIL, hoping that the infighting between jihadis would come to an end, but ultimately to have seen no other option than presenting the evidence of al-Baghdadi's transgressions, which he says go against the pre-scribed method of the Prophet Mohammed. He challenges IS's understanding of takfir (excommunication), and warns against ways in which religious zealotry can turn to tyr-anny. In presenting the Muslim Brotherhood as being too compromising and weak, and IS as being too extreme, Zawahiri thus charts a clear "middle way" for Al-Qaeda and its understanding of the world, which he claims will ultimately be victorious.

Al-Sahab Media presents
New address by Sheikh Ayman Al-Zawahiri, leader of Al-Qaeda

In the name of God, the Most Gracious, the Most Merciful and peace and prayers upon his Messenger, his relations and supporters.

Dear brothers everywhere, may peace, mercy and blessing be upon you. I would like to start this series about the coming Islamic Spring, God permitting. Despite the intensity of the crusaders' campaign against Muslims, from Waziristan to the Islamic Maghreb; despite the apostate regimes' onslaught on the Arab people's revolutions; despite the failure of the groups who attempted to establish the Sharia law through non-Sharia rules, including secular and nationalist laws; despite all this, I believe that, with the help of God, the Islamic Spring will emerge.

However, before starting this series, I would like to raise a certain number of issues: first, Israel's attempts to Judaise al-Aqsa Mosque. This crime will ignite the spirit and energy of the Muslim *ummah* [nation or community] and will prove, with the will of God, that the methods of negotiations and agreement with the international community, and all means of reaching alliances with the secular traitors, are destined to fail. The *mujahidin* had in fact warned against these methods, because they clearly contradict Sharia and Islamic belief and lead to the loss of faith as well as worldly life. A crime such as this should prompt us to unite our efforts and rise above all arguments, bickering and accusations which are raised by some individuals with no evidence, sometimes contradicting the evidence. We must rise above these arguments and differences and unite our ranks against the crusader Zionist enemy, who is currently joining in alliance with the crusaders, the Safavids [Shia], the Nusayiris [Alawite] and the secularists. The importance of jihad in Al-Sham [Syria] is a priority. Our duty is to prevent *fitna* [sedition/strife] and internal [strife] and political conflicts within this blessed country. Victory in Al-Sham is a prelude to the liberation of Beit Al-Maqdis [Jerusalem], God willing. I shall dedicate one episode of this series to Palestine and the *ummah*'s jihad against Israel.

The second matter is to offer condolences following the death of Sheikh Mukhtar Abu-Zubair,[10] God have mercy on him. Let me congratulate the Muslim *ummah* and the *mujahidin* across the entire world, in the eastern southern land of Islam in particular [probably referring to Somalia or Yemen], and our beloved loyal brothers including the *mujahidin* and the lions of Islam in East Africa and in the land of the two migrations [north-east Africa] on the death of the beloved, learned scholar, emigrant [*muhajir*], commander—as we believe he is—the Amir and leader Sheikh Mukhtar Abu al-Zubair, may God have ample mercy on him and house him in the highest of his paradises with the prophets, the righteous, the martyrs and the virtuous who are the best of companions. I pray God reunites me with him in the highest of heavens, remaining forever not disgraced or repentant.

> *They shouted "a knight fell from his horse"*
> *I asked if Abdullah was the one who fell?*
> *If Abdullah hadn't left his place*
> *He wouldn't have faced disaster*
> *Wrapped in a creased cloth*
> *With half his leg visible*
> *Forever resilient and overcoming obstacles*
> *Rarely complaining about misfortunes*
> *Well-versed today in tomorrow's events*
> *You see him with a drawn-in stomach*
> *Despite the abundant food around him*
> *Gaining strength from hunger and energy from fatigue*
> *God shall make his presence felt in life and death*
> *Whereas others seem far, even if they are a corner away*

May God have mercy on you, Sheikh Al-Zubayr. You were such a devoted brother, a loyal supporter, a true ally and a faithful colleague. In Ramadan of the year 1434 [July 2013], he sent me, may God have his mercy on him, a letter in which he expressed concern about:

the brothers' mismanagement of the [Islamic] State; we pray God to forgive them and guide them to the right path. The arguments they had come up with to justify their breaches and violations were not expected of people like them; especially when we claim day and night to be doing our utmost to establish an Islamic caliphate all over the world. Sheikh, I am inviting you to be patient, forgive them, accept our failures, try to prevent and put them right, paving the way for reforms.

I also sent him a letter in Jumada al-Uwla of the year 1435 [March 2014] in which I said:

I know how sad you are about what has been happening in Al-Sham, including the eruption of *fitna*, the violation of legitimate sanctities, the negation and deceit of established matters such as the pledge of allegiance to Al-Qaeda, and allowing the [declaration of] *takfir* [excommunication] [against] their opponents. I even found, in one of the network's recordings, a tape proclaiming the *takfir* upon this poor slave [referring to himself]. Regardless whether this tape is genuine or not, it does however show the level to which those who instigate *fitna* have fallen. He who is willing to pronounce this poor slave [referring to himself] a *kafir* [disbeliever] and blow up Abu Khaled al-Suri, may God have mercy on him, will not refrain from doing the same to anyone who challenges or opposes his plans.

I am asking you to communicate with all the brothers and urge them not to stir *fitna*—"he who cannot say good should remain silent".[11] I also ask you to convey to all the other brothers, including those of the State [IS] and the [Nusra] Front, that unity is mercy and disunity is torment. I previously asked Sheikh al-Golani not to take part in any assault against the *mujahidin* and ordered the Front to stop attacks on Muslims and *mujahidin*. In an address, which is about to be published, I implored the State to return to Iraq and unite ranks, even if they consider this return as an oppression, in order to put an end to this pouring bloodshed.

May God have mercy on you, Abu Zubair, and compensate us for your loss. Our only consolation is that you met martyrdom attacking the crusaders, not fleeing from them. I pray that God accept your and the brothers' martyrdom, forgive your sins and grant you the highest of His paradises. We only say what pleases God, He is the Most Merciful.

> *These are the vicissitudes of time*
> *None has any command on time*
> *Be patient even if patience has been exhausted*
> *Misfortunes could happen for a reason*
> *We were struck by the loss of those who*
> *Are mourned by heavens and earth, lands and seas*
> *Glory to Him [God] who makes his people appealing to death*
> *As though death longs for revenge*
> *He selects whom he wants amongst his people*
> *He who has high wisdom*
> *He who ordains and forbids*
> *There are my brothers on every front*
> *Dying and being buried in trenches*
> *Their graves are unknown in the middle of trenches*
> *Separated by plains, hills and mountains*

As for my brothers, the lions of Islam in East Africa, those who have been fighting with their hearts and souls to defend the south-eastern land of Islam, I am telling these beloved loyal and patient brothers to remain steady on the path of jihad, because their steadfastness is the price for victory that our Lord has informed us about. *Or do you think that you will enter Paradise while such [trial] has not yet come to you as came to those who passed on before you? They were touched by poverty and hardship and were shaken until [even their] messenger and those who believed with him said, "When (will come) the help of God?" Unquestionably, the help of God is near.* {Sura 2 (The Cow), 214}

I approve of their choice of Sheikh Abu Obaida Ahmed Umar as their Amir [of Al-Shabaab] and pray God to grant him success in his endeavours to be the custodian of jihad. I shall ask him to do his utmost to implement a

Sharia-based governance and establish the sovereignty of Islam in East Africa. I urge him to defend the sanctity, honour and dignity of Muslims in East and Central Africa. Sheikh, you are responsible, in the name of God, for protecting the sanctity, dignity, honour and security and safety of Muslims; please work day and night, spare no effort, and sacrifice your soul and heart to protect and defend them. May God help you in your efforts and grant you His grace, strength and victory. I am asking Him to empower the Sharia courts, whose rules should be applied to all people regardless of their status or class, and to look after the *mujahidin* brothers and fulfil their needs and provide a good living to them and their families.

I also urge him to care for the martyrs' widows, their orphans and relatives, and ensure their welfare and wellbeing. I entrust him with promoting knowledge and supporting educational institutions. They represent the fortresses of jihad and the incubators of lions; I shall ask him to provide them with the necessary help and assistance; look after our scholars and callers, ensure they are well provided for so they can dedicate their time to the noble *dawa* [benediction] and [issuing] statements.

I advise him to take up *shura* [consultation] as a method and deep core approach. I advise him to be patient and lenient and forgiving, as these are the best virtues for a fair ruler. I request him to have mercy on the poor and the deprived and fulfil their needs. I know that this is a big task. For this reason, I invite him to seek help from the people of honesty, wisdom, honour and morals; [and] more importantly [to] dedicate time to his Lord, confide in Him, seek His help and ask Him to accept his prayers. *And Noah had called us, and [We are] the best of responders.* {Sura 37 (Who Stand Arrayed in Rows), 75}

I reiterate to him that we are all, including his good self, the other Amirs and all the other leaders in the Qaeda Al-Jihad organisation, that we are all soldiers to our Amir, the Amir of the faithful, Mullah Mohammed Omar; we obey his orders and guidance according to the Book of God and the *hadith* [tradition of the Prophet] of his Prophet Mohammed, may peace and prayers be upon him. We shall not disobey him, break our promise or renounce our pledge. May God help me and you and all Muslims to obey Him [God].

The third issue is to offer my condolences and console our brothers in Libya for the loss of their Amir Mohamed Zahawi,[12] God have mercy upon him. I pray God to compensate them fully for his loss and guide them to his obedience, and continue their march in jihad in order to make the word of God supreme and make the word of infidels degraded, so that the supremacy of Sharia prevail all over Libya. Libyans will be able therefore to govern, not be governed; rule, not be ruled; and lead, not be led.

The fourth matter I would like to mention before I start this series is to express our thanks to brother Abu Nasser al-Wuhayshi, deputy leader of Al-Qaeda and the Amir of Al-Qaeda in the Arabian Peninsula, as well as brother Abu Musab Abdul Wadud, the Amir of Al-Qaeda in the Islamic Maghreb, for their statement supporting the end of fighting in Iraq and the Levant. May God reward them for their blessed endeavours to put an end to the Muslims' bloodshed and unite their ranks against the crusaders, the Safavids and the secularist common enemy. Unfortunately, this invitation to unite was rewarded by [Abu Bakr] al-Baghdadi and his supporters by calling the *mujahidin* in Algeria and Yemen to split their ranks and renounce their oath of allegiance, which he and his supporters had done before. They have incited those *mujahidin* to jump from one allegiance to another in the same way they would change clothes or sell and buy items. The two honourable Sheiks wanted to put out the flames of *fitna* in Al-Sham, whereas al-Baghdadi was keen to transfer the *fitna* from Al-Sham to the rest of the Muslim world.

I would also like to thank our Al-Qaeda brothers in the Arabian Peninsula for the address by the venerable Sheikh Harith bin Ghazi al-Nadhari,[13] God have mercy upon him, entitled "Statement regarding the content of Sheikh Abu Bakr al-Baghdadi's address", subtitled "Even if the disbelievers dislike it".

Here I pause to ask God, all almighty, to bestow His mercy and blessings on the honourable *mujahid* Sheikh Harith al-Nadhari, who had set an excellent example to scientists and students martyred in the field, mixing the scholars' ink with the martyrs' blood, thus setting arguments against those who failed in their duty of obligatory jihad to confront the crusaders all over the land of Islam. God will compensate us and the Muslim *ummah* for his loss, and grant his family and relatives and all the brothers patience and resilience. May God reunite us with him in his everlasting heavens.

Going back to the *fitna* that al-Baghdadi and his supporters inflamed amongst the *mujahidin*, I would like to state that, just before the start of the current crusade against Iraq and Syria, I had organised this series in a number of episodes. In these episodes I examined in detail the forensic, historical and concrete evidence, as well as all the documents, papers and correspondence relating to the events that took place in Syria and Iraq which led to the announcement of Abu Bakr al-Baghdadi as caliph, and during which his official spokesman called on all the jihadist groups to renounce their allegiance and hurry to swear allegiance to a caliph [al-Baghdadi] whose nomination came as a surprise to everyone. I had completed a substantial amount of [episodes based upon] this evidence and was about to start filming it.

However, due to the crusaders' campaign, I decided to leave out these details and focus on the discourse of unity, aiming to put an end to disputes, bring together the *mujahidin* and unite their ranks against the crusaders; unfortunately, al-Baghdadi's campaign subtitled "Even if the disbelievers dislike it" came to emphasise the same ideas which he and his supporters had advocated previously.

Despite this, I am determined to continue my efforts to resolve the situation in Syria and Iraq. I am keen for the unity between the *mujahidin* ranks to be achieved so that they are able to thwart the crusaders' campaign in the region. For that reason, I hope that "the pious and wise" appreciate my position and don't compel me to go into details about the serious facts which I sparingly touched upon. I call on the brothers to unify their ranks and renounce the views they had formed against their other brothers. I had informed my jihadist brothers in different branches of the jihad community to declare and focus only on the best way to stop the fighting between the *mujahidin* in Al-Sham, and to do their utmost to put an end to this *fitna*. I also empowered my honourable brother Sheikh Basir Nasser al-Wuhayshi, deputy leader of the community [Al-Qaeda], to do everything in his power to bring an end to the fighting between the *mujahidin* in Al-Sham.

We have endured much abuse and harm at the hands of Abu Bakr al-Baghdadi and his supporters; we chose to respond in the least harmful manner possible in order to smother the flames of *fitna* and pave the way to action from well-doers and reformers amongst the *mujahidin*. However, al-Baghdadi and his supporters left us no choice: they called on all the *mujahidin* to renounce their documented allegiances and swear oath to their supposed caliphate. They went even further and appointed themselves guardians over the Muslims without proper consultation or consideration for their brothers' anguish and miseries. All they were after was to gather oaths of allegiance and split the ranks.

While our brothers in Somalia were subjected to a fierce crusaders' campaign at the hands of a domestic and international enemy coalition, and as they were struck by the martyrdom of the *mujahid* leader Sheikh al-Zubair and his two companions, may God have mercy on them, these brothers' [al-Baghdadi and his followers] main concern was to call on Al-Shabaab soldiers, to incite them to split from their emirate and urge them to pledge allegiance to their so-called caliphate without consultation or advice from other Muslims. At a time when our brothers in Islam in the Maghreb were languishing under the French and American crusaders' campaigns, who were mobilising forces and building bases to fight them, these brothers' main concern was to call on the brothers in the Islamic Maghreb to persuade them to split from their emirate and pledge allegiance to their so-called caliphate without consultation or advice from other Muslims.

While our brothers in the Arabian Peninsula were subjected to a malicious Safavid and secular crusade, these brothers' [IS's] main worry was to call on the jihadist brothers in the Arabian Peninsula to incite them to split from their emirate and pledge allegiance to their so-called caliphate without consultation or advice from other Muslims. Al-Baghdadi went even further and declared that the Houthis had encountered none who were able to confront them.

At a time when Gaza was burning under Israeli bombs, Abu Bakr al-Baghdadi did not utter a word of support. He was mainly concerned with the *mujahidin's* pledge of allegiance to him after appointing himself a caliph without prior consultation with other Muslims. At a time when Waziristan was on fire due to the traitorous Pakistani army campaign allied with the American spy planes—the same campaign was officially announced twenty days before al-Baghdadi appointed himself as a caliph without prior consultation with other Muslims—during this time, al-Baghdadi did not bother to mention a single word of support in favour of Waziristan; his main concern was to get the soldiers of Al-Qaeda to split from it, and swear loyalty to the supposed caliph they had appointed without prior consultation with other Muslims.

At a time when our brothers in Afghanistan proudly waded in to the greatest battles in Islamic history, achieving glorious victories under the leadership of their Amir, the commander of the faithful Mullah Mohammed Omar *mujahid*, who is also our and al-Baghdadi's Amir, to whom al-Baghdadi renounced allegiance; during this time, al-Baghdadi did not utter a word of support to the brothers who were languishing under the American bombardments and under NATO's offensive campaign, nor did he show any sympathy towards the tens of thousands of the captives who filled Afghanistan's and Pakistan's prisons.

Al-Baghdadi and his followers were only interested that the soldiers of the [Afghan] Emirate renounce their loyalty to the commander of the faithful, who was forever patient and always relied on God and who was able, with the blessing of God, to achieve victory for Islam in Afghanistan. The soldiers of the Islamic State of Iraq used to repeat and cheer the name of this ascetic faithful Amir in their chants and recordings. Yet al-Baghdadi, his supporters and soldiers in Afghanistan, Pakistan, Central Asia, the Indian subcontinent, together with all the other groups—who swore loyalty to him including

Al-Qaeda with its various branches in Iraq including the Islamic State of Iraq—had the audacity to call on all these brothers, inciting them to break their allegiance to their Amir Mullah Omar, who is also the Amir of al-Baghdadi and his inner circle, defect from their cause, split from their ranks and show loyalty to al-Baghdadi's alleged caliphate. The latter was announced without prior consultation with other Muslims, and endorsed by anonymous people hiding behind false aliases whose real names still remain unknown.

At this point I would like to ask all those who have retracted their allegiance to the commander of the faithful Mullah Mohammed Omar *mujahid*, may God protect him: what is the legitimate reason that led you to break your allegiance? What unlawful offence, if any, had the Islamic Emirate committed which prompted this break of allegiance? Can you produce any legitimate evidence you may have to support your decision? We pledged allegiance to the Islamic Emirate commander according to the Book of God and the Sunna [Practice of the Prophet] of His Messenger, peace and prayers be upon him; if the Amir or the Emirate had committed an obvious offence that explains this break of allegiance, our course of action would be first to advise them, and then leave them if they didn't respond to our advice. We did not pledge allegiance to them for material or political gains. Breaking allegiance in this way is therefore an obvious violation of the Quran and the Sunna.

Some would argue, especially those who are merely looking for justifications, that the [Afghan] Islamic Emirate did not have a clear stance regarding issues that concern the Muslims. Whoever has made this statement is blatantly denying history and the facts. We, in Al-Qaeda, are a living proof that the Emirate had showed fierce enmity to America and its Western-led crusaders' coalition and Arab and Persian infidel agents, and fought hard to defend the *mujahidin* and the emigrant [*muhajirin*] brothers. The Amir Mullah Mohammed Omar, may God protect him, together with the Emirate's officials, sacrificed their Emirate and authority to protect and preserve the safety of their fellow *mujahidin* and emigrant brothers in general and Al-Qaeda's brothers in particular. To reiterate, whoever stated that the Islamic Emirate's stance with regard to the Muslims' issues is not clear is blatantly denying history and the facts, as this saying suggests: *"Minds may not be right if the obvious needs to be proven."*

The commander of the faithful, Amir Mullah Mohammed Omar, has expressed on many occasions his sympathy and support towards his fellow brothers in Palestine and all over the Muslim world. However, al-Baghdadi never showed any support to the Muslims in Gaza, Afghanistan, Pakistan or

Waziristan at a time when the Islamic Emirates continue to have noble, good-hearted, clear, praiseworthy stands both in theory and in practice. The Amir Mullah Mohammed Omar sacrificed his power and authority to keep his promise, whilst al-Baghdadi broke his pledge to gain power; that is the difference between the two.[14]

I would like to pause here to talk about the noble attitude of the commander of the faithful Mullah Mohammed Omar and his brothers, may God grant them victory and help them to support Islam, which is as follows: At the beginning of the crusaders' invasion of Afghanistan, when the Islamic Emirate decided to change war tactics from conventional confrontation to guerrilla warfare, and decided to redeploy its troops in mountains and villages and suburban areas—a method which proved later on to be highly successful, and was, thanks to God's help, one of the main reasons behind the crusaders' defeat in Afghanistan—when the Emirate took this course of action, it also made the decision to depart from Kandahar, which was the declared capital of the Emirate. Refusing to surrender the town to the crusaders and their agents, it opted instead to hand it over and leave it in the good hands of Mullah Naqib, a former *mujahid* and a member of the Islamic Society [Al-Jamiat-e Islami]. [Hamid] Karzai went along with this agreement, which was rejected by the Americans afterwards. Under these tough circumstances, when bombs poured over Kandahar like heavy rain, the commander of the faithful, may God protect him, postponed day after day the handover of Kandahar until he made sure, after three days, that all the Arab families had left Kandahar.

Such a delay was a serious risk on Mullah Omar's life and the lives of the Islamic Emirate's other officials and soldiers. More importantly, the whole agreement could have collapsed because of this delay. Once Mullah Omar was completely reassured about the evacuation of the Arabs and the emigrants [*muhajiroun*] and their families, he left Kandahar with his soldiers, including the emigrants. This is one of the many examples of the glorious accomplishments of this noble hero; may God keep him steady on the right path and grant him His immense rewards.

Here he is [al-Baghdadi] today rebelling and renouncing his allegiance to the commander of the faithful, and calling on people to follow his steps in rebellion and broken promises. At a time when our brothers in the Indian subcontinent [*shab al-qarat al-hindia*] were subjected to continuous suffering and torture, particularly in Kashmir, India, Burma and Bangladesh, al-Baghdadi and his supporters' main concern was to urge these brothers to renounce their allegiance and divide their group ranks.

While our brothers in the Muslim Caucasus, including our brothers in the Caucasus Islamic Emirate [*Imrat Al-Quqaz Al-Islamiya*], were fighting the toughest battles and enduring oppression and injustice at the hands of Russia, an oppression they had been facing for four and a half centuries, al-Baghdadi and his followers' main concern was to call on these brothers to split their ranks, renounce allegiance and show loyalty to his alleged caliphate which he established without prior consultation with the Muslims.

At this point, and in contradiction to this bad attitude, I would like to pay tribute and praise the stance of the commander of the faithful, Mullah Mohammed Omar *mujahid*, may God protect him, who was the only head of state in the world to recognise the Islamic Republic of Ichkeria[15] and officially received its former martyr, President Zelimkhan Yandarbiyev,[16] as we believe he is, God have mercy upon him, and assured him that all of Afghanistan's capabilities were at his disposal. The commander of the faithful [Mullah Omar] has been doing his utmost to provide support to his brothers the Chechen *mujahidin*, at a time when al-Baghdadi and his group were calling on the Caucasus Emirate soldiers to renounce their allegiance and follow their example in breaking allegiances and promises.

Glory to God, why split the ranks? Who will benefit from it? A legitimate Caliph, rightfully chosen by Muslims, with their full consent and agreement, is not allowed to have such an attitude because it would mean and lead to the weakening of the *mujahidin's* ranks at a time when they are engaging in fierce battles against the enemy. We don't exactly know who had sworn allegiance to him [al-Baghdadi]; the *mujahidin* were stunned with his appointment. Is it not the responsibility of the caliph to preserve Muslim unity and protect their homes? This caliph did not, however, bother to say one word to comfort the *mujahidin* brothers who have been in the path of jihad centuries before him and remained, with the help and bounty of God, dedicated and steadfast until now. This caliph did not [offer] any support towards the *mujahidin* in the Maghreb of Islam, Somalia, Gaza, the Arabian Peninsula, Afghanistan, Indonesia, the Indian subcontinent or the Philippines. His main interest was to call on people to swear allegiance to him.

Here I would like to raise an important question: who will benefit from al-Baghdadi's declaration, of pretending to be a caliph, when he decides to cancel [disband] the Islamic groups in areas where he has [received] sworn allegiance [from] one of these groups or some members of these groups? Before that, his official spokesman [al-Adnani] declared that the legitimacy of all the Islamic groups and Emirates have ended with the pledge of allegiance to al-Baghdadi's anonymous Consultative Council.

Who will benefit from the decision of the so-called caliph to disband a large number of jihadist groups and Emirates whose followers reached thousands and millions of jihadists, all of whom spent decades in jihad, making huge sacrifices and fighting in Afghanistan, Hama [in Syria or in the jihadist *Intifada* [uprising] against Sadat, decades before al-Baghdadi took part in jihad? With the grace of God, these groups have remained steadfast in their struggle against the global and local apostasy, offering tens of thousands of jihadists in martyrdom. The apostates, on the global and local level, have spent years and invested billions in an attempt to eradicate these jihadi groups but failed in the end.

On what book or law did al-Baghdadi audaciously base his decision to revoke the Islamic Emirate in Afghanistan? Millions of Muslims in Afghanistan, Pakistan, India, Central Asia, Eastern Turkmenistan, Iran and other countries, as well as all branches of Al-Qaeda, had already pledged allegiance to the Emirate, including the *mujaddid* [renewer] Imam Sheikh Osama bin Laden, may God have mercy on him, who swore loyalty to the Emirate and called on Muslims to follow suit. Al-Baghdadi himself had sworn loyalty to the Emirate, but later rebelled, retracted his action and broke his promise.

How could al-Baghdadi allow himself to revoke the Caucasus Islamic Emirate simply because of his so-called appointment as a caliph by an unknown Consultative Council? How dare he take that decision at a time when the Afghan *mujahidin* had set off, in the last phase of jihad, jihad that goes back twenty-four years, and before then a long history of struggle against the Russians, which has being going on for four and a half centuries? How could he give himself the right to be elected by three or four unknown people, having himself broken his oath of allegiance and blatantly disobeyed his Amir? How dare he demand that the jihadists, who have been fighting for decades before him, should "dissolve" themselves? Is this improvement or distortion? Is this unity or division? Is this justice or injustice?

Al-Baghdadi allows himself to act in this way because he claims to be a caliph, who deserves to be fully obeyed. The reality is of course very different; none of the previous statement is correct. He is clearly not a caliph who deserves the right to be obeyed and listened to; on the contrary, he is of all people the least worthy of obedience and respect since he himself is a rebel who defied obedience and respect. *Do you order righteousness of the people and forget yourselves?* {Sura 2 (The Cow), 44}

Anyone could follow the same argument, call himself Abu al-Himsi or al-Musali for instance and claim that some unknown "people of authority" [*ahl al-hal wa al-aqd]* have convened and agreed to get rid of Abu Bakr al-Bagh-dadi. This is because "the people of authority" are allowed to dissolve the caliphate in the same way that they have the right to elect it. From that point of view, if asked about the identity of "the people of authority", these people would certainly reply: Who are al-Baghdadi's "people of authority"? The sword will then rule in the same way it did when the Umayyads rebelled against the Abbasid [caliphate]. The latter took power "by the sword", which led Abdulrahman al-Dakhel to flee to Andalusia and appoint himself caliph "by the sword". The *ummah* became, subsequently, governed by two cali-phates. The caliph who was most entitled to governance was the one who caused the greatest destruction.

Here I would like to raise another question: Al-Sham [Syria] and Iraq are currently facing a fierce campaign at the hands of the crusaders who target every single *mujahid* in these countries. The *ummah* has essentially been sub-jected to this brutal campaign all over the Muslim world, from Chechnya to Mali. One would wonder, what would benefit Islam and Muslims the most? Is it to unite the *mujahidin's* ranks and defer their disputes? Or invent new ill-founded arguments? Would Islam and Muslims benefit from Al-Baghdadi's actions in inciting other groups to retract their allegiance on the basis of untenable grounds, and labelling them later as non-compliant aggressors and defiant at a time when the same groups are being continuously bombarded by the crusaders? Is this the behaviour of someone who is keen to unite Muslims against the enemy?

I am sorry to dwell on the subject, but al-Baghdadi and his supporters have left us no choice but to do so.

> *I told Ared and Ared's fellow friends*
> *And the group of Bani Sawdaa and people were my witnesses*
> *They openly had faith in the thousands of noble armoured leaders*
> *Soon they saw them attacking in every corner*
> *When I saw the horses coming forward like locusts*
> *I advised them in the corner of Liwa [name of the place where the battle took place]*
> *They did not take up my advice until it was clear to them*

There is also another important question, a question of extreme impor-tance: Under the current climate and in the midst of our struggle to push back the crusaders, is the rift between the *mujahidin* a good or a bad thing for the Americans? Is the rebellion of al-Baghdadi and his supporters against the [Afghan] Emirate of jihad, their renouncement of the established alle-giance, their obvious insurgence against the Amir, their aggression against

Mullah greatest destruction Omar—whose name was vehemently cheered by them before—their declaration of an allegiance pledged by very few unknown people and their call on these people to retract their oaths of loyalty, split their ranks and stir up *fitna* and disputes: will all of this please or displease the enemy?

Dear brothers, I would like at this point to clarify a very important matter: we do not recognise this caliphate [Islamic State] because it is not based on the Prophetic method; it is an illegitimate takeover without proper consultation. Muslims should not swear allegiance to this caliphate and we do not deem al-Baghdadi fit or qualified to run it. Let me reiterate, we do not recognise this caliphate because it was not established on the Prophetic method.

The above statement has been endorsed by the rightful, steadfast jihad scholars, despite the numerous sacrifices they had made for the sake of God, such as the honourable Sheikh Abu Mohammed al-Maqdisi, the honourable Sheikh Abu Qatada al-Filistini, the honourable Sheikh Hani al-Sabaaee and the honourable Sheikh Tarik Abdulhalim, may God protect them all.

I would also like to address a message to the Muslim *ummah*. The actions of al-Baghdadi and his supporters do not represent the common direction of the jihadist movement in general and the direction of the Al-Qaeda group in particular. Our aim is not to rule Muslims using a secret allegiance and subject them to bombings and explosions. This is not what our beloved sheikhs, God grant them His mercy, had sacrificed their lives for over the decades. They sacrificed their lives and everything they owned for the sake of restoring a rightly-guided caliphate whereby the Imam, who had to fulfil all the required legitimate conditions, was selected and held accountable by a caliphate based on the election of "the people of authority", on the basis of consent and the *shura* [consultation], not on the basis of saying: "we take this by force and by way of fighting, bombings and explosions".

Dear Muslim *ummah*, our opposition to al-Baghdadi and his supporters is not a dispute between two groups or two organisations. It is fundamentally a clash between the Muslim *ummah*, which endeavours to establish a rightly-guided caliphate, and those who want to impose a flawed governance supposedly based on the Prophetic methodology. I do apologise for making this statement, but al-Baghdadi and his followers obliged us to do so.

However, the fact that we do not recognise al-Baghdadi's caliphate and view it as a caliphate that is not based on the Prophetic methodology does not mean that we do not acknowledge the numerous accomplishments achieved by al-Baghdadi and his supporters. I must say, though, that they have also made grave mistakes. Despite those mistakes and our non-recognition of the legitimacy of their state, let alone their caliphate, I would like to confirm that, had I been in Iraq or Al-Sham, I would have cooperated with them in fighting the crusaders, the secularists, the Nusayiris [Alawites] and the Safavids [Shia] because the jihadist's interest is far more important than what I think of them [al-Baghdadi and his supporters] or the authenticity of their caliphate.

This is the case where an *ummah* is being subjected to a raging campaign at the hands of the crusaders. The *mujahidin* should unite and intensify their efforts in order to confront the enemy. I will talk in detail, with the will of God, about the necessary attitude we should take towards the crusaders and the main characteristics of "the prophetic" caliphate in due course.

The fifth issue I would like to mention is to congratulate the Al-Qaeda organisation in the Indian subcontinent[17] on their operation against the Pakistani and American marines. In their statement regarding the operation, they confirmed that they had targeted America because it was responsible for Muslims' bloodshed in Syria, Iraq, Yemen, Mali, Burma, Bangladesh, Afghanistan, Pakistan and India and all over the Muslim lands. I pray to God to bless their endeavours and make them a means to liberate the Indian subcontinent from oppression, humiliation and subjugation.

The sixth matter I would like to raise is my sincere thanks and gratitude to the honourable Sheikh Abu Mohamed Daghistani, the Amir of the Caucasus Islamic Emirate, for the letter he addressed to the *ummah*'s scholars in general and to the honourable Sheikhs Abu Mohammed al-Maqdisi, Abu Qatada al-Filistini, Hani al-Sabaaee, Tarik Abdulhalim and Abu Mundir Al-Shanguiti in particular. Sheikh Daghistani had gracefully honoured me twice in his letter: first by having faith in me, and second when he mentioned my name amongst the names of such learned respectable scholars. I love knowledge, but I am by no means a scholar or an academic. I listened to his latest lecture in which he addressed our brothers in Al-Sham, and warned against raising *fitna* and shedding Muslims' blood and harming their honour and sanctities. He ended his address by saying: "Be aware that this *fitna* will not die away until each one of you makes concessions; you should engage in dialogue, be attentive and obey the supreme command orders or comply with the Sharia court rulings."

I would like to extend my sincere thanks to the honourable sheikh for the trust he put in me and hope that I deserve it. I would like also to thank him for his valuable advice to our *mujahidin* brothers in the beloved Al-Sham and his dignified stance and efforts to reconcile the *mujahidin* during this time of *fitna*. He set an exemplary and noble model which should be followed. God blessed you with success and guided you to do good, so praise God repeatedly for His bounty and grace. God is my witness when I express my affection towards you and towards all the *mujahidin* brothers in the Muslim Caucasus. Caucasus has a special place in my heart. You may already know that I spent nearly six months in Dagestan; most of it was in Sizzo Edine prison in Mahaj Al-Kala, may God help us to recover it. This happened when I was arrested while on my way to Chechnya. During that time, I met several honourable brothers to whom I send my warmest regards and beseech God to grant them the best of rewards.

In the second edition of my book *Knights under the Banner of the Prophet*, may God's prayers and peace be upon him, in the chapter titled "Dagestan—relief after cessation of means" I talked about my love and affection for those brothers in Islamic Caucasus. God preferred for me not to complete my journey to Chechnya; after leaving prison I went to my beloved Afghanistan, where I was warmly received by the renewer Imam Sheikh Osama bin Laden, God have mercy on him. God bestowed his grace upon me and gave me the chance to accompany our beloved sheikh on several occasions.

Your letter, where you kindly mentioned my name, proves that we are one *ummah* and that we all share the same joys and the same unhappiness. It also proves that brotherhood between Muslims is long-lasting, despite all attempts from the enemy of Islam to divide and split their unity. God and His Prophet, may peace and prayers be upon him, is responsible for these brothers. *But if they intend to deceive you—then sufficient for you is God. It is He who supported you with His help and with the believers. And brought together their hearts. If you had spent all that in the earth you could not have brought their hearts together; but God brought them together. Indeed, He is exalted in might and wise.* {Sura 8 (Spoils of War), 62–63}

I implore you kindly to keep providing me and all the brothers with your valuable advice and guidance and not to forget us in your prayers. I am pleased to bring you glad tidings; we are, with the will of God, on the verge of great conquests and a bright phase in the history of Islam. I am longing to meet with you in the near future to benefit from your knowledge and wisdom. I am sure God will make this easy for me.

The seventh matter I would like to tackle in this series is to remind my Muslim brothers of their duty towards our captive brothers, those patient content and isolated brothers who are languishing under the burden of shackles and enduring degradation and humiliation behind prison bars for the sake of their faith and in support to their *ummah*. Those include our captive sisters everywhere, in particular our sister Hasnaa, the widow of Sheikh Abu Hamza al-Muhajir, may God have mercy on him, and her follow sisters detained in the American Safavid prisons in Iraq; our sister Aafia Siddiqui[18] in America, our sister Heela Al-Qasir and her fellow sisters in the Arabian Peninsula, and all the captive sisters worldwide. I am urging our brothers, who are in the process of negotiating the release of hostages, to give the issue of the captive sisters priority in their demands, and do their utmost to avoid making any concessions unless forced to, even if they have to detain a hostage one thousand years and even if they have to detain one thousand captives in exchange for the release of one of our sisters.

At this point I would like to pay tribute to our brothers in Khorasan who demanded, as one of the conditions for the release of the American Warren Weinstein, the release of our captive sisters including Aafia Siddiqui and Hasnaa, the widow of Sheikh Hamza al-Muhajir, may God have mercy on him. I also praise, thank and pay tribute to our brothers on the Al-Nusra Front, may God make our faith victorious at their hands.

I also pray to God that their jihad, and the jihad of their fellow brothers, "the lions of Islam", will help restore the rightly-guided caliphate. Such a caliphate is established on the "Prophetic method" and based on the implementation and empowerment of Sharia law, whose rules should be applied to all people regardless of their status or class; a caliphate based on *shura* [consultation] and consent and set up to protect Muslim sanctities, increase their faithfulness and adherence to their faith, and ordain them to keep their promises, refrain from getting involved in facilitating *takfir* and causing explosions in pursuit of authority and power and self-indulgence. May God grant long lives to the lions of Al-Nusra who exchanged the Maloula nuns[19] for 152 captive sisters, including a mother with four children, who all used to be detained in the prisons of the criminal Bashar [al-Assad]. May God grant long lives to the lions of Al-Nusra who are currently demanding the release of our captive sisters detained by the Lebanese government. I pray God, in the name of Islam and Muslims, to reward them with the best of his rewards and to help them in their endeavours to free all Muslim prisoners. They have set the best example which should be followed and acted upon by all of us, may God accept their deeds, grant them victory and success and strengthen their faith.

[Footage shows the release of prisoners which include families, women and children]

Short interview with a masked man:

Q. What is your comment about this operation where nuns are exchanged for 250 female captives, including a mother with four children?

A. Praise be to God, praise be to God; we are thanking God and hope to be able to free all the prisoners. I swear by God that we will not rest until we free all our captive sisters from the apostates' prisons.

[Al-Zawahiri continues:]

I would also like to remind the Muslim and *mujahidin* brothers everywhere of our captive brothers in America, including our reverent Sheikh Omar Abdul-Rahman, may God protect him and speed up his release. He courageously stood up before the judge, while the prosecutors were demanding his execution, and in a firm and powerful manner shouted in a voice that made the courtroom shake: "President of the Supreme State Security Court, the case has been proved, the truth has come out, you have to rule according to the Sharia of God and apply the ruling of God; if you don't, you are an unfair tyrant, a *kafir* [disbeliever, infidel]."

Lastly, I would like to remind you of our captive brothers held by the Safavids and all our prisoners detained by the apostate regimes in Afghanistan, the Arab Peninsula, Russia, the Islamic Maghreb, Al-Sham, Iraq, Somalia and every part of the world.

Jihadist and Muslim brothers, the only way to liberate our captive brothers and sisters is by force, so seek help from God and do not lose strength.

I have reached the end of this talk and hope to see you, God willing, in the next episode.

The last of our supplications is praise to God the Lord of the creations.

THE ISLAMIC SPRING, PART 2

SEPTEMBER 2015

By Ayman al-Zawahiri

In the second part of the series on the "Islamic Spring", and following a traditional division between "far" and "near" enemies, Zawahiri separates the "internal" struggle in Syria, Iraq and neighbouring regions from the external battle targeting Western heretics. Echoing the laissez-faire approach to violence adopted by IS, albeit within the boundaries of legitimate targeting, Zawahiri urges followers to carry out improvised attacks using whatever means are at their disposal, whilst warning believers that if they do transgress and commit sin, the fact that they were following orders will not absolve them when it comes to answering for their deeds before God.

In the name of God, praise be to God, peace and prayers be upon God's Messenger, his family and companions and whoever supported him.

O Muslim brothers everywhere, peace and God's compassion and blessings be upon you!

This is the second part of the Islamic Spring in a series in which I would like to talk about the forthcoming Islamic victory, God permitting. The Muslim *ummah* [nation or community] in its search for liberation from humiliation, disgrace, defeat and dependency, moral decline and social disintegration, political corruption and economic degeneration has discovered the illusion by which some were deceived under the name of the Arab Spring, and brought it back again to the abyss of distrust and corruption in a more severe and extreme way. It has led to the victory of the forces of evil that the *ummah* hoped to eradicate. The *ummah* has realised that secularism, people's rule, tyranny, the nationalist state and the union of nationalisms—to which many Islamic movements allegedly involved with Islamic work have pushed the *ummah*—have only led to the loss of faith [*deen*] and the worldly life. Perhaps it has become clear to the *ummah* by now that the path of the *mujahidin* and the trustworthy callers—those who long advised and warned Muslims that jihad is the only way to salvation—is the right path as it is evidenced by the texts of the Book and the Sunna and demonstrated by history and facts.

The loyal *mujahidin* and trustworthy callers [i.e. those who call people to Islam] have therefore a duty to clarify this issue beyond any doubt so that the *ummah* can move forward on the right path guided by the Book and the Sunna of the Prophet, PBUH.

I believe that there are two other issues that the loyal *mujahidin* and trustworthy callers have to clarify to the *ummah*. First, the movements engaged in jihad to make God's word the highest will not try to excommunicate the general public and exclude them from the denomination [i.e. Sunni Islam] based on random suspicions, which are mostly insignificant or incorrect, especially [when] these people are obedient or close to the jihadi movements.

The second issue is that the jihadi awakening endeavours to establish the righteous caliphate on the method of Prophethood and does not endeavour to return the irascible rule which took power through a bloodbath of Muslims and a pile of their skulls and bodies. To be clear, we want the return of the rule of the righteous caliphs whose rules our Prophet (PBUH) ordered us to cling to stubbornly, as he (PBUH) said: "I advise you to fear God and be obedient, even if it were a Habashi [Ethiopian] servant [to be appointed leader]; whoever lives after me will see great differences, so remember my rule and the rules of the righteous caliphs and hold onto them and cling to them stubbornly."

We want the rule that follows the method of the righteous caliphs (may God be pleased with them), whom the Prophet endorsed before he died; not the rule that is guided by Hajjaj bin Yusuf and Abu Muslim al-Khurasani.[20] We do not want the rule of the people who wave their swords and say "this is our Amir [leader] of believers, and if he dies the sword will prevail and will threaten whoever refuses to obey"; nor the rule of the people who say "whoever opposes us will be butchered by what is inside this sheath [the sword]"; or the rulers whose hero says "determination and courage have replaced my whip with a sword. Its handle is in my fist, its pouch around my neck and its edge in the neck of whoever disobeys me"; or the rulers who claim that they took it [power] forcefully with the edge of the sword, with explosion, detonation and destruction.

The truthful callers should make it clear to the *ummah* that the rule they must implement is the rule of Sharia which commands of us consultation and gives the *ummah* the right to choose their rulers and hold them accountable. The truthful callers have to explain to the *ummah* the dangers of excesses and shortcomings, such as the call of some Islamic movements, like the Muslim Brotherhood and the Salafi group serving [Egyptian president] Sisi, who promote the implementation of Sharia through the ruling of non-Sharia principles.

The other call is that of those who advocate the establishment of an Islamic caliphate in a secret pledge of allegiance carried out by ignorant people to a man who has not been chosen or approved by the *ummah*. They surprise it [the *ummah*] by alleging that a caliph has come to you from where you do not know or consider. You have to obey him and the punishment of the one who disobeys him is to shoot him in the head, whoever he is, without any dignity, because the ignorant ones imposed themselves on the *ummah* and [decided to establish the] caliphate forcefully through explosion, detonation and destruction. The role of the *ummah*, the people of authority[21] and the people of jihad and benediction was simply to follow the media to know who the caliph was, what were his instructions and who appointed him as leader. Those who did not do this have only themselves to blame.

The truthful callers should clarify the exact meaning of the prophet's succession and the difference between this succession and the irascible rule which the Prophet (PBUH) warned against when he said "the first who will change my rule is a man from the people of Umayyad". Edited by al-Albani (may God have compassion on him) who said "perhaps the purpose of the Hadith is to change the Caliphate's selection system and make it hereditary". The Prophet (PBUH) said that the one who grabbed the caliphate by force would be the one who will change his [the Prophet's] rule. So how could he [al-Baghdadi] brag about it today, knowing that he had taken it by force; how could he allege that he is following the method of Prophethood?

Conquering and enforcing are two features of the irascible rule and were the main reasons behind the degeneration, collapse and fall of the caliphate and the defeat of the Muslim nation. I will, God willing, talk about some of the characteristics of the caliphate on the method of Prophethood in the next episode. We must know why the caliphate fell, and why it degenerated and why it was defeated. We did not awake suddenly to find that the caliphate had fallen under the strikes of the allied forces in WWI. However, it was the vices of the irascible rule that decayed the bones of the nation until it collapsed; had it not been for the good people in this *ummah*, such as religious scholars and the worshipping faithful, *mujahidin* and righteous people, this *ummah* would have collapsed earlier and could not have lasted fourteen centuries. The caliphate was confronting superpowers that were weaker than the criminal superpowers of today.

We are faced today with the harshest crusader campaign in history, and the forces that confront us are a thousand times as powerful as us. However, the *ummah* today in terms of religious scholarship, faith and jihad is weaker than in the first centuries. If we didn't pay attention to the grounds of vice that led to the fall of the caliphate before, then our fall this time will be faster, nastier and harsher. The caliphate collapsed and it declined from the method of Prophethood to cantankerous rule, founded upon depriving Muslims of the right of consultation, and upon despotism, injustice, attacking sanctities and banning the commanding of good and the forbidding of evil.

The Prophet (PBUH) said: "You will annul the obligations of Islam one after another, and whenever an obligation is annulled, people will appeal to the next one, and the first one annulled is the rule and the last one is the prayer." Based on the glad tidings of the caliphate on the method of Prophethood and the rejection of injustice and corruption, I would like to review together with my brothers, through this series, the situation in the Muslim land and give them glad tidings that the true spring is the victorious spring of Islam, which is undoubtedly coming, God permitting! The Muslim *ummah* is going through a strong jihadi awakening, which has revived all parts of the world and given them a new spirit and a different life that wipes out the age of humiliation, meekness, submission and inferiority, and paves the way to the establishment of an age of Sharia rule, justice, consultation and the liberation of the Muslim lands, God permitting.

There is no doubt that nations are like people. In the process of their growth and recovery from problems, similarly to [how humans deal with their] problems, they evolve through several stages. At this particular stage we have witnessed some failed and distorted experiences, like the failed experience of the Islamist military group in Algeria, the internal struggle between the *mujahidin* after the withdrawal of Russia from Afghanistan and the *fitna* [sedition/ strife] between the *mujahidin* in Syria, which led to the claim of the caliphate without prior consultation with Muslims. However, the general constitution of the Muslim *ummah*, God permitting, is growing and rising. After each stumble, the *ummah* became stronger, more determined and more focused. So, after the internal strife in Afghanistan, the Islamic emirate came into being, and after the failure of the Islamist military group, the Salafist Group for Preaching and Combat [GSPC] came into being to join the blessed caravan of jihad and the auspicious union, and then it became the Al-Qaeda Organisation in the Islamic Maghreb.

The *fitna* in Syria will make the Syrian jihad stronger and more focused, God willing, in order to establish an Islamic state that promotes justice and consultation agreed upon by both the *mujahidin* and all Muslims, God willing.

However, before talking about the countries of the Islamic Spring, I need to speak first about the secular crusader-Safavid [Western–Iranian] campaign against Iraq and Syria. My dear brothers, the brutal crusader campaign, which is waged today on Iraq and Syria, is part of a brutal crusader campaign extending from the Philippines to West Africa, and from Chechnya to Somalia and Central Africa, and from eastern Turkmenistan to Waziristan and Afghanistan. It is a war against Islam under the name of a war against terror. The crusaders' campaign that descended upon Syria and Iraq does not have a particular group as a target, instead the real target is the jihadi uprising of the Muslim *ummah* against its enemies. Understanding fully this concept would allow us to comprehend this campaign and be able to confront it.

It is a campaign in which the enemies went beyond their disagreements against us, so we have to unite in one rank against them. I would like to put forward to my brothers a call for cooperation between the *mujahidin* in Iraq and Syria. However, before that I want to explain an important issue which is that our non-recognition of al-Baghdadi's claim to the caliphate and our vision that it is not a caliphate on the method of Prophethood does not mean that we deny his or his brothers' achievements. We will support them if they erect Sharia courts among themselves; but if they run away from being judged by the Sharia among themselves and others, then we will be against them. We will support them if they kill the big criminals; but we stand against them if they say they did not order, nor intend to kill Abu Khalid al-Suri (may God have compassion on him). We will be with them if they fight the crusaders, Shia and secularists; but if they conquer the bases of the *mujahidin* and destroy them and seize the Sharia committees' monies, then we will be against them. We will be with them if they extend the schools, religious knowledge circles and committees for commanding good and forbidding evil; but if they slander the *mujahidin* and us with lies and false accusations and allegations that we are seculars and Brotherhood [members] and we implement the policy of Sykes—Picot and that we are like the adulterer who hides her pregnancy when she is in her ninth month, then we will be against them. We will support them if they free the Muslim captives and release them from prison; but if they kill a [formerly] disbelieving captive who surrenders to Islam, then we are against them. And if they refer to the Amir of believers, Mullah Mohammed Omar (may God protect him), and chant his name as before, then we will support them; but if they break their pledge to Al-Qaeda and to the Amir of believers, Mullah Mohammed Omar (may God protect him), and lie to Abu Hamza al-Muhajir (may God have compassion on him) and to themselves and to their confirmed pledges and allege that there were no such pledges, then we will be against them. We will support them if they aid and abet their Muslim brothers everywhere; but if they try to divide the ranks of the jihadi groups under the claim of the caliphate which is not approved, then we are against them. We support them if they try to revive the caliphate; but if they want to impose the caliphate on Muslims by force, explosion, destruction and detonation and not by consultation, then we will be against them. If they wrong us, we will be fair to them, and if they disobey God in us, we will obey God in them with His aid.

In spite of all these grave mistakes, I call upon all the *mujahidin* in Syria and Iraq to cooperate and coordinate their efforts to stand in one rank in the face of crusaders, secularists, Alawites [Assad's religious sect] and Iranians, even if they do not recognise the legitimacy of al-Baghdadi's state and his group, let alone their caliphate. The matter is bigger than not admitting the legitimacy of their state or their allegation of the establishment of the caliphate. It is about an *ummah* that faces a brutal crusader campaign, and we must rush to defend it against the assailer. Here, I want to confirm without any ambiguity that if the war is between the crusaders, secularists, Iranians and all Muslim and *mujahidin* sects, including Abu Bakr al-Baghdadi's sect and whoever is with him, then our only choice is to stand with the Muslim *mujahidin* even if they wronged us, slandered us, broke promises and deprived the *ummah* and *mujahidin* of their right of consultation and choosing their caliph, and even if they run away from judging by Sharia when they disagree.

We continuously beseech God to support and grant victory to Muslim *mujahidin* everywhere. As we call to cooperate with Abu Bakr al-Baghdadi and his brothers against the secular crusader and Iranian–Alawite campaign, we do not call for that because he is the caliph of the Muslims or because those with him are representing the caliphate state, as that claim has not been approved. However, we call to cooperate with them against the enemies of Islam and shielding the attacks of the enemies of Islam on Muslims. When we call for the support of our brothers in the Nusra Front, we do not do that only because they are our brothers and partners in the Al-Qaeda organisation whom we are proud of, but also because they are Muslims and *mujahidin*. When we call for support to the jihadist groups in Syria and Iraq, we do it regardless of any disagreement between us and because it is an individual duty that Islam has imposed on us, as God almighty says: *Fight the polytheists collectively, as they fight against you collectively. But know that God is with those who are the pious.* {Sura 9 (Repentance), 36}

Our choice is clear and shining like sunlight, and bare and decisive like the edge of the sword. We are with every Muslim *mujahid* in Iraq and Syria, and every Muslim *mujahid* from eastern Turkmenistan to Mali and from the Caucasian peaks to the forests of Africa and from Indonesia to Nigeria; we support them against the enemies of Islam, the crusaders, secularists, Shia Iranians, the atheist Russians, the polytheist Hindus and the Chinese unbelievers. We support and aid them whether they were good or bad to us, whether they were fair or unfair to us. But we are not with them if they escape from judgement by the Sharia or label the Muslims as disbelievers or slander them or break their promises or try to divide their ranks or violate their sanctities.

We have a good opinion of the great majority of *mujahidin* in Syria and Iraq and all the Muslim countries, and we consider that they have taken up arms to support their religion and tried to rule according to their lord's law and to return the caliphate on the method of Prophethood. I ask God to accept their virtuous deeds and forgive them and grant them honour in life and winning the afterlife. We consider that most of the corruption in these movements is committed by a tiny ruling minority who mix a virtuous deed with a bad one. I ask God to forgive us and them and to give us and them guidance and gather us together on what He wishes and accepts.

After this clarification, I would like to move on from the general call to practical procedures, and I call my Muslim and *mujahidin* brothers to support the Muslims in Syria and Iraq against the secular crusader–Iranian campaign. I divide these procedures which I call for into procedures outside the regions of Syria and Iraq, and the internal ones. For the external procedures, I call upon every Muslim who can cause harm in any crusader coalition country not to hesitate in doing so. Why? Because the Western crusader countries are leading this campaign, and the rest take orders from them. So if we hit the head, the wings and body will fall down; and if the war reaches the heartland of the big criminals, God permitting, they will stop the war and revise their policies. I see that we should focus on moving the war to the heartland and cities of the Western crusaders, and especially to America.

They have to know that as they bombard, so they will be bombarded; as they kill, they will be killed; as they injure, they will be injured; and as they destroy, burn and wipe out, they will be destroyed, burnt and wiped out. They have to know that the war is a common fate, and punishment comes from their deeds. I consider that most young Muslims are desperate to be called to take up arms in the jihad battlefields, and they are hurt by the pictures of destruction and killing in Afghanistan, Waziristan, Iraq, Syria, Palestine, Yemen, Somalia, Kashmir, Chechnya and all other Muslim lands. I consider that many of them wish for a martyrdom operation to make their religion victorious. So why don't they do it in the crusaders' heartland, in their cities, facilities, and their economic, industrial and financial centres? The martyrdom operation doesn't always need explosives, and even if it needs explosives, they don't have to be traditional explosives. There are various means other than explosives that can be thought of, experimented with, searched for and invented. The hero brothers Ramzi Yusuf and his brothers, Mohammed Atta and his self-sacrificing eagles, Mohammed Sidiq Khan, Shahzad Tanwir, Nidal Hasan, Omar al-Faruq [Abdulmutallab], and the brothers Tamerlan and Dzhokhar Tsarnaev, Mohammed Merah and finally, the valiant knights of the battle of Paris [*Charlie Hebdo* attackers] are strong examples in this respect. So why don't we continue on this critical front and increase it until it becomes several more fronts?

You might not be needed to take arms to go to the battlefields of jihad, as the battlefields might be just a few steps away from you. However, the effort to try to call to take up arms might make you vulnerable to being discovered by the crusaders' intelligence agencies. So depend on God and don't feel weak; perhaps in the Al-Sahab Foundation tape, "Fight in the path of God, you are not held responsible except for yourself", and in the volumes of *Hardh* [Incite] and *Inspire* magazines which are published by the al-Malahim Foundation of the Al-Qaeda organisation in the Arabian Peninsula, there are ideas which can help develop thinking about these means.

O you the Muslim *mujahid* in the Western crusader country, learn what the religious rules are in battle, then search for the targets that Sharia will permit you to hit; look for the suitable means, try hard to make preparations for it, keep it quiet from your nearest people, be careful of the infiltrating spies among the Muslims, make up your mind and go forward to victory, God permitting. Here I have to greet my Muslim brothers in the bosom of Jerusalem who attack the Zionist occupiers with the simplest weapons. They have satisfied the required duty and given an exemple to their *ummah* despite their weakness and lack of means.

As for the procedures inside the regions of Iraq and Syria, I call all the *mujahidin* in the regions of Iraq and Syria to cooperate and help one another until the two regions become one battlefield and one jihad field where the *mujahidin* can move freely, manoeuvre with their forces, store their weapons and machinery, treat their wounded, shelter their prisoners, and get their provisions and ammunitions. This will make the war for the secular crusader–Zionist campaign complicated, but to be realistic and not live by emotions and apart from reality, we have to confess that wish will be difficult to achieve at present because of the severe crisis of confidence that prevails among the *mujahidin*, because of the *fitna* that happened in Syria and Iraq: 7,000 were killed and double this number were wounded, and this has led to an unknown minority declaring a caliphate for a caliph who has not the consent of a majority of the *mujahidin* or other Muslims. To make matters worse, some have declared it an obligation to pledge allegiance to the alleged caliph, denying the legitimacy of all groups and emirates, and have encouraged their followers to split the head of whoever disagrees with bullets.

This painful history might obstruct their cooperation because of the bitter experiences amongst the *mujahidin*, which will make some of them worried about letting the other side's weapons and machinery into their territories. There must be, therefore, urgent procedures to restore confidence among the *mujahidin* to enable them to achieve full cooperation in the jihad against the secular crusader–Iranian campaign in Iraq and Syria.

The first of these procedures to which I call the *mujahidin* in the regions of Iraq and Syria is to stop immediately the fighting between jihadi groups. Second is to stop the calls to kill those who disagree and split their heads with bullets by claiming that they are breaking rank and other similar nonsense, which actually leads to breaking Muslim ranks at a time when they are most in need of uniting their efforts and mobilising their energies in the face of an enemy who has gathered itself against them from the east to the west. Bringing about *fitna* and disagreement between the *mujahidin* in Syria and Iraq was a strong blow to jihad. This, undoubtedly, will serve the interests of the enemies of Islam.

My brother *mujahidin* everywhere! The crusader war against us is long and getting longer, and we must wage it unified, not start it with conflict and disagreement. We were united before, with God's blessing. All or most of the jihadi groups either pledged allegiance to or supported Mullah Mohammed Omar (may God protect him) and the Al-Qaeda organisation, until Abu Bakr al-Baghdadi and his brothers came and escaped from being judged by independent Sharia courts and left the door wide open to the *fitna*. They refused attempts to put it out and lied to Abu Hamza al-Muhajir (may God have compassion on him) and alleged that he broke his pledge of allegiance to Al-Qaeda at the time of Sheikh Osama (may God have compassion on him) unilaterally, and it is a pure lie. They then lied to themselves and denied their confirmed repeated pledges, like al-Baghdadi's letter to me dated 7 Dhu al-Hijja 1433 [equivalent to 23 October 2012], which he starts with: "In the name of God, praise, prayers and peace be upon God's Messenger. To our Amir, Sheikh Dr Abu Mohammed Ayman al-Zawahiri (may God protect him), peace be upon you," and continues:

> Our blessed sheikh, we would like to make it clear to you and declare to you that we are part of you and we are from you and for you, and we are indebted to God that you are the guardian of our affairs, and we owe you obedience as long as we are alive, and that your advice and mention are rights we have from you. Your orders are obligatory to us, but some matters may require clarification as we live the reality of the events in our battlefield. I hope your heart is wide open to our points of view and you will have the order afterwards. We are only arrows in your quivers.

This was the end of the letter.

But, unfortunately, this is who is indebted to God as long as he is alive. He didn't resist for six months, and declared his union even without notifying his Amir, and whoever was with him disobeyed their Amir publicly and they insisted that the whole of Sham is under their emirate. They claimed that they chose the consent of God over the consent of their Amir. When the Sheikh [Abu Mohammed al] Golani (may God protect him) disagreed with him and raised the matter with their Amir, they described him with the worst fabrications and they lied to their Amirs and sheikhs and to the Al-Qaeda organisation and pelted it with accusations that led to *takfir* [excommunication]. They said it fell into secularism, Brotherhood and the policies of Sykes–Picot and that it took the side of the majority and was supported by the secularists and traitors. They then got into swearing and described it as the adulterer who claims her chastity while she is in her ninth month. They suddenly declared a caliphate by [the will of] some unknown people, for a majority of *mujahidin*

and Muslims do not consent to it. They then alleged that all the jihadi groups'
legitimacy had expired and they had to dismantle themselves while they were
under fierce bombardment and in continuous confrontation with the crusader
enemy, and whoever disagreed with them would get a bullet in his head,
because they reached their caliphate by force with explosions, destruction and
detonations. They claimed, after all this, that they have done this to unify the
divided ranks of the *ummah*. Their spokesperson then scandalously said: but
no, [we] are the oppressed State, and "he hits the one who is in ordeal and
laughs at him" [Arabic proverb].

The third of these procedures is to establish the independent Sharia court
and affirm its power, authority and clout in the regions of Iraq and Syria on
all the *mujahidin*. Without this independent Sharia court, all the cooperation will be up in the air, tossed by the wind and vulnerable to being played
out by any player and to aversion and criticism by whoever wishes. The honourable religious scholar Sheikh Abu Mohammed al-Maqdisi (may God
protect him) tried in this respect with his initiative, and I sent him my support. He became disappointed after that, for reasons which he declared and
which all know. This initiative and the likes of such blessed calls should be
enlivened anew, practised and implemented. And escaping from it is to focus
on dividing our ranks and energies. We, in the Qaeda Al-Jihad organisation,
put our trust in the sheikhs and scholars of jihad whose sincerity, strife and
compassion were proven, like our beloved Sheikh Abu Mohammed al-
Maqdisi, Sheikh Abu Qatada al-Filistini (may God protect them), Sheikh
Abu Walid al-Filistini, Sheikh Mohammed al-Zawahiri, Sheikh Salem al-
Murjan and Sheikh Ahmad Ashosh (may God release them), Sheikh Hani
al-Sabaaee and Sheikh Tariq Abdulhalim and the likes of these truthful invocators, as we consider them thus and they don't need to be recommended to
God; then the sheikh of the jihadi sect, its mentor, teacher and educator, the
tied up and handcuffed lion, the honourable Sheikh Omar Abdulrahman
(may God release him). These people are our wealth and capital, our provision and valuable treasure of this age. So for whose interest do we disrepute
them and allege against them and show disrespect? Who benefits from this
disrepute? I have the answer. The beneficiaries are two sorts of people: the
first is the secular crusader–Iranian campaign; and the second is the people
of political greed who disrepute and slander anyone standing against their
political and authoritarian ambitions.

The fourth of these procedures is the attempt to give a general amnesty. I
call all virtuous people and supporters of jihad and those who care about the

victory of Muslims in Iraq and Syria to try to mediate between the jihadi groups in parallel with establishing an independent Sharia court, without disbanding it to reach a general amnesty among the jihadi sects and groups, and start a new page of cooperation and turn the page on the past and its despicable *fitna*, without revoking the right of anyone who wants to settle judgements in the Sharia courts.

The fifth of these procedures is the initiative to cooperate at any possible level, like treating the wounded, sheltering families, storing equipment, supplying provisions and ammunition and [carrying out] joint operations. I present this initiative to the *mujahidin* in Iraq and Syria to try to unite their ranks against their enemy which is united against them, even if some have rejected it or undermined it or claimed that he does not need it. It suffices that I tried my best and advised my brothers. The Messenger (PBUH) said: "religion is advice". We said to whom? He said: "to God and His Book, Messenger and to the whole of the Muslim *ummah*".

Before I conclude, I would like to pause and talk about some footage I saw on tape which was an attack by a group in Syria against a religious committee of another group. The words of a brother at the end of the tape brought me to a halt [when he said]: "By God, we have to take our revenge!" I say to this brother: O my dear littlest brother or my dear son, my son would have been at your age or near your age had he been alive; O my dear son, who are you taking revenge upon? You take revenge on your brother *mujahid* the monotheist, who wants to bring the rule of Sharia and establish the caliphate on the method of Prophethood? You try to take revenge on him while the crusader missiles drop on his head and your head? I am not saying that you are the wrongdoer or the wronged one, but I say to you, my dear son, if you have a grievance you should direct it to the independent Sharia court set up by your beloved uncle, the active scholar, *mujahid*, fighter and educator, our dear Sheikh Abu Mohammed al-Maqdisi. Sheikh al-Maqdisi (may God protect him) who called and endeavoured for the establishment of this court supported by your uncles the sheikhs of jihad who spent their lives in jihad, preaching monotheism and struggling against tyrants, and are still doing so, all praise to God; *"God shall raise them by degrees"*. {Sura 58 (She Who Disputes), 11}.

This independent Sharia court was called for by your uncles, the sheikhs of jihad, so that none of us should take revenge on one another and not direct our weapons against the chest of one another, since the crusader bombardment doesn't distinguish between one and another. Your uncle, Abu

Mohammed al-Maqdisi, and your uncles, the sheikhs of jihad, did not intend with this initiative to harm anyone. But they wanted to spare the blood of Muslims and put out the *fitna* between them, so that the *mujahidin's* weapons are directed towards their enemies the crusaders, Iranians, Alawites and secularists. My dear son, ask yourself and let your brothers ask themselves, who are those that Sheikh Abu Mohammed al-Maqdisi (may God protect him) testified against that they escaped from settling judgements by the Sharia? What is it that pleases and what is that saddens the crusaders? Is it when we point our weapons at the chest of one another, or when we settle our problems and grievances in an independent Sharia court and we direct our weapons at the chest of the enemies of Islam?

I ask God to gather us together on what He pleases and accepts, and to unite our ranks and reconcile us, gather us together with the most pious person amongst us, and accept our deeds and free us from dissidence, disagreement and conflict.

My last advice to every *mujahid* is to be careful not to get involved in shedding any impermissible blood. He has to know that his Amir's orders will not exempt him from the sin, and he will face God alone. He will not find the Amir to defend him, and his Amir will then be most in need of being defended. Every *mujahid* should know that when he leaves his home to fight the enemies of Islam, he should not get involved in any of the Amir's political aspirations. If his Amir ordered him to kill a Muslim or a disbeliever who has submitted to Islam or to kill someone [where the reasoning] is suspect, such as the notion that his commitment to Islam is doubtful, or he is a heretic, or has joined the Sahwat, or supports the apostates or cooperates with them and any other claims, he should not accept them just because he heard them. He must ask for decisive proof that is clear of doubt. The *fitna* and conflict of leaders and groups around you have increased. So there must be firmness, and you should not go ahead shedding blood unless its religious acceptability is ascertained. If he finds himself in doubt or suspicion, he must not obey his Amir and he should prefer peace. The sin of killing a Muslim is great, and he must remember the words of God almighty: *"And whoever kills a believer intentionally, his recompense is hell to abide therein, and the wrath and the curse of God are upon him, and a great punishment is prepared for him."* {Sura 4 (The Women), 93}

The *mujahid* should know that he took up arms to protect the sanctities of Muslims and not to attack them. If his Amir ordered him to attack a jihadi group or take their money or occupy their bases or whatever they have of

Muslims' money, under the pretext that they are oppressors or that his Amir and group are more entitled to this money or that they are the guardians, that they have the right to take the money of those who disagree with them, all these claims cannot be permitted just because they are Muslims' money, provisions and ammunitions. The saying of the Prophet (PBUH) should be remembered: "every Muslim's money, blood and honour is impermissible for another Muslim [to take]". I ask God to gather the *mujahidin* and Muslims together and unite their ranks to establish a caliphate on the method of Prophethood, on the method of the righteous caliphs with justice and consultation and submission to the Sharia.

And after Syria and Iraq, I want to move to the crime that is happening silently to our brothers in Waziristan. The treacherous Pakistani forces carry out a joint operation with the crusader American enemy, who bombard from the air the people of Waziristan, the *mujahidin* and migrants [to the land of jihad]. The Pakistani forces attack them with their artillery and aircraft from air and land, killing thousands of women, children, Muslims and young people and displacing about a million refugees outside Waziristan. They are begging for aid, and suffer from lack of shelter, hardship in getting food, housing and drugs from Afghanistan and Pakistani cities in the midst of the summer heat and cold winter. The rulers of Pakistan, including politicians and military men, treat them like insects so that their master the Americans will approve of them and fill their pockets with *haram* [impermissible] money.

All this, to no avail, is to secure the exit of the occupier crusader from Afghanistan. The media also join them in covering up the crime; it is rather done with their blessing under the name of war on terror. And God, almighty, gave the truth: *Verily, those who disbelieve spend their wealth to hinder (men) from the path of God, and so will they continue to spend it; but in the end it will become an anguish for them. Then they will be overcome. And those who disbelieve will be gathered unto hell.* {Sura 8 (Spoils of War), 36}

All this and your brothers from the migrants [to the land of jihad] and the *mujahidin* are standing firm like unshakable mountains, despite the flow of blood that streams from them. They attack God's enemies, with His blessing, and the campaigns of the traitors and their master crusaders collapse in the face of their resistance and jihad. They wait for the dawn of victory, the light of which has risen, even if the disbelievers despise it. Waziristan writes a new epic in Islamic history and crushes the slaves of the English as it crushed their masters before, with God's blessing. This is the Islamic emirate with its strikes rising against the crusaders and their cronies from the Arab and non-Arab traitors. It pounds Kabul with its continuous strikes. So, congratulations to the Muslim *ummah* for this victory which is made in Afghanistan, the bastion of Islam. This victory will soon open a new page of Islam's victory, conquest and empowerment, God permitting.

I finish with this, and in the next part, God willing, I will talk about the main characteristics of the caliphate, that is on the method of Prophethood. I entrust you to God's custody, whose trust cannot be lost. Our final prayers, praise be to God, the lord of the two universes, prayers be upon our master, Mohammed and on his family and companions. Peace, and God's compassion and blessings, be upon you.

[The credit on the screen after the speech reads: Omar al-Faruq (may God be pleased with him) said: "We are a nation whom God has honoured with Islam; we will not seek honour from anything else."]

THE ISLAMIC SPRING, PART 3

SEPTEMBER 2015

By Ayman al-Zawahiri

In the third part of his "Islamic Spring" series, Zawahiri expands upon the necessary preconditions for the declaration of a legitimate caliphate and the duties that the caliph will have to respect as well as the qualities that he will have to represent. He then follows each point in seeking to demonstrate how IS and its declaration of a caliphate is unjust and in violation of scripture and the Prophetic method. He addresses questions concerning some of these points in more detail in the fourth instalment which, for the sake of space, I do not include here.

In the name of God, praise be to God. Peace and prayers be upon God's Messenger, his family, companions and whoever supported him.

O Muslim brothers, wherever you are! Peace, God's compassion and blessings be upon you.

I talked, last time, about the dutiful stance regarding the crusaders' campaign against Iraq and Syria and about the Pakistani—American crime against Waziristan. I stressed earlier that the crusaders' campaign is targeting Islam under the name of war on terror. We are with all the *mujahidin*, whether they are good or bad to us, fair or wrong to us, show contempt or generosity to us, assault us or refrain, deny or affirm our right and whether they are impolite or polite to us. The matter is bigger than all this; it is the matter of a nation facing a crusader campaign that requires us to be united to confront it.

I come back and reiterate so that this speech does not get carried away from its meaning. Our vision of what Abu Bakr al-Baghdadi declared is that it [IS] is not a caliphate on the method of Prophethood and it does not oblige Muslims to pledge their allegiance to it. This vision has nothing to do with our call for all the *mujahidin* to stand in one rank in the face of the secular crusaders and the Iranian–Alawite campaign.

We have been calling on Muslims and *mujahidin* to unify ranks and stand up against the crusaders in the West, Russia, Africa, Asia and America, in particular to confront Israel and the secular apostate treacherous rulers who dominate most of the Muslim lands, and face up to Safavid Iran and its followers, as well as all the enemies of Islam.

In this part, I would like to talk, briefly and concisely, about the caliphate that is on the method of Prophethood and its main characteristics. Whoever wants to go deeper should refer to the books of jurisprudence, especially the books of political Sharia and the history of Islam. I will mention general rules, God permitting, without referring to details. I would like to divide the talk on this matter in the following way.

First, clarifying what the caliphate on the method of Prophethood is. Second, [asking] what are the main characteristics of the caliphate on the method of Prophethood? Third, what is the religious way to choose the caliph? Fourth, what are the main qualities of the caliph? Fifth, replying to some doubts and queries.

First then, clarifying what the caliphate on the method of Prophethood is. Imam Ahmad (may God have compassion on him) thus defined the caliphate on the method of Prophethood: "Every pledge of allegiance that took place in Medina was a prophetic caliphate." For that reason, Imam Zarkashi (may God have compassion on him) commented on it in his search for the authoritative nature of the people of Medina and said it is clearly the creed of Ahmad. To him, what the righteous caliphs established is what should be followed, and Ahmad said that every pledge of allegiance that took place in Medina was a prophetic caliphate. It is clear that the pledges of allegiance to al-Sadiq, Omar, Othman and Ali were in Medina, and after that no pledge of allegiance took place there.

So any pledge of allegiance held on the method of the pledge of allegiance of the righteous caliphs is a pledge of allegiance on the method of the Prophet. And any pledge of allegiance contrary to the method of the pledge of allegiance of the righteous caliphs is a pledge of allegiance to a caliphate that is contrary to the method of the Prophet. You can call it the kingdom of conquest or the emirate of confiscation or the caliphate of explosion, detonation and destruction, coercion and conquest, call it whatever you wish. But it is not a caliphate on the method of Prophethood.

Second, what are the main characteristics of the caliphate on the method of Prophethood? The main characteristic of the method of the Prophet is arbitration by Sharia, and whoever is summoned to it must say I hear and obey and act by what God almighty says: *The only saying of the faithful believers, when they are called to God and His Messenger, to judge between them, is that they say: "we hear and we obey". And such are the prosperous ones (who will live forever in Paradise).* {Sura 24 (The Light), 51} Whoever was testified against by the established religious scholars and escapes from being called to be arbitrated by Sharia is not on the method of Prophethood; he is not even suitable for an allegiance to be pledged to him.

Imam al-Mawardi (may God have compassion on him) mentioned that the duties of the caliph are ten, and briefly they are: memorising the creed, arbitrating disputes, guaranteeing security, imposing punishments, fortressing the trenches, jihad against the enemies, collecting booties and charities, estimating donations and spending them, appointing the trustworthy ones and managing affairs. Imam al-Mawardi (may God have compassion on him) then said: "If the Imam satisfied what we have mentioned of the rights of the *ummah* [nation or community], he will have satisfied their due rights to God and what He has on them." Pay attention to this, so if he satisfied this right, then he has done what is expected of him. After he has done this, they then owe two duties to him; obedience and support, if his condition has not changed.

If there is no one who can claim the caliphate and be capable of satisfying all these duties in the territories which he claims to control, and these are the smallest Muslim territories; that is, if he cannot guarantee security in all of them, nor collect alms and distribute them to the needy and liberate them from the enemy, but his power is variable and in some parts it increases and decreases every day, then how can he claim that he is the caliph of all Muslim lands? In many of the Muslim lands, even in those where he assumes dominion, there is the power of other jihadi groups and emirates which meet most of the religious duties, such as ruling with Sharia, commanding good and forbidding evil and jihad. He does not have any power in their territories and they have not pledged allegiance to him, so how can he claim that he is more entitled than them to guardianship? He declared himself a caliph only with the pledge of allegiance of the individuals surrounding him. If he was not capable, before his claim to the caliphate, of supporting the Muslims and satisfying their rights in most of the Muslim lands, how can he then demand their pledge of allegiance, support and obedience? And if the two pillars of the caliph could not be met, which are the pledge of allegiance and the ability to meet his duties, then the most he can claim is that he has conquered some of the Muslim lands and his emirate is the emirate of conquest. He is not permitted to assume any position if he has not met the first condition, which is the pledge of allegiance; and he has not been able to meet the burdens of the second condition, which is to manage the duties of the caliphate. The caliphate, which is the grand leadership, is not just a claim without proof or an illusion without a reality. It is a reality that should be achieved on the ground, so it deserves its religious descriptions and achieves its purposes that have been legislated for. It [the caliphate] is not hopes or desires that could be achieved just by issuing names; Sharia takes into account facts and not simply names. The main question that arises here is: Why do they race to claim titles and descriptions while the realities have not been achieved? Why do we not admit the fact that we are at the stage of defence against an enemy who assaults the Muslims, and that the *mujahidin*, in some places, achieved things that cannot rise to the status of a caliphate which we try, with God's help, to establish?

Instead of racing to claim titles and descriptions that have no basis in reality, we should strengthen and empower the existing Islamic jihadi entities, and at the top of them is the Islamic Emirate in Afghanistan which is led by the Amir of believers, the *mujahid* Mullah Mohammed Omar (may God protect him). So don't rebel against it, break the pledge, be supreme and unfaithful to it and try to overtake it, and even demand tht its soldiers break their promises based on claims that are not supported by facts or proofs. For whose interest [do you do] all this? God is sufficient for us and He is the best disposer of affairs.

I will talk, God willing, about whether the appropriate circumstances have arisen to establish the caliphate; and if they have not, what is the alternative and what is the practical way to establish it, God permitting?

Third, what is the religious way to choose the caliph? We assume that the caliphate has to have the consent of Muslims and that this is the way of the righteous caliphs, whether it is by selection or succession. When al-Siddiq (may God be pleased with him) objected to the supporters [*ansar*], he said in the al-Bukhari narration: "this matter is not known to anyone but to the people of Quraysh [tribe]". And in Abdulrazaq's collection: "the Arabs will not know this matter apart from the people of Quraysh, as they are the best of

Arabs in terms of land and descent". This is a narration that is supported by a chain of trustworthy imams, thanks to God! The majority of people, mostly Arabs at the time, objected because they would not accept a man [as caliph] unless he was from Quraysh. This was supported by the gracious *hadith* [narration], meaning that the Muslim population that is represented by the People of Authority [those who have the authority to elect and depose the caliph] have the right to choose among those who meet the religious conditions of the caliphate, and this is what was emphasised by our master Omar (may God be pleased with him) in his collective speech in Medina. Imam al-Bukhari edited the saying of our master Omar narrated by Ibn Abbas (may God be pleased with them) and said:

> I used to teach [the Quran to] some people of the emigrants, among whom was Abdulrahman bin Auf. While I was in his house at Mina, and he was with Omar bin Al-Khattab during Omar's last Hajj, Abdulrahman came to me and said, "Would that you had seen the man who came today to the Amir of the believers, saying, 'O Amir of the Believers! What do you think about so-and-so who says, "If Omar should die, I will give the pledge of allegiance to such-and such person, as by God, the pledge of allegiance to Abu Bakr was nothing but a prompt sudden action which got established afterwards"?' Omar became angry and then said, 'God willing, I will stand before the people tonight and warn them against those people who want to deprive others of their rights.'"

Pay attention to this: "warn them against those people who want to deprive the others of their rights". Abdulrahman said:

> I said, "O Amir of the believers! Do not do that, for the season of Hajj gathers the riff-raff and the rubble, and it will be they who will gather around you when you stand to address the people. And I am afraid that you will get up and say something, and some people will spread your statement and may not say what you have actually said and may not understand its meaning, and may interpret it incorrectly, so you should wait till you reach Medina, as it is the place of emigration and the place of Prophet's Traditions."

Pay attention to this: "it is the place of emigration and the place of Prophet's Traditions". And there you can be in touch with the learned and noble people, and tell them your ideas with confidence; and the learned people will understand your statement and put it in its proper place.

> On that, Omar said, "By God! God willing, I will do this in the first speech I will deliver before the people in Medina." Omar sat on the pulpit and when the callers to the prayer had finished their call, Omar stood up, and having glorified and praised God as He deserved, he said, "Now then, I am going to tell you something which [God] has written for me to say. I do not know; perhaps it portends my

death, so whoever understands and remembers it must narrate it to the others wherever his mount takes him, but if somebody is afraid that he does not understand it, then it is unlawful for him to tell lies about me."

He then said:

I have been informed that a speaker amongst you says, "By God, if Omar should die, I will give the pledge of allegiance to such-and-such person." One should not deceive oneself by saying that the pledge of allegiance given to Abu Bakr was given suddenly and it was successful. No doubt, it was like that, but God saved [the people] from its evil, and there is none among you who has the qualities of Abu Bakr. Remember that whoever gives the pledge of allegiance to anybody among you without consulting the other Muslims, neither that person, nor the person to whom the pledge of allegiance was given, are to be supported, lest they both should be killed.

And he said about the pledge of allegiance to our master Abu Bakr (may God be pleased with them):

Then there was a hue and cry among the gathering and their voices rose so that I was afraid there might be great disagreement, so I said, "O Abu Bakr! Stretch your hand out." He stretched his hand out and I pledged allegiance to him, and then all the emigrants gave the Pledge of allegiance and so did the supporters [ansar] afterwards.

I repeat for its importance: "He held his hand out and I pledged allegiance to him, and then all the emigrants gave the Pledge of allegiance and so did the ansar afterwards."

In a different narration of Ibn Abi Shaiba's (may God have compassion on him) collection: "I came to know that there are people who say 'the caliphate of Abu Bakr was sudden and it was like that, but God saved people from evil'. There is no caliphate without consultation." Pay attention for its importance: "There is no caliphate without consultation." This is a correct ascription to a chain of trustworthy people, thanks to God!

And in the narration of Ahmad (may God have compassion on him), in the Musnad [hadith] according to a correct ascription: "Whoever pledged allegiance to an Amir without consulting the Muslims, neither he nor the one who pledged allegiance can have the pledge." I repeat for its importance: "Whoever pledged allegiance to an Amir without consulting the Muslims, neither he nor the one to whom the pledge of allegiance was given can have the pledge, lest they both should be killed."

We should note here that our master Omar, on the advice of our master Abdulrahman bin Auf (may God be pleased with him), delivered this sermon in Medina (God glorify it), which was a platform for the leaders of the *ummah* and the people of tradition, jurisprudence and religious knowledge. Our master Omar warned Muslims of the importance of the sermon and asked those who fully understood it to do their utmost to report its content to a wider audience. It was an important and a significant event which was delivered in the presence of a large number of companions (may God be pleased with them), who are the People of Authority, and it is not known if anyone objected to it; it is narrated in the most correct books of tradition and it is tantamount to consensus or the companions' consensus and no one objected to them.

In this significant speech, our master Omar (may God be pleased with him) warned of some important matters. Firstly, he who pledges allegiance to a man without consulting the Muslims has deprived them [Muslims] of their rights. Secondly, the *ummah* should be warned of this person. Thirdly, he should not qualify for a pledge of allegiance, and any pledge of allegiance to him should not to be accepted. Fourth, he should not be held accountable for his actions. Fifth, the pledge of allegiance of our master, Abu Bakr, was a general pledge of allegiance by the emigrants and the supporters [*ansar*]. Sixth, the matter of electing and deposing is exclusive to the people of knowledge, jurisprudence, the mighty honourable of Islam and the Prophet's companions in Medina; and not for the ignorant people, since nobody knows their names, history or number and they would monopolise the matter without the [consent of] Muslims. He (may God be pleased with him) also said in Abdulrazaq's (may God have compassion on him) collection: "the emirate is consultation." This narration is correct according to the chain of ascriptions of trustworthy imams, thanks to God! Imam al-Baihaqi (may God have compassion on him) in his Great Rules said: "Our master, Omar bin al-Khattab (may God be pleased with him), said to his companions while he was on his deathbed: "Deliberate on it, if anything happened to me, let Suhaib, the chief of the sons of Juda'n, pray to the people for three nights, then collect on the third day the honourable people and commanders and commission one of you. And if anyone wanted to command without consultation, then strike him on the neck." Pay attention to this: "And if anyone wanted to command without consultation, then strike him on the neck." This is a correct ascription, thanks to God! In the pledge of allegiance of our master, Othman (may God be pleased with him), Abdulrahman bin Auf said to our master Ali (may God be pleased with them) in the narration that is edited by Imam Bukhari (may God have compassion on him): "And now, O Ali, I looked into people's affairs and I didn't see that they were fair to Othman." Pay attention to its significance: "I looked into people's affairs and I did not see that they were fair to Othman. Do not give them the chance to do the same to you, and he said: 'I pledge allegiance to you on the tradition of God and His Messenger and the previous two caliphs.' Abdulrahman pledged allegiance to him and then the emigrant [*muhajiroun*], supporter [*ansar*] people, commanders and Muslims pledged allegiance to him." Pay attention to its importance: "Abdulrahman pledged allegiance to him and then the emigrant, *ansar* people, commanders and Muslims pledged allegiance to him."

There is a significant meaning in this narration, which is that it does not suffice that the person is qualified to be the caliph and meets the conditions to assume the caliphate, but he will not be a caliph unless he is chosen by the Muslims who have the right to choose among those who are qualified for this position. The six [people] whom Omar (may God be pleased with them) selected were all qualified for the caliphate, but they selected two among them, Othman and Ali (may God be pleased with them). Our master, Ali, was more qualified to be a caliph, but the Muslim people decided not to select him but to select another who is also qualified for the caliphate.

This is the biography of the righteous caliphs (may God be pleased with them). The *ummah* is represented by the People of Authority; if they agree, then the *ummah* will agree; and if they refuse, then the *ummah* will refuse. They will select their caliph among those who are qualified to assume the position of the caliphate. The Sheikh of Islam, Ibn Taymiyyah (may God have compassion on him), stressed this when responding to the Shia, who fraudulently claimed that the pledge of allegiance to Abu Bakr al-Siddiq (may God be pleased with him) was made by a minority of the companions (may God be pleased with them). That means that the pledge of allegiance cannot be established without the People of Authority, who represent the *ummah*. The Sheikh of Islam, Ibn Taymiyyah, said when responding to the Shia al-Hili[22] regarding Abu Bakr's matter that the Shia al-Hili claimed that the pledge of allegiance to our master, Abu Bakr (may God be pleased with him), was only made by a minority of the companions. Ibn Taymiyyah denied this and refuted his claim and said: "If it was the case that Omar and a segment of people with him pledged allegiance to him and the rest of the companions restrained from doing that, he would not have become a leader with that. But he became the leader with the pledge of allegiance of the companions." Pay attention to this: "He would not have become a leader if the rest of the companions restrained from the pledge of allegiance; he became the leader with the pledge of allegiance of the companions, who are the people of authority and might." So whoever says he will become the leader with the consent of only one, two or four and they are not the People of Authority, then his might is mistaken. The people who pledged allegiance to the Prophet in Medina are the same who pledged allegiance to Abu Bakr. As for Omar, Abu Bakr left him in charge of the *ummah*'s rule and the Muslims then pledged allegiance to him after the death of Abu Bakr. He became the leader when he attained power and capability with their pledge of allegiance. Who pledged allegiance? The Muslims pledged allegiance after the death of Abu Bakr. He then became the leader when he attained power and capability, with what? With the pledge of allegiance to him. It is also said that Othman did not become a leader with the selection of some of them, but with the pledge of allegiance of the people and all the Muslims who pledged allegiance to Othman bin Afan and no one abstained from pledging allegiance to him. If it was the case that only Abdulrahman pledged allegiance to him but not Ali and the other companions and the people of might, he would not have reached leadership. It has also been said that Othman became caliph after people pledged allegiance to him, not because some had selected him. All Muslims pledged allegiance to Othman and no one failed to do so. He would not have become caliph if Abdulrahman and Ali and other people of might had not pledged allegiance to him.

Let me say to those who allege that the Prophet's caliphate can be established with a secret pledge by a small number of ignorant people to a person who is not selected by the *ummah*, slandering Muslims and people of jihad, knowledge, grace and leadership; let me say to them that what they are alleging is exactly the same as the Shia al-Hili alleged before when he said that the Prophet's companions—may God bless them—stated that Abu Bakr al-Siddiq became caliph with the allegiance of a small number of companions. This is what you alleged and which is denied by the Sheikh of Islam, Ibn Taymiyyah [in response to] al-Hili, the Shia, and refuted his allegation. He explained and cleared that the People of Authority from the companions and emigrants have pledged allegiance to the righteous caliphs. So, whoever claims that the pledge of allegiance to a person by an ignorant minority who does not have the consent of the *ummah* is a religious way will provide a justification to the likes of al-Hili, the Shia.

Look at what dilemma they are in; they say they fight the Shia, but they provide them with justifications for these allegations of false doubts. The pledge of allegiance will be made only by consent and not coercion. For that reason, Imam Malik issued a fatwa to the people of Medina that their pledges of allegiance to Mansour were null because they were taken by coercion. Ibn Kathir mentioned the pledge of allegiance of the people of Medina to Mohammed ibn Abdullah, known as the clever spirit, as he referred to the events of the year 145 [Islamic calendar] when Mohammed ibn Abdullah delivered a speech to the people of Medina on that day and he spoke about things that he blamed on the sons of Abbas. He told them he never went to any country and did not receive the pledge of allegiance with obedience. All the people of Medina then pledged allegiance to him apart from a minority. Ibn Jarir narrated from Imam Malik that he issued a fatwa to the people to pledge allegiance to him. They told him that they had pledged allegiance to Mansour. He told them that since they were coerced, the pledge of allegiance cannot be taken from the coerced. What did Ibn Jarir narrate from Imam Malik? He issued a fatwa to the people to pledge allegiance to him, and the people told him that they are bound by the pledge of allegiance to Mansour. Imam Malik told the people: you are coerced and the coerced are not eligible to pledge allegiance. People then pledged allegiance to him according to what Malik said.

What can inform this matter is the pledge of allegiance of the Sultan of Egypt and Sham, Rukin al-Din Baibars and the great religious scholars like Sheikh Izaddin ibn Abdulsalam (may God have compassion on him) to the Abbasid caliph Al-Mustansir, when he went to Egypt in 659 [Islamic calendar], three and a half years after the fall of the Abbasid caliphate when the Tatars invaded it, which was a famous day in the history of Islam as the historians have recorded. The caliph Mustansir was given the pledge of allegiance before him as the ruling caliph blessed by God in 658 [Islamic calendar], by the ruler of Aleppo and a minority of Muslims. The Sultan of Egypt and its religious scholars did not challenge that pledge, but pledged allegiance to Al-Mustansir because Egypt was the centre of Islam's power and its Sultan was the ruler of Egypt, Sham including Aleppo, Hejaz, coasts of Yemen and the Red Sea, and therefore the centre of international trade was under his reign; this is the economic side of it. As for the ideological side of it, he was the custodian of the three holy mosques; the two holy places in Mecca and Medina and Al-Aqsa Mosque, and also because most of the religious scholars and honourable people were at that time in Egypt. The ruler then pledged allegiance to Al-Mustansir Bi-lah. The moral of this story is that the great religious scholars who do not fear the blame of blamers, like the Sultan, religious scholars, other kings and Sheikh Izaddin ibn Abdulsalam (may God have compassion on him) did not believe in a pledge of allegiance to a ruler by a minority of people.

Although not formal proof, this should be taken as a reference. There is another point to the story which is that the caliph Al-Mustansir, after he was given the pledge of allegiance, commissioned the Sultan Baibars to make a public covenant in front of the people. This makes us stop at every secret pledge of allegiance; did it include secret conditions not proclaimed to the public? Sometimes a person says things that are later contradicted by his followers; does it mean that he is in opposition with his followers? Is he changing stance? Or were things imposed on him that we are not aware of [by his followers]? The examples of the conditional pledges of allegiance are the conditions which Sheikh Abu Hamza al-Muhajir put on Sheikh Abu Omar al-Baghdadi (may God have compassion on them). He conditioned his pledge of allegiance to him that Sheikh Abu Omar should be subordinate to Sheikh Osama (may God have compassion on him), and through him he pledged allegiance to Mullah Mohammed Omar. Sheikh Abu Omar (may God have compassion on him) agreed to that and Sheikh Abu Hamza communicated this to us. This is the matter which the caliphs after him confirmed.

Fourth, what are the main qualities of the caliph? Scholars have listed a number of conditions required in a caliph. I will only focus on one of them: justice, which has long been forgotten in recent times and which covers all the other conditions. Justice is a requirement in any religious ruling; for that reason, it is an essential condition that the People of Authority should possess and a necessary requirement for anyone to be elected to the caliphate. He who lacks this condition is not fit to be among the People of Authority, let alone be a caliph. And that is for what God almighty says: "When the Lord of Ibrahim tried him with (certain) Commands, which he fulfilled. He said (to him), 'Verily, I am going to make you a leader (Prophet) of mankind.' (Ibrahim) said, 'And of my offspring (to make leaders).' (God) said, *My covenant (Prophethood, etc.) includes not the wrong-doers.*" {Sura 2 (The Cow), 124}

Imam al-Qurtubi quoted Ibn Khwariz Mindad (may God have compassion on them) in the interpretation of this verse and Ibn Khwariz Mindad said: "An oppressor is not a prophet or a caliph, not a ruler or a Mufti, not the imam of a prayer and his words are not accepted which he quotes from the religion and his testimony in matters of judgement is not accepted. He who is not just is not fit for religious leadership, such as the rulership of an Emirate or membership of the People of Authority." Examples of this would be that if it is proved against him that he escapes from settling judgements according to the

Sharia or that he lies or he breaks promises or he insists on the disobedience of his Amir or engages in extreme excommunication of the Muslims or accuses them of wrong accusations or shows contempt to their blood and sanctities or warns the honourable ones whose invocation and truth telling are testified and who do not fear the blame of blamers.

I would like here to advise my brother *mujahidin*, and I am in great need of giving this advice. I say to every brother *mujahid*: do not fight unless you are confident that he [the target] is the enemy of Islam and that he deserves to be fought. Know that your Amir will not spare you from anything on the Day of Resurrection, and be warned that your Amir has a political aim or hostility with a rival or a race for power or clout and he uses you for his disagreements. Do not label anyone an infidel unless you have ascertained his disbelief; and do not think you will be with him [the Amir], as you will be questioned alone on the Day of Resurrection. Your Amir will not release you from anything on the Day of Resurrection, but he needs someone to save him from the Judgement. Remember what God almighty says: *And whoever kills a believer intentionally, his recompense is hell to abide therein, and the wrath and the curse of God are upon him, and a great punishment is prepared for him.* {Sura 4 (The Women), 93}

Also remember what al-Bukhari narrated from Osama bin Zaid (may God be pleased with them) who said:

> God's Messenger (PBUH) sent us to Huraqa, where we attacked the tribe in the morning and defeated them. A man from the group of supporters [*ansar*] and I chased one of them and when we caught him, he said "There is no God but God." The *ansari* man withdrew, but I stabbed him with my spear until I killed him. After we had advanced he told the Prophet (PBUH) and he said: "O Osama, did you kill him even after he said (There is no God but God)?" I said: "He said that only to save himself." The Prophet (PBUH) kept on repeating that so often that I wished I never became a Muslim before that day."

With this I finish and in the next part, God willing, I will briefly reply to some doubts and questions on this subject. I entrust you to God's custody whose trust can never be lost. Our last prayers are praise be to God, the Lord of the two universes, peace and prayers be upon our master Mohammed, on his family and companions. Peace and God's compassion and blessings be upon you.

THE ISLAMIC SPRING, PART 5

SEPTEMBER 2015

By Ayman al-Zawahiri

In the fifth episode of the "Islamic Spring" series, Zawahiri continues to explore the conditions necessary to establish a caliphate. In doing so he seeks to undermine the appeal of IS's leadership by lauding Abu Musab al-Zarqawi, whom IS recognises as its forefather, and other leaders of the Islamic State of Iraq, whom Zawahiri had of course criticised in the past. He demonstrates their apparent loyalty towards the Al-Qaeda leadership (represented, of course, at that time by bin Laden), whilst reiterating his vision for the creation of a caliphate through solidifying existing "emirates" in Afghanistan and the Caucasus that are loyal to Al-Qaeda.

In the name of God, praise be to God. Peace and prayers be upon God's Messenger, his family, companions and whoever supported him.

O Muslim brothers, wherever you are! Peace, God's compassion and blessings be upon you.

I talked, previously, about the stance towards the crusaders' campaign against Iraq and Syria and about the Pakistani–American criminality against Waziristan and the main characteristics of the caliphate on the method of Prophethood.

I would like, in this part, to talk about two questions. First, are the current circumstances ready to declare the establishment of the caliphate? Second, if the circumstances are not ready now to declare the establishment of the caliphate, what is the alternative to trying to establish it?

Regarding the first question—which is, are the current circumstances ready to declare the establishment of the caliphate?—I will start, before answering it, with an introduction which is that the Islamic movements since the fall of the caliphate [all] strive to restore it and they have undertaken extensive endeavours in this respect. Al-Baghdadi and his group, all the branches of Al-Qaeda, including the Islamic state of Iraq, are nothing but one of the many outcomes from these endeavours.

To be brief, I will give one example [regarding this], which is to mention briefly the efforts of Sheikh Osama bin Laden (may God have compassion on him) in establishing the caliphate on the method of Prophethood. One of these efforts [was] his support of jihad in Afghanistan in the hope that Afghanistan would become the fortress of Islam, and his support of many jihadi movements in the world to help them establish Islamic states in their territories. Another effort was to support the government of Sudan in aiming to create an economic base on which any Islamic movement could rely. The sheikh thought [that] if any Islamic movement was able to hold power, the crusader West would wage an economic war against it, but Sudan with its agricultural capabilities would be able to supply the necessary food to any Islamic state facing economic embargo. He [made the case regarding] the importance of the economy, in that the Israeli state was created based on the financial support of the Jews.

His other project which he hoped to complete was to create a hajj land route that extended from Nigeria to Sudan, so that the Muslim African countries [would be] economically, culturally and demographically linked together. After that, [there is] his second migration to Afghanistan [1996 CE] and the attempt to unite the *ummah* [nation or community] around the jihadi movement in the face of one target, which is the American enemy. That is why he started to encourage jihad against America after he studied all the previous jihadi movements and experiences to gather the *ummah*, jihadi and Islamic groups around one uniting cause as a main step in the attempt towards the [establishment of the] caliphate. He then participated in the jihad, in the ranks of the Islamic emirate under the banner of the Amir of believers, the *mujahid* Mullah Mohammed Omar (may God protect him), against the emirate's enemies, whom he considered America's cronies, and saw in them the hostility to the *mujahidin's* unity and the establishment of the caliphate. This is what the events and Congress's report[23] confirmed regarding the events of

11 September, which the Al-Sahab Foundation has documented in its many publications.

The next important and perilous step was Sheikh Osama bin Laden's pledge of allegiance to the Amir of believers, Mullah Mohammed Omar. This was one of the signs of his mental vision which God granted him. He called on Muslims to pledge allegiance to the Amir of believers, the *mujahid* Mullah Mohammed Omar, considering that he has the power of the greatest Imam in Afghanistan and over those who pledged allegiance to him, including the Al-Qaeda (Al-Jihad) organisation with its various branches and the Islamic State of Iraq.

The most important soldiers of the Al-Qaeda organisation were the two martyred heroes (as we consider them thus), Sheikh Abu Musab al-Zarqawi and Sheikh Abu Hamza al-Muhajir (may God have compassion on them). From what school did these two heroes graduate? Sheikh Abu Musab grew up in Abdullah Azzam's jihadi school, was raised at the hands of Sheikh Abu Mohammed al-Maqdisi and became a soldier in the Al-Qaeda group. Here I would like to give two excellent examples of loyalty to his pledge to become an exemplar for the *mujahidin* [displaying] high morals and behaviour.

The first example is what he said in an audio tape to Sheikh Osama: "I am a soldier under the command of your emirate; if you wish, you can remove me and test me. What the Dr [Zawahiri] wrote to me in his letter were only queries; if they were decisive orders, I would have committed to them." These are the words of Sheikh Abu Musab to Sheikh Osama (may God have compassion on them). The second example is that Sheikh Abu Musab al-Zarqawi sent a messenger to his brothers in Khorasan and met some leaders, including Sheikh Mustafa Abu Yazid (may God have compassion on him). One of the things that the messenger told them about was that when Sheikh Abu Musab proposed to one of the jihadi groups a matter for the *mujahidin's* consultation, one of the jihadi groups [made it a] condition that the Al-Qaeda organisation in the countries of the two rivers [Tigris and Euphrates, i.e. Iraq] should cut off their relations with the headquarters of the Al-Qaeda. When the matter was taken to Sheikh Abu Musab, he said: "God forbid that I break my pledge to Sheikh Osama."

Whoever wanted more [information] should go back, for example, to the two speeches by Sheikh Abu Musab al-Zarqawi: the declaration of the pledge of allegiance to Al-Qaeda under the leadership of Sheikh Osama bin Laden, and the second speech being the message from a soldier to his Amir. As for Sheikh Abu Hamza al-Muhajir, he grew up in the [Egyptian] Al-Jihad Group and he was one of its most loyal soldiers. I considered him as my younger brother, and he accompanied and guarded me many times. He and Sheikh Abu Islam al-Misri pledged allegiance to Sheikh Osama in Afghanistan and sometimes he was sending letters to me, Sheikh Osama and Sheikh Mustafa and calling us by the names of paternal uncle, father and maternal uncle [i.e. terms of respect]. He put conditions on Sheikh Abu Omar al-Baghdadi in his pledge of allegiance to affirm that he was a soldier of Sheikh Osama and, therefore, to the Amir of believers, the *mujahid* Mullah Mohammed Omar. Before that, Sheikh Abu Hamza al-Muhajir said in a statement which he issued in the aftermath of the killing of Sheikh Abu Musab al-Zarqawi:

> Our Sheikh and leader Abu Abdullah, Osama bin Laden, God is generous and has granted us with audacious and distinguished brothers, gathered with us in the *mujahidin's Shura* [consultative] council. They were the best helpers and support-ers, we vowed for victory and promised to keep the method of the predecessors (may God be pleased with them). May God reward them from us and all the Muslims with all goodness. Sheikh Abu Abdullah, Osama bin Laden, we are wait-ing for your orders and we obey your commands, and we give you the glad tidings about the high morale of your soldiers and the kind brave souls who came under your banner and about the first victories soon, God willing!

Would it be rational that these two faithful martyred heroes break their pledges of allegiance to Sheikh Osama bin Laden unilaterally? The facts, events and documents prove the falsity of this allegation, and for whose interest would Abu Hamza al-Muhajir do that? Does this support the unity of the *mujahidin* or destroy it, and why does Abu Hamza al-Muhajir disobey the Amir of the Islamic emirate, Mullah Mohammed Omar? And what will be the result if every branch of Al-Qaeda or those groups who pledged allegiance to the Amir of believers, Mullah Mohammed Omar, break it as they alleged against Abu Hamza and even themselves? The result is the disintegration of the ranks of the *mujahidin* and their separation. Is the one who does this entitled to claim that he calls for the unity of the *mujahidin*? And what is the benefit [of a] group in insisting on spreading the slander that Abu Hamza broke his pledge unilaterally with Sheikh Osama, with Mullah Mohammed Omar?

The answer is: it is al-Baghdadi's group that is trying to expand by avoiding to settle judgements through Sharia and usurping the rights of Muslims with-out consultation or obedience; it labels whoever objects to its expansion—including the group's predecessors—with perversion, secularism, democracy and [*Muslim*] Brotherhood [association]. May God have compassion on you, O Abu Musab and Abu Hamza, the ordeal has become greater with your loss; we are from God and we will return to Him!

To return to Sheikh Osama bin Laden's steps in the effort toward [establishing] the caliphate, in addition to what I have mentioned, Sheikh Osama bin Laden tried to unite the Islamic movements by establishing the international Islamic front to fight the Jews and crusaders, then establishing the Al-Qaeda (Al-Jihad) organisation under the banner of the Islamic emirate, and expanding the Al-Qaeda organisation by forming various branches of it, which can all be gathered in one jihadi entity under the banner of the emirate of one Amir, who is the Amir of the believers, Mullah Mohammed Omar. This is in brief Sheikh Osama bin Laden's way, step by step towards the righteous caliphate. Despite these blessed and giant steps, Sheikh Osama and his brothers saw that the time was not suitable to declare the establishment of Islamic emirates, let alone the caliphate.

The Americans have published some of Sheikh Osama's correspondence, which imply this meaning. I do not want to refer to this correspondence as an argument, but I would like to make a point that no one, among those interested in jihad, will have an excuse if he fails to see these important documents. If it is only the domination of those brothers [that] provide[s] an excuse to declare the caliphate, the Al-Qaeda organisation would have priority over them, because it has national and international branches in many countries and it has dominion, with God's grace and help, over wide areas.

The Amir of believers, Mullah Mohammed Omar, has priority over all, as the whole of Al-Qaeda is his soldier. Here two scepticisms might emerge. First, it might be asked, is it a sin to decline to give the pledge of allegiance because the circumstances are not suitable? The answer is No. The evidence regarding this is the attempts of many companions to dissuade Hussein [ibn Ali] from rebelling and demanding pledges of allegiance for himself, and it was proved that their opinion was correct. Hussein received pledges of allegiance before he rebelled, and he did not ask for pledges of allegiance after he declared himself the caliph; and among those who opposed him were the great followers of his father, the pillars of his state who had fought under his banner, such as our master, Abdullah ibn Abbas (may God be pleased with them all). The second scepticism is that someone might say that you see the inappropriateness of the circumstances for the declaration of the establishment of the caliphate, but we see its appropriateness; that is your interpretation, and this is our interpretation. The answer is that if the mass of Muslims were agreeing with you on that, you would have been right; but since they did not agree with you, then you did not have the right to oppress the Muslims without their consultation.

The second question which I would like to talk about is that if the circumstances are not ready now to declare the establishment of the caliphate, what is then the alternative to attempting its establishment? Before answering this question, there are important issues which I must explain and re-emphasise. First, we are bound by a pledge of allegiance to Mullah Mohammed Omar, with which we will not tamper. Second, a caliphate cannot be established by bypassing the Islamic emirate's consultation in Afghanistan, knowing that it is the biggest and oldest existing legitimate emirate for the Muslims. It cannot also evade the Caucasus emirate's consultation, as well as the jihadi groups who are steadfast in the trenches of jihad, because if the Islamic emirate, Caucasus emirate and the jihadi groups are legitimate entities, then how can they be evaded and the matter suppressed without [engaging with] them? If those who claim the caliphate do not consider them legitimate, this is then coming from [a position of] extremism [the advocates of which] are not suitable at all for the caliphate. If the purpose behind [the one] who claims the caliphate for himself is to declare it only himself, it is then his duty to go back and join the Islamic Emirate in Afghanistan whose pledge he broke, and not to claim the caliphate with the pledge of some ignorant people, without the consultation of the *mujahidin* and Muslims and after demanding that others dismantle.

After this explanation and emphasis, I will answer the following question. What [should be the] way to choose to establish the caliphate? The way is: first, strengthening the Islamic Emirate in Afghanistan and the Caucasus Emirate; second, supporting the jihadi groups and trying to unite the *ummah* around them in the face of the greater enemy, alongside confronting the local lackeys in every country; third, widening consultation among the *mujahidin* about the availability of appropriate circumstances to declare Islamic emirates in different places, and widening consultation about two important issues. First, are the circumstances suitable to declare the caliphate and are its foundations complete? Second, if the mass of *mujahidin*, virtuous invocators and notables among the Muslims agreed that the foundations of the caliphate are complete and the circumstance is suitable to declare it, the consultation then will centre on whoever is suitable to assume this position and who has the consensus of the People of Authority;[24] he will be given the pledge of allegiance for the [position of the] caliphate.

At the end of this part, I deliver two messages. First, to the scholars of jihad and benediction, I ask them and I emphasise that they should concentrate on those parts which are neglected, because of their war against the enemies of the Muslim nation, the infidels and apostates; for example, concentrating on self-purification and moral education, warning the Muslims about the repulsiveness of the sin of lying and slandering and making up accusations against people in general, Muslims in particular and, especially, the *mujahidin*. Whoever slanders a Muslim or infidel without proof, he himself is a liar. God almighty says: *"Since they (the slanderers) have not produced witnesses! Then with God they are the liars."* {Sura 24 (The Light), 13} They should concentrate on the sanctities of the Muslims, their money, blood and honour and to remind the Muslims of what God almighty says: *"And whoever kills a believer intentionally, his recompense is hell to abide therein, and the wrath and the curse of God are upon him, and a great punishment is prepared for him."* {Sura 4 (The Women), 93} Also, they should concentrate on alerting those who are engaged in excommunication [*takfir*] and warn them against it and to clarify to the *ummah* that we are the callers of consultation, justice and fairness and we don't want to occupy it in the name of Islam, but we want the *ummah* to be ruled by Islam. They should explain to the *ummah* that we are not excommunicating them, but we are the most compassionate with them and caring about their guidance and we are the first defenders of their sanctities and we do not violate them.

The second message is to repeat the call for the *mujahidin* to settle disputes by an independent Sharia court, and whoever stood against it should go back to it. The call [is] for all the *mujahidin* in Syria and Iraq to cooperate and coordinate in confronting the secular crusaders and Alawite Shia campaign and in opening the door for the pious and rational people to get engaged, and in distancing the rampant and alarming people who try to deepen the differences and push for more stubbornness. And they should continue to try to establish the caliphate on the method of Prophethood, which is based on acceptance and consultation and not on explosion, detonation and destruction. How wonderful life is when my people are all together, their issues not separated by desires. This will now suffice and I will meet you in the next part, God willing.

Our last prayers are praise be to God, the Lord of the two universes, peace and prayers be upon our master Mohammed, on his family and companions. Peace and God's compassion and blessings be upon you.

THE ISLAMIC SPRING, PART 6

SEPTEMBER 2015

By *Ayman al-Zawahiri*

In this sixth episode of the "Islamic Spring" series, Zawahiri seeks to address some of the issues that IS became famous for spearheading, particularly the question of Shia dominance in the MENA region and the rise of Iran. He warns of a broad coalition of adversaries, including Shia forces and crusaders, which will undermine the interests of Sunni Muslims, and blames al-Baghdadi for the disunity among the latter.

In the name of God, praise be to God. Peace and prayers be upon God's Messenger, his family, companions and whoever supported him.

O Muslim brothers, wherever you are! Peace, God's compassion and blessings be upon you.

I previously talked about the stance on the crusaders' campaign against Iraq and Syria, the Pakistani—American criminality against Waziristan, the main characteristics of the caliphate on the method of Prophethood, and the suitability of current circumstances for declaring the caliphate. If the circumstances are not now ready to declare the establishment of the caliphate, what is the alternative in order to try to establish it?

In this part, I would like to talk about an issue which I find highly dangerous for the Muslim *ummah* [nation or community], which is the danger of the

Iranian—Safavid cooperation with the new crusaders' campaign. I will start this part by offering my condolences to our beloved honourable brothers in the Nusra Front, may God make His religion and Book and the Muslims victorious with them, for the loss of the honourable brother, the leader Abu Hamam al-Shami and his honourable brothers who were martyred by the crusaders' bombardment. I ask God to cover the honourable brother Abu Hamam al-Shami, his comrades and all the Muslim martyrs with His grace, and to heal their wounded ones and take care of their widows and orphans and all the Muslims.

My honourable brothers, there is a truth which we notice today, and it is that the crusaders' coalition cooperate and make a secret understanding and ally with Safavid Iran and its followers. This cooperation was obvious in the American wars in Afghanistan and Iraq, as admitted by the Iranian leaders themselves. This cooperation was documented by an Al-Sahab tape, with the title "Reviewing the events, truths of jihad and falsities of hypocrisy".[25] On the blessed Syrian front, the Safavid Shias[26] are waging an overt war that cannot be hidden from the people of Islam and Sunna. They declare publicly that they defend the Assad regime, and their forces move to Syria from Afghanistan, Iraq, Lebanon and other places. They cooperate and coordinate on the one hand with the Russians, and on the other with NATO. You see that the US Secretary of State [John Kerry] declares that there must be an agreement with Bashar Assad to solve the Syrian problem.

Whilst they are uniting against us, there are, unfortunately, those who insist on starting their war against them by infighting between the *mujahidin*. Instead of us all trying to end the disunity between the *mujahidin* by uniting their ranks in the face of their united enemies, some insist on creating new disunities and reasons for disagreement and claim names and positions which they don't deserve based on reality and the religion. The destruction of jihad in Syria by disunity, extremism and excommunicating the *mujahidin* with suspicion or half suspicion and even, sometimes, without any evidence or, sometimes, against the evidence will only serve the interests of the secular crusading Safavid Alawite[27] campaign.

There are some who believe that in order to build up themselves they have to destroy others, and that they must try to destroy all other jihadi entities so that they can declare themselves the only pure Islamic entity. For that reason, they accuse others of oscillating between apostasy, treason, wrongness and relapse and don't see that they are the first loser and the one who will be hurt in this. The previous jihadi entities confronted and still confront the secular crusaders and Safavid campaigns against Islam and the Muslims. He [Abu Bakr al-Baghdadi] is nothing but a fruit of their work and people knew him through them. He fawned on them and insisted on demanding that they recommend him and mention him in their publications. Instead of all of us building on what their brothers built who preceded him in jihad and migration [to the land of jihad]; and instead of trying to mobilise the *ummah* and all or the majority of the *mujahidin* to bring them to an agreement and unity to achieve the Islamic state which is built on consultation, as our master Omar (may God be pleased with him) declared in the correct *hadith* [saying], "The emirate is consultation"; instead of this righteous method, some insist on declaring one a caliph not only without consultation but also without informing anyone.

After he [Abu Bakr al-Baghdadi] declared himself a caliph and collect[ed] the pledges of allegiance, he turned things upside down. What we know from the traditions of the righteous caliphs is that the pledges of allegiance are first collected with consent and choice, and if the Muslim people agree the pledges of allegiance, they are then accomplished. But we see the opposite, and he who promotes this opposition insists that it is a caliphate on the method of Prophethood. And he who propagates this opposition got used to the propagation of contradictions. He demands that others be obedient to him, whereas he is disobedient to his Amir [Zawahiri and Mullah Omar].

He makes reference, on the duty to obey him, to Imam Ahmad (may God have compassion on him) who talks about the duty to obey the master who calls himself the Amir of believers, but he does not apply this saying to the Amir of believers, Mullah Mohammed Omar (may God protect him), whom he described as the towering mountain and whose name was chanted by his followers. He collects the pledges of allegiance for himself, while he breaks his pledge of allegiance made previously to his [Mullah Omar's] Emirate.

So imagine the complex corruption. He insists on fuelling a big problem which disunites the *mujahidin* and leads to infighting and bloodshed between them. His spokesperson calls for the destruction of all the groups apart from themselves, and strikes the heads of those who disagree under the pretext of dividing the ranks, whereas their enemies are united against them. So have we not learnt anything from our enemy? I am not here addressing the stubborn, extremist and intimidating people for whom I ask God for guidance. But I address the people of piety, ethics and reason and those who care about the unity of the Muslims and their victory against their united enemies. I call them in the ranks of the *mujahidin* and in all the jihadi gatherings to try to stop the internal destruction of jihad and work towards directing the energy of the *mujahidin* against their enemies who have gathered against them.

Is there anyone listening and is there anyone answering? I have offered a proposal in this regard with certain clauses which I will briefly repeat as a reminder. First, the immediate stop to infighting between the *mujahidin*. Second, stop the calls for killing him who disagrees and striking his head with bullets under the pretext of dividing the ranks and other similar myths which lead to the division of the Muslim ranks. Third, establish the independent religious [Sharia] court and affirm its power, presence and prestige in Iraq and Syria over all the *mujahidin*. Fourth, try to issue a general amnesty. Fifth, take initiatives to cooperate at every possible level, such as treating the wounded, sheltering families, storing the machinery, providing rations and ammunition and carrying out joint operations.

Jihad in blessed Syria is the hope of the *ummah*, which has long been waiting for it, because Syria and Egypt are the gates of conquest for Al-Quds [Jerusalem]. The destruction of jihad in Syria is the destruction of the *ummah*'s hope; and exhausting the *mujahidin* with internal fighting is an end which their enemies would wish for.

As for Iraq, the Safavids started to wage war against the people of Sunna when they entered Baghdad on the back of the US tanks. It is not a war only against he who installed himself as caliph without consultation, but it is a much bigger, wider and older one than this; it is a war against the people of Sunna in the region. It was the forces of the sectarian Shia government which attacked the protest camps in Anbar before the [creation of the] alleged caliphate, and the Shia militias perpetrated the most hideous crimes against all the people of Sunna even before the declaration of that alleged caliphate.

The popular mobilisation ["awakening"] forces are the ones which perpetrate atrocities against all the people of Sunna, whether they support the alleged caliph or oppose him. It is, therefore, a war against all the people of Sunna without discrimination, and if these forces were able to control the areas of the people of Sunna, they would give no regard to ties or covenants. As I mentioned before and despite our non-recognition of this alleged caliphate, I called and I repeat the call for the cooperation of all the *mujahidin* in Iraq and Syria in the face of the secular crusader–Safavid Alawite coalition: whoever was bad or good to us, whoever wronged us or was fair to us, whoever was polite or impolite with us and whoever slandered against us or was truthful to us. It is because the matter is bigger than us; it is the matter of the secular crusader–Safavid Alawite campaign that is waging [war] against Islam and the Muslims.

The people of the alleged caliphate are publicly calling for our destruction and the destruction of the Islamic emirate and everyone else apart from themselves, under the pretext of incoherent claims. Despite this, here we are extending our hand of cooperation to the people of piety and reason amongst them, based on judgements in accordance with the Sharia court, and that is out of caring for the victory of the Muslims against their united enemies.

O Muslims and *mujahidin*, the Pope's deputy has called for an international campaign against the extremists [*al-Mutatarifeen*]. It is, therefore, the crusaders' campaign which confronts us, while some of us excommunicate others and some of us destroy others and some of us kill others. Aren't these practices what the crusaders are wishing for? O people of reason and piety, we call for issuing judgements in accordance with the Sharia court under the supervision of independent notable people to judge either in favour of us or against us. So why do they escape from that? We also call for the unity of ranks of *mujahidin*, so why do they destroy that? We call for matters to be by consultation on the tradition of the righteous caliphs, so why do they escape from that? We call for being loyal to the pledges, so why do they escape from that? Have we not listened to God almighty's saying: *The only saying of the faithful believers, when they are called to God (His Words, the Quran) and His Messenger, to judge between them, is that they say: "We hear and we obey"?* {Sura 24 (The Light), 51} And also God almighty's saying: *O you who believe! Fulfil your obligations!* {Sura 5 (The Feast), 1} And His saying: *And do not dispute (with one another) lest you lose courage and your strength depart.* {Sura 8 (Spoils of War), 46}

I ask God almighty to grant us strength over the unbelievers, and humbleness for the believers, and to bring us back to harmony and unite our ranks and save us from disagreement, division and disunity. The Shia Safavids use the Houthis today as their arm in Yemen and they occupied Sanaa and other places, and they cried that they will arrive in the two holy lands after a few years. They declare that their first enemy is the *mujahidin* and they cooperate with the Americans to bombard them and follow them. The notables of Yemen, its proud tribes, freemen and brave *mujahidin* and on top of them the Qaeda Al-Jihad organisation in the Arabian Peninsula are the solid rock on which the efforts of the Houthis, the lackeys of the Shias and the conspiracies of the secularists, the partners of the Americans, are wrecked with God's blessing and will. It is no wonder, because they are the students of the *mujaddid* [renewer] Imam, Sheikh Osama bin Laden (may God have compassion on him), and they were raised in his school and their notables lived with him and they were his close loyalists and carried his banner to Mohammed's Peninsula.

Their commanders and notables have, one after another, sacrificed themselves for God's religion, like Khalid al-Hajj, Yusuf al-Uairi, Turki al-Dandani, Sheikh Abdullah Rashid, Abdulaziz al-Muqrin, Salih al-Oufi, Abu Ali al-Harithi, Anwar Awlaqi and Saed al-Shihri (may God have compassion on them). And hundreds more in the caravan of martyrs, may God accept them and settle them in His wide paradise. They brought themselves closer to their Lord: hundreds were injured and thousands taken captive, with some of them spending many years in prison and solitary confinement and some dying in prison, while the Shia captives were released straightaway because the Saud family and America's allies in Sanaa bow to Iran's pressure, defending its followers.

Our brothers in the Arabian Peninsula have offered all this and they are still offering more, so that the Arabian Peninsula, the land of revelation, is cleansed and the saying of the Prophet Mohammed (PBUH) is fulfilled: "Expel the unbelievers from the Arabian Peninsula." They confronted and are still confronting, with God's grace, the Saud family rulers, the crusaders and their secular allies and the Shia and their tails [the] Houthis in the Arabian Peninsula. May God grant them success in moving the operations to the heart of the crusader West. The last thing that God blessed them with is that they were honoured with avenging the Prophet (PBUH) against those who insulted him in the blessed battle of Paris.[28]

Despite all this honourable history, which I ask God to accept, someone comes and says to them, dissolve your group and break your pledge as I broke it and come under my authority. He [al-Baghdadi] further says that the Houthis did not find anyone who could confront them. He should have told them: may God reward you with good for your precedence, you went before us to jihad and migrated, and may God reward you for your good performance and let us cooperate on confronting the secular crusader–Safavid Alawite onslaught against Islam and the Muslims. Let us agree with all the *mujahidin* on an independent Sharia court consisting of notable scholars of jihad, whose true saying and deeds are testified for by everyone, so that all our efforts are directed towards our enemy and not wasted in creating disunity between us.

This is the careful way that should be taken for the victory of the Muslims against their united enemies. The rulers of the Arabian Peninsula, like the Saud family, the partners of America and Britain before and the slaves of their Lord, the US, and the sheikhs of oil markets on the Gulf coast whose fathers Sir Percy Cox[29] appointed to protect themselves with the wall of American bases. They work as service providers, whether clean or dirty, to their soldiers. These people will not protect the two holy places, because they and their grandfathers before them sold themselves and their country to the British and then to the Americans. These people will be the first to run if the Shia Safavids invade them, just as the Amir of Kuwait escaped before them when Saddam [Hussain] invaded his country. These people look to the US to protect them, but the US will only defend its interests. Iran makes an agreement with America based on mutual interests, and lets the Gulf rulers go wherever they want.

No one will defend the two holy places except for the honourable *mujahidin* from the Islamic world in general, and the Arabian Peninsula in particular. They are the descendents of the [Prophet's] companions (may God be pleased with them) and the descendents of the conquerors who spread Islam to the east and west, and those fifteen heroes, the martyrs came from their children, from God's Messenger's family and from the tribes of Ghamid, Zahran, Bani Shihr and Harb. They are [the ones] who pounded the Defence Ministry [Pentagon] and the twin towers in America [9/11 attacks], may God grant them great compassion.

Our honourable courageous brothers in the Qaeda Al-Jihad organisation in the Arabian Peninsula are leading the way, about whom the renewer Imam Osama bin Laden gave the good news when he said to our people in Palestine: we give you the glad tidings that the reinforcements of Islam are coming and Yemen's reinforcements will continue with God's blessing.

O Muslim *ummah*, the honourable beloved grandsons of the free companions, the active scholars, the proud respected tribes, the trustworthy traders and courageous leaders and the Muslims in the Arabian Peninsula and in all Muslim lands, do support your brother *mujahidin* in their battle to defend the Arabian Peninsula, the Peninsula of Mohammed (PBUH). Defend the two holy places against the Shia Safavid march towards them from the east in Kuwait, Qatif, Damam and Bahrain and from the south in Najran and Yemen and from the north in Iraq and Syria. The new Safavid organisations exist now in the city of the Prophet (PBUH). These are the Houthis who carry out their operations on the Saudi border. So do support your brother *mujahidin* by joining arms with them and supplying money, information, rhetorical support and prayers and all you are able to offer. Do support them before the traders of religion and the collectors of one fifth from the sources of misguidance get mastery over you and they violate your sanctities and your esteem, just as they violated the sanctities of your brothers and sisters in Iraq and Syria. Do support them before you openly hear the insults of the companions and the believers' mothers (may God be pleased with them) near the holy places.

Support them before the new Safavids do what the Safavid Ismael[30] did to your Sunni brothers in Iran. Support them before you regret it, when there will be no use in regretting. This will now suffice, and I will meet you in the next part, God willing!

Our last prayers are praise be to God, the Lord of the two universes, peace and prayers be upon our master Mohammed, on his family and companions. Peace and God's compassion and blessings be upon you.

LET US UNITE TO LIBERATE AL-QUDS [JERUSALEM]

NOVEMBER 2015

By Ayman al-Zawahiri

In times of crisis and turmoil, Zawahiri revisits a traditional rallying call to make the case for Al-Qaeda's continued relevance: the "liberation" of Jerusalem. This process, he argues, will have two components. The first would be to target the West, especially the United States and their interests across the world, as it is this support that is key to Israel's survival. The second component is the establishment of an Islamic state, centred in Egypt and the Levant, to create powerful staging posts to conquer Palestine. The purpose, of course, is to remind audiences that the major jihadi objectives remain unfulfilled and have become side-tracked due to the infighting in Syria.

The video starts with the recital of a verse from the Quran, which is recited by the martyr of the bombardment of the crusaders and Pakistani betrayal in Waziristan, the martyred leader—as we believe him to be—the reciter, Sofian al-Maghrebi Abu Essam al-Andalusi (Abdulkarim Hussein), may God have compassion on him:

They ask you (O Mohammed!) about the spoils of war. Say: "The spoils are for God and the Messenger." So fear God and adjust all matters of difference among you, and obey God and His Messenger, if you are believers. The believers are only those who, when God is mentioned, feel fear in their hearts and when His verses (this Quran) are recited unto them, they (i.e. the verses) increase their faith; and they put their trust in their Lord (alone); who perform prayers and spend out of that we have provided them. It is they who are the believers in truth. For them are grades of dignity with their Lord, and forgiveness and a generous provision (Paradise). {Sura 8 (Spoils of War), 1–4}

[A clip featuring Osama bin Laden plays]

The wound of Quds still burns inside me
The burning of the wounded man is like the flame that ignites inside
I haven't betrayed the pledge of God as the states betrayed
I engaged in battlefields of jihad when most of the people deserted
When the hands of sacrifice are chained and all the paths cut off
I marched as a mujahid *with whom one would be honoured*
Sons of Afghans, do not bow defencelessly if [the battle] breaks out
On the bonfire of sorrow, they became inflamed and on its hell they were matured
They embraced grief and from them it never separated
These are their homes washed with bursting pendulum
Under the thunder of air raids, they are burning on fire
These are the skulls of children crushed and it celebrates
Their pride has not been subdued and defeat was not welcome with them
The head of the nation rises high and the tide of sacrifice continues

[Ayman al-Zawahiri's address begins]

In the name of God, praise be to God. Peace and prayers be upon God's Messenger, his family, companions and whoever supported him.

O Muslim brothers, wherever you are! Peace and God's compassion and blessings be upon you.

Muslims everywhere have suffered and been bereaved by repeated Jewish aggression on the blessed al-Aqsa mosque, and by their successive crimes against our people in Palestine in general, and in al-Quds [Jerusalem] in particular. What is happening today in Quds is a new epic jihad. Blessed be the jihadi martyrdom hands, who defend Palestine and al-Aqsa with knives, cars and stones and with whatever they have. I ask God to bless these martyred people, who dare to stab the Jews when they are almost certain that they will be killed at the hands of the Jews. O God, accept their martyrdom and raise their position among the highest and make their sacrifices an exemple, incentive and motivation for every Muslim earnestly concerned with his religion, nation and sanctities.

LET US UNITE TO LIBERATE AL-QUDS [JERUSALEM]

My Muslim brothers, those who are eager to liberate al-Quds! The liberation of Quds and al-Aqsa mosque must have two components, though God knows best. The first component is to strike the West, especially America, in the heart of their land and attack their widespread interests everywhere. The supporters of Israel must pay the price in blood and treasure for their support of Israel's crimes against Islam and the Muslims. We must continue what the *mujahidin* did in the blessed battles of 9/11 and the battles of Madrid, Bali, London and Paris. We must follow the thorny path of Ramzi Yusuf, Mohammed Atta, Emrouzi [bin Nurhasyim], Shahzad Tanweer, Nidhal Hassan, Omar al-Faruq, Mohammed Marah, and the two brothers [Dzhokhar and Tamerlan] Tsarnaev.

The second matter is the establishment of an Islamic state in Egypt and Sham [the Levant/Syria], to gather the *ummah* [nation or community] to liberate Palestine; and in order to do that, there must be unity, removal of disagreements and an end to the infighting between *mujahidin*.

My Muslim brothers and *mujahidin* in all groups and everywhere, from Kashgar to Tangiers and from Grozny to Mogadishu! O people of jihad, O people of piety, O people of morality and principles among all the jihadi groups! We are facing today an American, European, Russian, Rafida [Shia] and Nusayriya [Alawite] aggression, which reminds us of the alliance between the Shia and the Tatars against the Abbasid caliphate and their alliance with the French against the Ottoman Empire. We have to stand united, from eastern Turkistan to the Islamic Maghreb, in the face of the satanic alliance against Islam, its nation and land.

The Americans, Russians, Iranians, Nusayriya and Hezbollah have coordinated their war against us. Have we failed to stop the infighting between us so that we direct all our efforts against them? Imam Bukhari, may God have compassion on him, narrated from Abu Musa who said:

> I heard al-Hassan saying: "Hassan bin Ali, by God, confronted Muawiyah with brigades like mountains." Amr ibn Al-As said: "I see brigades that cannot be destroyed before their matched opponents are killed." Muawiyah told him—and he was the best of the two men, i.e. Amr—"If these people killed those people, and those killed these, who will look after people's affairs, their women and loss?" He sent him two men from the Quraish [tribe] and said: "He didn't ask them a thing until they said: 'we assure you [of] that'. He then reconciled with him." Al-Hassan said: "I heard Abu Bakra saying: 'I saw the Prophet (PBUH) on the podium and Hassan bin Ali next to him and he was turning to the people once and to him another time and saying his son is a master [saint], may God make him a reconciler between two great sects of the Muslims.'"

My brother *mujahidin* in all the Muslim lands! The Syrian front is a crucial front in the liberation of Palestine, and the unity of the *mujahidin* in it under the banner of monotheism is the gate of victory, with God's permission. For that reason, the *ummah* generally and the *mujahidin* particularly have to generate public opinion and appeal for unity so that the *mujahidin* do not exhaust their energies in the fight against each other, whilst the Western crusaders are united against them and the Russians unite with the Safavids, Nusayriya and secularists. It is not only out of piety and logic [that we must] stop the war between the *mujahidin*, but so that all their efforts are directed against the satanic alliance, the attackers of the Muslim nation and invaders of Syria and Iraq.

Imam Ibn Kathir, may God have compassion on him, mentioned about our master Muawiyah, may God be pleased with him:

> When it was his rule, i.e. Muawiyah's rule and the rule of the leader of believers, Ali; in those days conquests didn't happen at all, neither at the hands of Muawiyah nor at the hands of Ali. The king of Rome wished for Muawiyah [his kingdom] after he feared him, humiliated him, defeated his soldiers and destroyed them. When the king of Rome saw Muawiyah was engaged in a fight with Ali, he sent great number of troops to some lands and wished for their conquest. Muawiyah wrote to him: "By God, if you don't stop and return to your country, curses be upon you; I and my cousin will gather forces and push you out of all your countries and will make the earth a small place under your feet." At that point, the king of Rome got scared and stopped, and asked for a truce.

All the *mujahidin* in all the groups and fronts, look! The king of Rome approached the Muslim lands with his army; but our master Muawiyah, may God be pleased with him, responded to him with this strong threat. However, we have been under the enemy's occupation for tens of years and the jihadi groups were formed under this occupation, but despite all this, infighting occurs between the Muslims. So, shouldn't the companions—may God be pleased with them—be our role models?

My Muslim brothers and the *mujahidin* in every country and every group and sect! Our war in Syria and Egypt—the two gates of Jerusalem throughout history—is a wide and comprehensive war. It is a war of armed jihad to stop the oppression of the apostate regimes and the crusader—Shia alliance which supports it. It is a war which the *ummah* must support with men, money, ammunition, expertise and prayers. It is a war by means of the jihad of prayers, to reveal that the accepted jihad which is legitimised by Islam is to raise the word of God, and not to empower secular and patriotic regimes. God almighty said: *And fight them until there is no more* fitna *(disbelief and polythe-*

ism: i.e. worshipping others besides God) and the religion (worship) will all be for God alone. {Sura 8 (Spoils of War), 39} The Prophet (PBUH) says: "Whoever fought to make the word of God the highest is in the cause of God."

It is a war by means of political jihad to persuade the *ummah* that our behaviour is in agreement with what we call for, and does not contradict it, nor turn the Muslim nation away from the *mujahidin*. We have to take our behaviour to a higher level to persuade our Muslim nation that we are really concerned with being arbitrated by the Sharia if we are summoned to it. We keep our promises and we don't attack the sanctities of the Muslims and do not over-emphasise *takfir* [labelling someone as unbeliever]. We are the most compassionate with our people, we do not try to be sovereign over the Muslims. But we want the *ummah* to choose its own Imam by consultation and consent, to return the caliphate on the method of Prophethood and the tradition of the rightly guided caliphs, may God be pleased with them. It is also a war by means of political jihad to reveal to our nation that there are groups which belong to Islamic activism—like the Muslim Brotherhood, the Salafists belonging to [Abdel Fattah el] Sisi and [Rached] Ghannouchi—who led them to lose this life and the hereafter. They allied with the enemies of Islam and the *ummah*, with the secular military and corrupt politicians. They beautified their distorted pictures and provided them with immunity and enabled criminals like Sisi, Mohammed Ibrahim[31] and Badji Kaid al-Sebssi[32] to hold the necks of Muslims.

They committed themselves to submissive agreements to Israel; they know that the price of holding power is to accept the secular constitutions and to submit to Israel. In order to keep Palestine away from these perverse methods, the people of piety, jihad and monotheism there have to mobilise our people in Palestine around the word of God's oneness [*tawheed*] and to call them to do their jihad to raise the word of God. They have to call them to reject the sellers of Palestine and call them to commit themselves to the sovereignty of the Sharia over any law, constitution, desire or majorities. They have to incite them to reject those perverse methods, which led to the loss of this life and the hereafter. Egypt, Tunisia and before them Algeria are the best examples.

O you the *mujahidin* in Palestine! Do you accept that the result of your jihad becomes a secular government that removes the Sharia, deviates from Islam and enforces on Muslims the rules and laws of the unbelievers [*kuffar*]? And how will the battle come together to liberate Palestine by legitimising the secularists, the sellers of Palestine? Do you want to sacrifice your lives for the sake of selling Palestine? Even the patriots and nationalists would not accept this who fight for the land, so how would a Muslim *mujahid* accept it? Today, there are some of your leaders who would lead you down the same dark tunnel in which their brothers in Egypt and Tunisia got lost. They misguide you that you will never have Palestine unless you have given up the doctrine of God's oneness and the sovereignty of Sharia. You have accepted unbelief [*kufr*], secularism and international legitimacy and you have established the nation state in which the *mujahid* is equal to the seller of Palestine, and the monotheist—who engages in jihad to make Sharia the sovereign—is equal to the secularist who rejects it. You will not achieve your independence unless you have acknowledged the legitimacy of the sellers of Palestine and helped them to achieve presidency, ministry and power. This dark tunnel will not lead to the return of Palestine, but it will lead to the giving up of the doctrine of monotheism and the loss of Palestine, i.e. the loss of this life and the hereafter.

My Muslim brothers and *mujahidin* everywhere, Quds is a responsibility on our shoulders, and to liberate it we have to make the supporters of Israel pay the price in blood and treasure for Israel's aggression against our *ummah*. We have to work to establish a Muslim government in the countries neighbouring Israel. It is a war of multiple fronts and inflaming disagreements between the *mujahidin* which will exhaust their power and delay their victory. We have to be united in the face of our enemies from Kashgar to Tangiers and from the tops of the Caucasus to Central Africa.

Our last prayers are praise be to God, the Lord of the two universes, peace and prayers be upon our master Mohammed, on his family and companions.

Peace and God's compassion and blessings be upon you.

[Clip featuring Osama bin Laden is shown]

"We are today, thanks to God almighty, redrawing the map of the Islamic world to become one state under the banner of the caliphate, with the permission of God almighty. We are today, thanks to God almighty, writing a bright history for the believers in this era in which oppression has increased and injustice, corruption and disbelief are widespread from east to west. The happy one is he whom God will make steadfast next to the banner of piety."

[Text graphic reads:]
"From Kashgar to Tangiers, we are coming, O Aqsa"

SHAM [SYRIA] IS ENTRUSTED
UPON YOUR SHOULDERS

DECEMBER 2015

By Ayman al-Zawahiri

Here Zawahiri touches upon another dynamic in the geopolitics of the region: the position of Saudi Arabia, at this stage engaged in fighting with Shia Muslim Houthi rebels in Yemen. The statement also comes in the wake of multiple Saudi-led efforts to consolidate opposition forces against the Assad regime in Damascus, including the December 2015 Riyadh Conference. Zawahiri uses the opportunity to remind his audience of Saudi treachery, listing the regime's crimes: from collusion with British colonial representatives to their harassment of the late bin Laden. He also weaves in his continued denunciation of IS, by now making very explicit comparisons between the group and the early transgressing Kharijites.

Al-Sahab Media Rabi' Al-Awal 1437 [corresponding to December 2015]
In the name of God, the most Gracious, the most Merciful
In the name of God and praise be to God, and prayers and peace be upon the Messenger of God, his family, his companions and those who support him.
O Brother Muslims everywhere, peace be upon you and the mercy of God and his blessings.

I am addressing you to today in relation to the Riyadh Conference[33] which was held recently; I will begin by offering my thanks to my brothers the

Muslim *mujahidin* everywhere, who are striving for the release of Muslim prisoners, both men and women. I would like on this occasion to mention in particular my noble brothers the "Lions of Islam" in the stronghold of Sham [Syria], and those in charge of Bayt Al-Maqdis [Jerusalem] in the noble and beloved Jabhat Al-Nusra, who endeavoured to free the men and women prisoners held by the Lebanese government. May God grant them great rewards, both in this world and in the hereafter. For they have reassured the believers and brought joy and happiness to their hearts. I implore God to take their good deeds into account on the Day of Judgement.

My noble brothers, this blessed deal was a victory from God; you have freed the prisoners, both men and women, and provided the emigrants [*muhajiroun*] with supplies, treatment and medication. You have established yourselves as the defenders of your *ummah* [nation or community]; you are eager to free this *ummah* from oppression and hardship and protect its sanctities. May God reward you the best of rewards. My dear brothers in the noble and dignified Jabhat Al-Nusra, you have set an eminent example for the *mujahidin* in every part of the world. So continue on this blessed path, striving to increase pious deeds and avoid sins; endeavour to achieve unity within the jihadist ranks and make them focus on the oneness of God [*tawheed*]. For unity is the gateway to victory, so open your hearts to all those who want to do good amongst the ranks of the extremists and the *takfiris*.

Dear Muslim *mujahidin* brothers, everyone followed the recent Riyadh Conference and the subsequent declaration by Saudi Arabia to establish an alliance to combat what they call terrorism in order to serve American interests. These are merely two links in a chain of attempts by Saudi Arabia and her wicked followers to divert the progress of jihad in general, and jihad in Sham in particular from the correct path. Saudi Arabia is also keen to throw jihad into the deceitful concept of the nation state and transform it into a dying flame in the same way they did with the uprisings of the so-called "Arab Spring".

For that reason, I implore my brother the *mujahidin* in the stronghold of Sham to be wary of this malicious government, and not forget its notoriously dark history in the service of the enemies of Islam. For Abdul Aziz al-Saud was in fact the one who signed the "Uqair Protocol" with Great Britain in 1915[34] and entered into the First World War against the Ottoman state. They agreed in the treaty that Britain would take on the defence of al-Saud in exchange for his commitment not to enter into any contract or treaty with any foreign government other than Great Britain. The first target of this treaty was the Ottoman state.

When the great revolution broke out in Palestine in 1936, Abdul Aziz al-Saud sent his two sons to calm down the revolutionaries. He issued, along with King Ghazi and Prince Abdullah, the famous declaration which says:

> The prevailing situation in Palestine has caused us great pain. We, in agreement with our brothers the Arab kings and with Amir Abdullah, ask you to resort to calm in order to avoid bloodshed; we rely upon the good intentions of our friend the British government and its desire to ensure justice. You may rest assured that we will continue our endeavours to provide you with the necessary help.

In 1945, towards the end of the Second World War, Abdul Aziz al-Saud met with [President] Roosevelt in order to transfer his allegiance from Great Britain to America. He consequently awarded America the wealth of the Arabian Peninsula, as well as the right to the exploitation of its land and air resources in exchange for America guaranteeing the house of al-Saud's reign over the kingdom [of the Arabian Peninsula] through Abdul Aziz's sons. Successive betrayals followed. When the Afghan jihad against the Russians was on the verge of victory, Saudi Arabia intervened alongside Pakistan to form a *mujahidin* government under the leadership of [Sibghatullah] Mojaddedi, an agent of America in Kabul. Then the Saudi government plotted the murder of Sheikh Osama bin Laden in Pakistan, after which Sheikh bin Laden emigrated to Sudan. As a result, the Saudi government put pressure on Sudan to throw out Sheikh Osama and his brothers from Sudan. As Sheikh Osama moved to be a guest of Sheikh Yunus Khalis in Jalalabad, Saudi Arabia demanded that the latter expel Sheikh Osama. This was followed by several demands to the Islamic Emirate either to expel Sheikh Osama and his brothers, or hand them over to America.

Ultimately, Turki al-Faisal[35] went personally to Kandahar and demanded that Mullah Mohammed Omar extradite Osama bin Laden, may God have mercy upon him, and his brothers. Mullah Omar kicked him [al-Faisal] out and insulted him using hurtful words. When the civil war broke out in Sudan, Saudi Arabia provided John Garang[36] with weapons, and supplied the Communists in South Yemen with arms. [King] Fahd, and after him [King] Abdallah, issued two malicious initiatives which both relate to conceding the right of Israel to the appropriation of what they had captured before 1967. It was from Saudi Arabia that the Crusader planes were launched which later destroyed and flattened Iraq and Afghanistan, and are today demolishing Sham and Iraq. When the popular Arab revolutions broke out, Saudi Arabia sheltered [former Tunisian president] Zayn al-Abdin bin Ali. They ordered that Abd Rabuh Mansour Hadi, deputy of the ousted president, take the place of the latter. They also supported [Egyptian president] Sisi in his coup against the [Muslim] Brotherhood.

Saudi Arabia persists to date in her evil role against jihad and the *mujahidin*. She has been striving to stir up *fitna* [sedition/strife] between the *mujahidin* in Sham, repeating the same in Afghanistan, hoping to tear apart the jihadi ranks and allow those like Mojaddedi, Abd Rabbuh Mansour Hadi, Sisi and Badji Kaid al-Sebssi to be in control of Sham in order to serve American interests and protect Israel's security. Fellow *mujahidin* brothers in Sham, experiences will tell and history will reveal to you that Saudi Arabia is mainly seeking to destroy Sham and protect Israel's security, as well as to abort any attempt to establish Islamic rule in Sham. So be wary of her [Saudi Arabia] and her conspiracies and conferences. No one would offer Saudi Arabia and America more than what [former president Mohammed] Morsi had offered. Nevertheless, he was overthrown by both of them. Take a lesson from it. Saudi Arabia will not provide you with freedom, dignity or power "because whoever does not possess something is unable to give it away".

Saudi Arabia and her followers are mere instruments of the crusader West to establish a secular nation state that complies with the international legitimacy in our current Islamic Arab world. For this reason, every *mujahid* must today be careful of the expressions: civil state, pluralist state and similar jargon which is used by the secularists to mean specific concepts that lead to the rejection of the faith, and the drift behind human fancies and worldly desires and pleasures.

Fellow *mujahidin* brothers in Sham and everywhere, the Noble Quran has determined the aim of jihad through the words of the almighty: *Fight them until there is no more fitna (sedition) and the religion is all for God* {Sura 8 (Spoils of War), 39}; and the Prophet—God's prayers and peace be upon him—specified it through his saying: "He who fights so that the word of God is supreme fights in the cause of God." Our jihad and endeavours should aim to establish a Muslim state, where the supreme legitimacy is for the ruling of the Sharia; a state which does not recognise national borders or state divisions, but strongly believes in the unity and fraternity of all believers. The emigrants [*muhajiroun*] in Sham and on every jihadi front cannot therefore be described as foreigners, but rather as brothers in faith and belief; those who had sacrificed their blood to make the religion of God victorious. Thus, their expulsion from Sham or from any other Islamic land is a clear and blatant infringement of the rules and regulations of Islam. How can this happen, when the Prophet—God's prayers and peace be upon him—described Sham as "the centre of the Abode of the Believers".

Fellow *mujahidin* brothers in Sham and everywhere, beware, then beware, and beware not to sacrifice yourself, your wealth and your migration [*hijra*], leaving your nation and family behind and spending years in prison to let a gang of secularists harvest the fruits of your great sacrifices. Beware of politicians haggling, which will result in the rejection of Sharia and religion. The drama which struck us for more than a century repeats itself. It seems that we have not learnt any lessons from those tragedies and from the outcome of the so-called "Arab Spring".

Lions of Islam in the stronghold of Sham, from every platoon and in every land of Islam: Sham is entrusted [as a responsibility] around your necks. Save it from the Nusayiris [Alawites], the secularists and the Safavids [Shia/ Iranians]; defend it against the attacks of the crusaders; don't leave it to the *takfiri* [excommunicating] fanatics, who have pronounced the leadership of Al-Qaeda as disbelievers, and falsely claimed that the Houthis have not been confronted by the *muwahiddin* [Monotheists], and who had the audacity to insult the soldiers of the [Afghan] Islamic Emirate labelling them as agents of the ISI[37] and pronounced most of the *mujahidin* in Sham as disbelievers. They are the ones who rejected the ruling of Sharia, at a time when the majority of the *mujahidin* in Sham agreed to it. Despite this rejection, they began to question the faith of the *mujahidin* who sacrificed their lives defending the reign of the Sharia. How can these people be trusted to implement the ruling of the Sharia? They then declared an alleged unknown caliphate based on a mysterious allegiance sworn in an unknown place by unknown people to a man unworthy to be caliph; yet this man found himself entrusted with the Islamic Emirate affairs. Furthermore, the news of the alleged caliphate was spread by untrustworthy, pitiful sources notorious for their lies and defamation. Just picture the mounting piles of corruption! They also claim that, by contradicting Sheikh Osama bin Laden, may God have mercy on him, they are following the steps of their ancestors [the Salaf]. Sheikh Osama declared that his oath of allegiance to the commander of the faithful Mullah Mohammed Omar was a supreme oath; he called upon the Muslims to follow suit and pledge allegiance to Mullah Omar. In so doing [reneging on their pledge], they [the IS leadership] are also opposing Sheikh Abu Hamza al-Muhajir, may God has mercy on him, who considers that he who breaks his oath of allegiance to Mullah Mohammed Omar has committed a great sin, significantly worse than fornication and drinking. He deemed his oath of allegiance to Mullah Omar a pledge of allegiance to the caliphate, as I shall, God willing, corroborate with documentary evidence. In his published notes he addressed Mullah Mohammed Omar as: "To Wali Amrna [Our Ruler/ leader] Mullah Mohammed Omar".

Then their [IS's] *takfiri* mania and extreme deviation reached a point where they dared defame the virtuous wives of the *mujahidin* of Jabhat Al-Nusra and others, and labelled them as whores. Before that, they insulted Al-Qaeda, comparing it to a prostitute who claims chastity. This is their level of degradation and the swamp of filth they are drowned in. Is this a caliphate that follows the method of the Prophet? As I mentioned before, the murder of Abu Khaled al-Suri,[38] may God have mercy on him, reminds me of the murder of the two Sheikhs, Mohammed al-Saeed and Abd al-Razzaq al-Rajam, and their fellow brothers in Algeria. The killings of these two sheikhs and their fellow brothers represented a moral defeat which was followed by a material defeat of the GIA group in Algeria.

In the same way, I believe that the killing of Abu Khaled al-Suri—may God have mercy on him—represents a moral defeat for his murderers, which should be followed by a material defeat. May God have mercy upon you, Abu Khaled.

> *Rest in peace for the armies, after your death,*
> *Offered their arms and necks [support and sacrifice] to God*
> *They vowed not to see, all over Sham, but the shining light of Sharia*
> *And agreed between them to sweep clean their countries with their blood*
> *O Sham be wary of Rawafid [Shia]*
> *They have been allies of the invaders for times and centuries*
> *Ba'athists are those who made our blood run like rivers and seas*
> *Those who protect the borders of Israel*
> *To please their guardian fathers*
> *And those who seek positions, and in so doing*
> *Openly and obscenely violate sanctities*
> *Their ancestors killed the third Caliph*
> *As he peacefully and patiently recites the Book*
> *They stabbed Imam Abu al-Hassan in the midst of his prayers*
> *A stabbing which stopped the sun and the moon from shining*
> *They will be bitterly disappointed in Sham*
> *God shall be for them the Best guide and the Best supporter*
> *God willing.*

The killing of Abu Khaled al-Suri—may God have mercy on him—revealed the evil side of the modern *takfiri* fanatics, which in turn highlighted the difference between them and the early Kharijites:[39] the early Kharijites used to make their actions public and boast of their activities. When Abd al-Rahman ibn Muljam struck Ali ibn Abi Talib—may God be pleased with him—with his sword, he shouted, "There is no rule except the rule of God, not yours, Ali, and not that of your companions." In contradiction, the modern Kharijites commit murders and assassinations but don't find the courage, unlike the early Kharijites, to declare their acts and reveal their true identity because they are cowards. The killers of Abu Khaled al-Suri—may God have mercy on him— are cowards; they incite others amongst the misguided ones to carry out the killing, while they keep their acts quiet. In addition to this disparity, exposed by the killing of Abu Khaled al-Suri, there are other differences between the two types of Kharijites: the early Kharijites considered lying as a form of disbelief, while the modern *takfiri* fanatics are used to lying. Their leaders are not embarrassed to lie, even amongst themselves. They would affirm something and openly and shamelessly deny it afterwards. The first Kharijites would consider breaking a promise as disbelief, whilst the modern *takfiri* fanatics consider leaping from one oath of allegiance to another as a political skill, in their eager pursuit of power. The first Kharijites are disbelievers because they commit sins, whereas the modern fanatics are disbelievers on account of their lies, deceit and pledge of allegiance to unworthy people. [For] the early Kharijites *takfirism* was doctrinal, whereas [for] the new fanatics *takfirism* is political, self-interested and utilitarian. Anyone who is in agreement or allied with the modern Kharijites derives benefit and praise but [is] requested to commend them in exchange so that they can gain status; those who disagree with them will suffer abuse, lies and defamation and be pronounced disbelievers by them. This coincides [with] their *takfiri* method, which focuses on bombings, expulsions and tyranny.

In this respect, the *Dabiq* magazine reminds me of Abu Abd al-Rahman Amin's message, "Guidance of the Lord of the Two Worlds", which indicates the collapse [of the *takfiris*]. In the same way, the bombing of Ariha mosque, after the liberation of Ariha and the killing of those fasting inside the mosque,[40] reminds me of the killing, by al-Khalifi and his followers, of people performing prayers in the Ansar Al-Sunna mosque in Omdurman, and their subsequent attack on the accommodation of Sheikh Osama bin Laden—may God has mercy upon him—in Khartoum.[41] When al-Khalifi was asked about the reason for his attack on the Ansar Al-Sunna mosque, he said it was because the mosque was a polytheists' temple. When asked why he had attacked the accommodation of Sheikh Osama, may God have mercy upon him, he replied that Sheikh Osama was the one who misguided people the most, and he deemed it right to attack him first. In Peshawar the fanatics pronounced me as a disbeliever because I would not pronounce the Afghan *mujahidin* as disbelievers. They then did the same to Sheikh Abu Mohammed al-Maqdisi—may God preserve him—because he would not denounce me as a disbeliever. These people claim that they follow the ideology of the Ahl al-Sunna wal-Jamaa and that they do not commit the sin of pronouncing *takfir*; unlike al-Baghdadi's group, who claim to conform to the ideology of the Ahl al-Sunna wal-Jamaa, yet use lies and false accusations and anything that does not lead to *takfir*, including the adherence to the Book and the Sunna, to pronounce *takfir*. For example, they pronounced *takfir* on Abu Saad al-Hadrami, may God have mercy on him, because he took oaths of allegiance from the Free Syrian Army engaged in jihad.

They also pronounced *takfir* on me and alleged that I follow the majority and did not pronounce *takfir* on account of tyranny. This is because I supported the revolutions of the oppressed and sympathised with the prisoner Mohammed Morsi as per the teaching of the Book and the Sunna and *dawa*. It became clear that the main reason behind this defamation was because I got in the way of their aspirations and endeavoured to spare the blood of Muslims.

I mixed with *takfiris* of all types and kinds in Egypt; I even sent a handwritten letter in the 1970s to challenge them as they were exploiting the enthusiasm of the young people for corrupt purposes, including the deviation from true Islam, while many believers joined them, seeking the truth. It was revealed that most of those who joined them then left them after a while, which was good news. More importantly, the majority of those who left became the people who conformed the most to the methodology [*manhaj*] of the Ahl al-Sunna [Sunnis], and defend the best the sanctity of the Muslims taking lessons from their previous experience.

This prompts us to persevere in our call to clarify the facts and expose their [IS's] deceitful media. The media will never be able to change facts, no matter how many lies and deceit it uses. The truth will always remain the truth, and lies will always be unmasked; loyalty will remain loyalty and betrayal will be uncovered.

Fellow *mujahidin* brothers in the stronghold of Sham, the current satanic alliance that includes the apostate Safavids, Nusayiris and secularist Rawafid [Shia], as well as crusaders in the East and West, are lying in wait for you, seeking to split the ranks of the *mujahidin* and stir turmoil between them. So be steadfast and hold on to your faith, rely on your Lord—and have trust in Him, He the exalted, all glory to Him—and after Him have confidence in yourselves and your *ummah*. Beware of the agents of the West, including the Gulf oil merchants who tempt you with "crumbs" so that you give up your faith and disown your brothers. God has made you steadfast, granted you success and protected you from their deceit. Seek help from God and be patient; for you are the hope of the *ummah*, so do not let her down. Suffice the misfortunes she is enduring at the hands of the *takfiri* fanatics who sacrifice the sanctities, unity and blood of Muslims to attain power. The agents of the West will try to hold you prisoners to the concept of the nation state, which was imposed upon us after the fall of the [Ottoman] caliphate. Don't ever succumb to their attempts, for you are the vanguards of the Muslim *ummah*, and her battalion [which is] heading, God permitting, towards Al-Aqsa. Your strength—in addition to the strength of God, may He be praised and exalted—is in your Muslim *ummah*. So fight [the enemies] to liberate Sham, then fight them to conquer Jerusalem, God permitting.

Fellow Muslim *mujahidin* brothers in Sham, Sham is entrusted [as a responsibility] around your necks. So do not surrender it to the secularists, nor should you give it up to the Rafida [Shia] including the Safavids, Nusayiris [or to the] *takfiri* fanatics. Persevere and do not stop jihad until an Islamic state is established, the ruling of the Sharia implemented and the banner of jihad raised high. You shall lead the march of the *ummah* towards Al-Aqsa, God permitting.

Finally, our last prayers are all praise is due to God, the Lord of the two worlds, and God's prayers and blessing be upon Mohammed, his family and his companions.

And peace be upon you, and the mercy of God and His blessing.

MARCH FORTH TO SHAM [SYRIA]!

MAY 2016

By Ayman al-Zawahiri

Zawahiri has noted on a number of occasions that he did not want Al-Qaeda's presence, via allies, on the ground in Syria to become known, as this would distract from the goal of toppling the Assad regime and serve as a propaganda victory for local Shia forces seeking to present the conflict in a more international light. This was part of his publicly articulated frustration with al-Baghdadi's declaration of the Islamic State of Iraq and Syria, initially as a merger with Jabhat al-Nusra, which Zawahiri rejected. In this statement, Zawahiri insists that he does not desire material or political power, in Syria and elsewhere. This goes back to his previous conceptualisations of Al-Qaeda as a "mode", message and mission, which he presented as bin Laden's legacy and ultimately his own legacy too. If the people of Syria and its mujahidin fighters came to an agreement regarding their Islamic leadership that would end the infighting, Zawahiri insisted, he would be happy to offer the consensus his backing. At the same time, of course, he continues to present IS and al-Baghdadi as illegitimate, praising instead the Nusra Front. The latter declared its independence from Al-Qaeda, with Zawahiri's acquiescence, in July 2016, potentially giving it more freedom to manoeuvre within Syria and garner local support.

Ayman al-Zawahiri: March forth to Syria [Sham]!

[The video begins with a recitation from the Quran]

O you who believe! What is the matter with you, that when you are asked to march forth in the cause of God (i.e. jihad) you cling heavily to the earth? Are you pleased with the life of this world rather than the hereafter? But little is the enjoyment of the life of this world as compared with the hereafter. If you march not forth, He will punish you with a painful torment and will replace you by another people, and you cannot harm Him at all, and God is Able to do all things. {Sura 9, (Repentance) 38–9}

[Recording of al-Zawahiri begins]

In the name of God, praise be to God, peace and prayers be upon God's Messenger and his family, companions and those who supported him.

O Muslim brothers everywhere, peace and God's compassion and blessings be upon you!

Today Syria is the hope of the Muslim nation, because it is the only popular revolution among the Arab Spring revolutions that follows the right path: the path of invocation and jihad to establish the Sharia and implement it, and to endeavour to establish the righteous caliphate, not the caliphate of Ibrahim al-Badri;[42] the caliphate of the method [*manhaj*], not the caliphate of Al-Hajjaj.[43] For that reason, the big criminals have gathered in the world to prevent the establishment of a jihadi state in the jihadi stronghold of Syria. The conspiracies, plots, pressures and allurements have started, but God almighty willed that a jihadi group remain among the best of the supporters [*ansar*] and migrants [*muhajiroun*], steadfast in the truth without moving away from it. The Muslim nation has gathered around it in Syria and realised the difference between their true method and the falsity of the method of the new extremist Khawarij *takfiris* [excommunicators], who the [Muslim] nation now know will be the successors of al-Hajjaj bin Yusuf and will carry the weight of their heads on their behalf [meaning to behead them].

My Muslim and jihadi brothers in the stronghold of jihadi Syria and everywhere! Our duty today is to defend the jihad in Syria against the conspiracies that are plotted against it, which are led by the stepdaughter of Britain and the servant of America, the state of the Saud family and its tails in the region. All these conspiracies are aimed at erecting a system that is presented as Islam in Syria, but it offers a false Islam that is in agreement with secularism and the nation state and tradition and with the system of big international criminals. It sheds the blood of hundreds of thousands of those who went out to demonstrate and shout naturally: [in support of] our everlasting commander, our master Mohammed.

The biggest problem for the international system and its criminals and for our rulers and their apostate regimes is that the *mujahidin* of Syria stand on the border of Palestine, threatening what they call Israel—the fifty-first state of the US or the biggest American base outside America. So, the criminals have to cooperate together to hit this jihad and bury it alive and divert its path towards secularism, patriotism and nationalism and to subject it to the international system, to the big criminals. They move from one conspiracy to another and from one plot to another: Geneva, Riyadh,[44] truce and the resolutions of the big criminals' [UN] Security Council, and an endless series of deception, lies, slander and deceit. Our duty today is to defend the jihad in Syria with all we can, and we march forth to its victory, whether you are healthy, young and wealthy or ill, old and poor. Our duty today is to urge the unity of the *mujahidin* in Syria until it is liberated from the secular Nusayiri [Alawite] regime and its Iranian Shia aides and the Russian and Western crusader allies, and until a righteous Islamic jihadi entity is established.

My *mujahidin* brothers in the jihadi stronghold [*ribaat*] [of] Syria and everywhere in the world! The matter of unity today is a matter of life and death for you. You either become unified to live as honourable and dignified Muslims, or you disagree and differ, then to be devoured one by one. There remains a matter in which many have engaged many times to try to avert the glance of the Muslim jihadi people in Syria from their real enemies, which is the matter of the association of the proud, strong and generous Nusra Front with which we [in the] Qaeda Al-Jihad organisation are proud to be associated. We ask God to increase their steadfastness and successes.

I will say some brief, clear and obvious words. We have said on many occasions and repeatedly that if the people of Syria and especially the courageous and blessed *mujahidin* have established their Islamic government and chosen their Imam, then whatever they choose is our choice too. We are not, with God's blessings, power seekers, but we seek the implementation of the Sharia and we don't want to rule the Muslims. Rather, we want to be ruled as Muslims by Islam. We were and still are calling for the unity of the *mujahidin* in Syria and for congregating to establish the righteous Islamic jihadi government that spreads justice, extends consultation, brings back rights, supports the oppressed, revives the jihad, liberates the country and tries to liberate Al-Aqsa [in Jerusalem] and returns the caliphate on the method of the Prophethood. The organisational ties should not, with God's permission, ever be an obstacle preventing the achievement of these great goals, which the nation hopes for as we are part of them; and we are not their guardians, nor have we jumped over them with the pledge of allegiance of a group of ignorant people or with the caliph of surprises.

After all, will the big criminals approve of Al-Nusra Front if it is dissociated from Al-Qaeda? Or will they force them to sit at the table with the criminals and murderers? They will then force them to submit to the agreements of disgrace and humiliation, and to the dependent and corrupt governments, and then to enter the rotten game of democracy and after that they will throw them in prison as they did with the Islamic Salvation Front in Algeria and the Muslim Brotherhood in Egypt. God almighty said truthfully: *Never will the Jews nor the Christians be pleased with you (O Mohammed!) until you follow their religion. Say: "Verily, the guidance of God that is the (only) Guidance. And if you (O Mohammed!) were to follow their (Jews and Christians') desires after what you have received of knowledge (i.e. the Quran), then you would have against God neither any guardian nor any helper.* {Sura 2 (The Cow), 120}

We in the Qaeda Al-Jihad organisation have not accepted any pledge of allegiance without consent. We didn't coerce anyone into it, we didn't threaten anyone with beheading or cutting throats, and we didn't excommunicate anyone who fought us, as the new Khawarij [referring to IS] have been imagining.

O our Muslim nation in the heartland of the believers and our honourable brothers, the lions of Islam in the territories of the Levant! We are from you and for you and part of you even if we were separated by lands and countries. Doctrine and religion have united us, and we are with you waging the same battle in various fronts against the big criminals of the crusaders and their apostate aides. Your victory is our victory, your glory is our glory and your strength is our strength. Be steadfast, O slaves of God, in the face of this brutal assault in which the crusaders from the West and East have allied with the secular Nusayiri and the turncoat Shia. Be patient, be steadfast and be strong, don't be terrified by the war machinery of the crusaders. They have been crushed before in Afghanistan and Iraq, and remember the words of the Amir, who depended only on God as we see it, Mullah Mohammed Omar, may God have compassion on him, when he said: "God promised us victory and Bush promised us defeat; we will see which of them is truer." Also remember his words when he said: "The matter about Osama is not the matter of a person; it has become the matter of the honour of Islam." And when he said to his brothers: "If I handed over Osama, you would hand over me tomorrow."

This dependency on God alone and placing confidence in Him and not anyone else is what crushed the Western and Eastern crusaders' war machinery in Afghanistan; and it crushed them in Iraq, and will, with God's permission, crush them in the Levant. Be aware of the temptations of the dependent, apostate and crony governments, who will not grant you freedom or honour or dignity, because whoever lacks something will not be able to give it. Let your actions corroborate your words when you said: "death and not humiliation". If you be patient and fear God, their ruses will not harm you. God is aware of what they are doing.

Our last prayers, praise be upon the Lord of the universe, peace and prayers be upon our master Mohammed and on his family and companions.

Peace and God's compassion and blessings be upon you!

[Script at the end of the broadcast]

"We are coming, O Aqsa."

Zaid bin Thabet al-Ansari, may God be pleased with him, said: "I heard God's Messenger saying: 'Blessed is Al-Sham [Syria]! Blessed is Al-Sham!' They said to the Messenger: 'Why is that so?' He said: 'Because the angels of the Lord have spread out their wings over Al-Sham.'" Edited by al-Tirmidhi.

WE SHALL FULFIL OUR PLEDGE

JUNE 2016

By Ayman al-Zawahiri

We end with Zawahiri's pledge of allegiance to the new leader of the Taliban, Mawlawi Haibatullah, which is combined in this statement with a eulogy of Mullah Akhtar Mohamed Mansour, who was killed in a US drone strike in May 2016. Zawahiri uses the opportunity to emphasise the loyalty and steadfastness of jihadi stalwarts within both the Al-Qaeda central command and the leadership of the Islamic State in Iraq, including Abu Musab al-Zarqawi, thus accentuating his depiction of the Islamic State organisation as a transgressor, disrupting a noble legacy of jihadi activism reaching, in modern times, back to the venerated conflict against the soviets and Afghanistan, and ultimately back to the precedent set by the Prophet Mohammed and his companions.

In the name of God, the Most Benevolent, the Most Merciful
There is no God but God, and Mohammed is the Messenger of God.

And hold firmly to the rope of God all together and do not become divided. And remember the favour of God upon you—when you were enemies and He brought your hearts together and you became, by His favour, brothers. And you were on the edge of a pit of the fire, and He saved you from it. Thus does God make clear to you His verses that you may be guided. {Sura 3 (The Family of Imran), 103}

[A clip of Osama bin Laden giving an address is played]

Our pledge of allegiance to the commander of the faithful is a greater pledge as supported by the texts and *hadith* [sayings] of the Prophet. Abu Hudaifa says, narrating on the authority of Muslim [*hadith* collection], that the Prophet, peace and blessings be upon him [PBUH], says: "hold fast to the group of Muslims and to their Imam". Narrating on the authority of Muslim, the Prophet PBUH says: "The one who dies without a pledge on his throat dies an ignorant death." At the time, this was addressed to the Sahaba [Companions of the Prophet], may God be pleased with them. Unlike nowadays, threats of dying an ignorant death were enough to make the Sahaba run away as one would run from a lion; this is because they had experienced life in Jahiliyya [pre-Islamic ignorance], an odious life which was far from the path of God, exalted is He. "The one who dies without a pledge on his throat dies an ignorant death." Every Muslim should therefore make a heart-felt intention to pledge allegiance to the commander of the faithful Mullah Mohammed Omar, and this is the greater pledge.

[Another clip from December 1998 of bin Laden is played]

We advise Muslims inside and outside Afghanistan to support this pledge. We also advise Muslims abroad that any efforts made in the absence of a Muslim state will bear no fruits. Our Prophet, PBUH, spent 13 years calling and preaching in Makkah; but only a few hundred migrants, may God be pleased with them, responded to his call. However, when the state of Medina was founded, despite its small size and being surrounded by the Persian and the Roman empires, as well as by the tribes—Abs, Thahban and Athathan and the other Arabian tribes which were tearing it apart—the Good was established nonetheless. We call upon all Muslims to use all their power, capabilities, ideas, money and *zakat* [alms-giving] to support this state, because it now represents, God permits, the banner of Islam. Any American offensive on Afghanistan today is not considered as an attack on Afghanistan as a country, but instead an assault on Afghanistan, the bearer of Islam and its banner which flies high over the Islamic world. This is the true Islam for which we are waging jihad.

[Ayman al-Zawahiri begins his address]

In the name of God, all praise is due to Him, peace and blessings be upon the Messenger Mohammed, his family and companions and those who supported him.

To the commander of the faithful Mawlawi Haibatullah,[45] God preserve him, support him with the truth and enable him to support the truth, uphold the faith [*deen*] and defend the Book of God and support His faithful servants.

May peace and God's mercy and blessings be upon you.

I pray God to guide you as well as your brothers, soldiers and supporters to a path that He is pleased with. I pray He grants you glory and success and protects you from evil and harm in both the worldly life and the hereafter.

To the great sorrow and grief of the Muslim *ummah*, *mujahidin*, migrants and the marabouts, we learned of the death of our martyr Amir (as we believe him to be), the commander of the faithful Mullah Akhtar Mohammed Mansour; may God—by His blessing and favour—have ample mercy on him, reunite us with him in the highest heavens, and not make us of the disgraced or bearers of heretic changes.

Our consolation is that he received death while being steadfast in the truth, waging jihad and leading the *mujahidin* until he was killed by the invader's crusader strike. He attained martyrdom for the sake of God, which is the highest level that every *mujahid* wishes for. He acquired this sublime status after spending his life fighting the Russians and Communists and their supporters as well as the Americans, their allies and followers. He dedicated his life, together with his and the life of our late Amir Mullah Mohammed Omar, may God have mercy on both of them, and their devout companions, ordaining good and forbidding evil. They steadfastly engaged in jihad to cleanse Afghanistan from the filth of oppression, corruption and tyranny that Muslims were subjected to. Mullah Akhtar met his Lord after a life full of endeavours to establish a strong foundation for the Islamic Emirate and get rid of the remaining enemies amongst the people of evil and corruption, and those who sold themselves to the West. They [Mullah Akhtar, Mullah Mohammed Omar and the rest of the *mujahidin*] also dedicated their time to defending the migrants and the oppressed, when they stood alongside their Amir to defend the honour of Muslims and refused to surrender the Muslims to the disbelievers. They remained firm in the face of the campaign of tyrant crusaders to which they vehemently refused to kneel down; they proclaimed that they would only prostrate to God, even if they had to sacrifice their lives, families and wealth. They set a noble example which has made the history of Islam proud, as well as the history of the free people all over the world. Mullah Akhtar Mansour, may God have mercy on him, spent his life refusing to recognise the tyrant treacherous government of Kabul. He asserted that it was a product of the infidel crusaders who invaded the Muslim land. He spent his life leading his brothers in the Islamic Emirate, taking care of them and attending to their interests until he joined his Lord after a long life in jihad and migration, during which he ordained good and forbade evil and stood in the face of falsehood and betrayal. I pray to God that he will be among those to whom God says:

So do not weaken and do not grieve, and you will be superior if you are [true] believers. If a wound should touch you—there has already touched the [opposing people] a wound similar to it. And these days [of varying conditions] we alternate among the people so that God may make evident those who believe and [may] take to Himself from among you martyrs—and God does not like the wrongdoers—and that God may purify the believers [through trials] and destroy the disbelievers. Or do you think that you will enter Paradise while God has not yet made evident those of you who fight in His cause and made evident those who are steadfast? {Sura 3 (The Family of Imran), 139–142}

May God have mercy on our martyr the Amir, *mujahid*, migrant, Mullah Akhtar Mohammed Mansour who enjoined good and forbade evil and strongly rejected oppression, corruption and subjection. While we accept God's will and destiny and submit to His decree, we pray that He makes us steadfast in the truth, the righteous deeds and the faith [*deen*] and the Sunnah of His Prophet, PBUH. We also pray that God, by his grace and divine providence, keeps us firm on the path of jihad. We shall continue in the path of jihad and unite the *mujahidin*, following in the footsteps of our devout martyred leaders, may God have mercy on them: our Amir, the lion of Islam Sheikh Osama bin Laden, our brother Abu Musab al-Zarqawi, Abu Hamza al-Muhajir, Mustafa Abu al-Yazid, Abu al-Layth, Atiyah God and Abu Yahya al-Libi and all the other devout sheikhs of jihad, as we believe them to be and leave the true judgement to God. I declare therefore, in my capacity as Amir of the Qaeda Al-Jihad organisation, my pledge of allegiance to you, renewing the way of Sheikh Osama, may God have mercy on him, in his call to the Muslim *ummah* to support and pledge loyalty to the Islamic Emirate.

We pledge allegiance to you on the Book of God and the Sunnah of His Prophet (PBUH) as well as the Sunnah of the right-guided caliphs, may God be pleased with them. We are pledging allegiance to you so that the Sharia prevails over all the land of Muslims, so that the Muslims will rule and not be ruled, lead and not be led, nor challenged by any authority. We pledge allegiance to you to be free from any rule, regime, situation, treaty, agreement, charter—such as the United Nations and similar institutions—that is contrary to the Sharia, either inside or outside the Muslim land. We pledge allegiance to you to wage jihad in order to liberate every inch of the stolen occupied Muslim lands from Kashgar to Andalusia, from the Caucasus to Somalia and the centre of Africa, from Kashmir to Al-Quds, and from the Philippines to Kabul, Bukhara and Samarkand. We pledge allegiance to engage in jihad against the infidel rulers who changed the Islamic laws, invaded Muslim lands and impeded the implementation of the Sharia rules.

They subjected Muslims to the rulings of unbelievers [*kuffar*], spread corruption and imposed on Muslims agent and apostate regimes. The latter despise the Sharia, elevate the unbeliever's creed and philosophies and surrender the Muslim land and its wealth to their enemies. We pledge allegiance to you to support the oppressed believers wherever they are. We pledge allegiance to you to ordain good and forbid evil as much as you can. We pledge allegiance to you to defend the Islamic Emirate according to the guidance of the Book of God and the Sunnah of His Prophet PBUH. We pledge allegiance to you to establish the caliphate on the Prophetic method, which is based on the acceptance and selection [of caliphs] by Muslims. It is also based on spreading justice, allowing *shura* [consultation], achieving security, ending oppression, recovering rights and raising the banner of jihad. We pledge allegiance to you on all the above and on obedience in pleasure and animosity, ease and hardship as much as we can. We pray that God helps us to fulfil our pledge and helps you to accomplish your tasks.

Commander of the faithful, Mawlawi Haibatullah, may God preserve and protect you, God, exalted is He, has honoured you by His grace as He honoured your predecessors: the commander of the faithful Mullah Mohammed Omar and Mullah Akthar Mohammed Mansour, may God have mercy on them both. God, exalted is He, has also honoured the Islamic Emirate with jihad against the Russian invaders and their Communist allies. God has blessed you by enabling you to establish the first and only religious Emirate since the fall of the Ottoman caliphate. It was set up to wage jihad, command good and forbid evil and establish the rule of Sharia. The *mujahidin* recognised the Emirate's establishment of truth and commitment to the faith and hastened to pledge allegiance, as did the mujaddid [renewer] Imam Sheikh Osama bin Laden. The latter declared that he had sworn "the great pledge of allegiance" and called on all other Muslims to do the same. All those who swore loyalty to Sheikh Osama bin Laden, may God have mercy on him, and his Al-Jihad organisation joined in this pledge. God, exalted is He, honoured you when He helped you confront the crusaders' campaign. He enabled you to protect and defend your migrant brothers, sacrificing yourselves, your power and authority, and wealth to protect them: "This is the favour of God, He bestows it upon whom He will". {Sura 62 (Friday), 4} Your Muslim brothers and sons are today facing a global enemy which seeks to eradicate Islam and corrupt the Muslims from Kashgar to Tangiers and from the Caucasus mountains to the centre of Africa. They consider the Islamic Emirate, given the catastrophes, wars and injustice it has been subjected to, as a stronghold for Islam and a refuge for Muslims. So seek help in God, the Owner of Majesty and Might, and be up to their expectations.

Strong resolutions are measured according to those who take them
And the like is true for nobility and generosity and their givers
Futile matters are deemed great by little minds
While grave affairs pale into insignificance in the eyes of the great

To conclude, I pray that God raises your ranks by obeying Him, establishing His Sharia, supporting His allies and waging jihad against His enemies. We are indeed your soldiers, supporters and one of your brigades. God has spoken the truth when He says: *And whoever fears God, He will make for him a way out and will provide for him from where he does not expect. And whoever relies upon God will accomplish his purpose.* {Sura 65 (Divorce), 2–3}

Your brother Ayman Al-Zawahiri, the Amir of the Qaeda Al-Jihad organisation

NOTES

GLOSSARY

1. Cf. Roel Meijer (ed.), *Global Salafism: Islam's New Religious Movement* (London: Hurst, 2009); John L. Esposito (ed.), *The Oxford Encyclopaedia of the Islamic World* (Oxford: Oxford University Press, 2009); John L. Esposito (ed.), *The Oxford Dictionary of Islam* (Oxford: Oxford University Press, 2003).

INTRODUCTION

1. A. Schmid and J. De Graaf, *Violence as Communication: Insurgent Terrorism and the Western News Media* (London: Sage, 1982), p. 1.
2. Montasser Al-Zayyat, *The Road to Al-Qaeda: The Story of Bin Laden's Right-Hand Man* (London: Pluto Press, 2004), pp. 16–17. Zawahiri denounced Zayyat publicly on a number of occasions, claiming he knew nothing about the events Zayyat wrote about in his book, e.g. in his "Open Meeting" media initiative which Al-Sahab, Al-Qaeda's premier media outlet, released in April 2008.
3. Ibid., p. 36; Lawrence Wright, *The Looming Tower: Al-Qaeda's Road to 9/11* (London: Penguin, 2007).
4. Cf. Wright, *The Looming Tower*. Ayman al-Zawahiri, *Knights under the Banner of the Prophet* [Fursaan taht rayat al-Nabi]; an early version of the book was released by the newspaper *Al-Sharq al-Awsat*, after being found in Afghanistan in 2001; Al-Sahab later published a "full" second version which is over 500 pages long.
5. Fawaz Gerges, *The Far Enemy: Why Jihad went Global* (Cambridge: Cambridge University Press, 2005), ch. 3, pp. 119–50.
6. Cf. Jeffrey R. Halverson, H. L. Goodall Jr, Steven R. Corman, *Master Narratives of Islamist Extremism* (Basingstoke: Palgrave Macmillan, 2011).
7. "Zawahiri's letter to Zarqawi" (English translation), available from Combating Terrorism Center (CTC), West Point, https://www.ctc.usma.edu/posts/zawahiris-letter-to-zarqawi-english-translation-2, accessed July 2016.

8. For an overview, see CTC's analysis in Nelly Lahoud, Stuart Caudill, Liam Collins, Gabriel Koehler-Derrick, Don Rassler, Muhammad al-'Ubaydi, "Letters from Abbottabad: Bin Laden Sidelined?'" 3rd edn (New York: Combating Terrorism Center, West Point, May 2012).

9. Ibid.

10. 8th Annual ASDA'A Burson-Marsteller Arab Youth Survey, "Inside the Hearts and Minds of Arab Youth", 2016, http://arabyouthsurvey.com, accessed August 2016.

11. No author, "Amongst the believers are men: Abu Junaydah al-Almani", *Dabiq* issue 12 (2015), p. 55.

12. Abu Jarir ash-Shamali, "Al-Qa'idah of Waziristan: A Testimony from Within", *Dabiq* issue 6 (2015), p. 53.

13. Ibid.

14. http://www.linguassist.co.uk. Note that I have adopted simplified transliteration of Arabic words where they are offered for consistency and ease. Transliterated Arabic words are given only to identify the original meaning and do not necessarily reflect the exact way in which they are pronounced (e.g. with respect to the 'ayn (Al-Qaeda versus Al-Qa'ida for example) and "sun" and "moon" letters (Al-Sahab versus As-Sahab, for instance) or macrons, aside from the name of certain Quranic verses).

PART 1: AL-QAEDA AFTER THE ARAB SPRING

1. One of the Prophet's companions.

2. Companion of the Prophet and Islamic warrior.

3. The Israeli Embassy in Cairo was attacked by a mob on 9 September 2011, forcing an evacuation of staff.

4. The senior Al-Qaeda commander was killed in a US drone strike in Pakistan in August 2011.

5. The helicopter was downed on 6 August 2011 resulting in 38 fatalities: 30 US and 8 Afghan service personnel.

6. The *Groupe Islamique Armé* emerged as a prominent fighting force during the Algerian civil war (1991–2002) but was ultimately discredited due to its excessive violence and targeting of civilians.

7. 2011 was a very bloody year for Coptic Christians in Egypt, starting with a terrorist attack in Alexandria on 1 January 2011 that killed 23 worshippers at a New Year's Eve service. There were then multiple cases of street violence and clashes with the military that resulted in dozens of fatalities.

8. As part of British imperial efforts to control Sudan.

9. An Egyptian woman said to have been seeking divorce from her Coptic priest husband and intending to convert to Islam. She was rumoured to have been incarcerated in a monastery in order to prevent her conversion and later killed. The case, and a

similar account involving another Egyptian woman, Camilla Shehadeh, has been used by extremists in Iraq, Egypt and elsewhere to orchestrate, call for and justify scores of attacks against Christians, targeting places of worship predominantly.

10. I.e. where Muslims are massacred.

11. Weinstein, an American academic and expert in international development, was kidnapped from the house where he was staying in Lahore on 11 August 2011; he was held by Al-Qaeda in the semi-autonomous Federally Administered Tribal Areas on the Afghan–Pakistan border, where he died in a US drone strike targeting Al-Qaeda leadership figures on 14 January 2015.

12. A US-educated Pakistani neuroscientist sentenced in the US for the attempted murder of US soldiers in Afghanistan. The case has attracted much political and media scrutiny due to allegations of false imprisonment and miscarriages of justice.

13. "Agreement on Provisional Arrangements in Afghanistan Pending the Re-establishment of Permanent Government Institutions", signed in Bonn, Germany, 5 December 2001.

14. Battle of Shubra Khit, 13 July 1798.

15. Zawahiri is here referring to the intellectual evolution within mainstream political Islam in the region, especially through the Muslim Brotherhood and those associated with its political and intellectual leadership.

16. Refers to a committee headed by Amr Moussa charged with amending the 2012 Egyptian constitution, passed when the Muslim Brotherhood was in power in Egypt, which introduced dedicated references to Islamic governance that have since been removed.

17. Founder and president of the Tunisian Islamic political party *Ḥarkat al-Nahda*, which gained political power after the revolution against Zine El Abidine Ben Ali in 2011.

18. Sendero Luminoso or "Shining Path", the radical communist organisation in Peru.

19. The doctrine of *hisba* (*al-amr bil-marouf wal-nahee an al-munkar*): commanding good and forbidding that which is evil or wrong.

20. Zawahiri is referring here to the National Salvation Front (Jabhat al-Inqadh [Inqaz in Egyptian Arabic] al-Watani), the Tamarod movement which emerged in opposition to President Morsi's rule, and Naguib Sawiris, whose "Free Egyptians" party formed part of the NSF.

21. Which bases Egyptian law on the "principles of sharia".

22. See above.

23. Former Grand Mufti of Egypt.

24. See note above.

25. See note above.

26. Secured via http://nokbah.com

PART 2: AL-QAEDA AND THE SYRIAN *FITNA*

1. See note 6 in Part 1.
2. Abu Mohammed al-Golani (or Julani), leader of the formerly Al-Qaeda-affiliated Jabhat al-Nusra (JN) in Syria.
3. Hassan Aboud Abu Abdullah al-Hamawi, leader of Ahrar al-Sham.
4. Abu Bakr al-Baghdadi, leader of what at this point was still Islamic State of Iraq and Syria/Levant (ISIS/ISIL). Weeks after Zawahiri's Al-Sahab interview was released, ISIL had captured Mosul and declared a caliphate, the Islamic state.
5. The Muhajiroun were the emigrants who followed the Prophet Mohammed out of Mecca in 622 CE. The Ansar were the local people of Medina who helped the newcomers and joined their ranks. In this context the terms are used as metaphors for those who arrived in Syria from abroad versus the locals.
6. Members of Al-Qaeda's inner core.
7. About the creation of ISIL as an Islamic State of Iraq–JN merger.
8. Hezbollah Secretary General.
9. Those who declare others non-Muslims, a reference in this context to extremist transgressors.
10. A play on words referring to the Islamist Nour party as "fakes" who are Sisi supporters.
11. A statement Zawahiri issued in April 2013.
12. Article 2 exists as a form of "sharia insurance" in the Egyptian constitution, intended to ensure that legislation rests on and respects the principles of Islamic law. But the true meaning of Article 2 for Egyptian law and society has always been open to debate. The Muslim Brotherhood's efforts to underscore the centrality of Sharia in Egyptian law through the introduction of Article 219, elucidating the principles of Sharia referenced in Article 2 in more detail, offered no greater clarity or consensus. Cf. Mohammed Fadel, "Judicial institutions, the legitimacy of Islamic state law and democratic transition in Egypt: Can a shift toward a common law model of adjudication improve the prospects of a successful democratic transition?" *I•CON*, Vol. 11, No. 3 (2013), pp. 646–65.
13. In 1985 the Egyptian Supreme Constitutional Court (SCC) concluded that it could hear challenges to new laws or amendments that were seen to challenge Article 2 of the Egyptian constitution. Cf. Clark B. Lombardi, "Designing Islamic constitutions: Past trends and options for a democratic future", *I•CON*, Vol. 11, No. 3 (2013), pp. 615–45.
14. Article 44 in the 2012 constitution, shaped in large part by Islamists, prohibited the insulting of prophets. It was since removed following the 2013 *coup d'état*.
15. See note 10, above.
16. Founder and first king of Saudi Arabia.
17. Founder of Al-Nahda, see note 17 in Part 1.
18. Mongol siege of Baghdad, 1258 CE.

19. Derogatory term for Alawites.
20. Reference to the Safavid dynasty and, by extension, Persian imperialism.
21. The question seems to concern Muslim casualties inflicted during the civil war in the Central African Republic, which broke out in 2012, as well as French military involvement in Mali, which began in January that same year, and potentially turmoil in Sudan and newly independent South Sudan too.
22. Al-Sahab's original transcript contained words underlined and in bold in order to emphasise particular points. This emphasis is retained here.
23. Aka Hani Mohammed Yusuf al-Sabaaee, an extremist Islamist preacher from Egypt, currently living in London.
24. Al-Maqreze Centre for Historical Studies.
25. Abu Hamza al-Muhajir and Abu Umar al-Baghdadi were leaders of the Islamic State of Iraq.
26. Aka Saeed al-Masri, Al-Qaeda leader.
27. Emphasis in original. Zawahiri is trying to emphasise here that the leaders of the Islamic State of Iraq recognised the clear and direct authority of the Al-Qaeda central command.
28. Hasan ibn Ali became caliph briefly after the death of his father in 661 CE, but abdicated to make way for Muawiyah I.

PART 3: AL-QAEDA AND THE "ISLAMIC STATE"

1. Derogatory term for the Alawite sect, see note 19 in Part 2.
2. The Kharijites were a group of zealots who abandoned their caliph, Ali ibn Abi Talib, after he sought to negotiate a truce with his rival, Muawiyah I, and his Syrian allies following the Battle of Siffin, which took place near the Euphrates river in July 657 CE. This angered those who sought to implement the Quran directly and saw the agreement as a "man-made" arrangement, not a divinely guided accord. Those who rebelled and seceded (*kharaja*) from Ali's authority in protest have since come to represent any extremist, fringe movement obsessed with doctrinal purity and the notion of excommunication (*takfir*) in Islam. The Kharijite label has since become a staple tool of delegitimisation and has featured prominently in denouncements of IS.
3. "Awakening" councils of local Sunnis who were supported against Islamic State of Iraq forces and were later encouraged to reform against IS.
4. Musa bin Nusayr, Uqba ibn Nafi, Tariq ibn Ziyad—all prominent generals in the Muslim conquest of North Africa and Spain.
5. Referring to the attacks on the offices of the French satirical newspaper *Charlie Hebdo* in Paris on 7 January 2015, which resulted in 12 deaths. The perpetrators, Saïd Kouachi and his younger brother Chérif, claimed links to Al-Qaeda in the Arabian Peninsula.

6. The latter attack is a reference to Amedy Coulibaly's attack on a Jewish supermarket in Paris two days after the *Charlie Hebdo* attack.

7. In relation to the controversial cartoons depicting the Prophet Mohammed published in the Danish newspaper, *Jyllands-Posten*.

8. Reference to the *Innocence of Muslims* film, by Nakoula Basseley Nakoula.

9. An extensive arms sales agreement between Britain and Saudi Arabia, where there have been accusations of financial irregularities.

10. Aka Ahmed Abdi Godane, leader of Al-Shabaab, who was killed in September 2014.

11. Part of a *hadith* attributed to Abu Hurayrah and recorded in Sahih al-Bukhari and Sahih Muslim.

12. Leader of Ansar Al-Sharia in Libya.

13. Harith bin Ghazi al-Nadhari was a leader of Al-Qaeda in the Arabian Peninsula, who was killed in a drone strike in January 2015.

14. The death of Mohammed Omar, the leader of the Afghan Taliban and the so-called Afghan Islamic "Emirate", was acknowledged by the Taliban and Al-Qaeda in the summer of 2015, and Zawahiri was quick to pledge allegiance to his successor, Akhtar Mohammed Mansour, who in turn was killed the following summer. The Islamic State had dismissed Mullah Omar's authority, suggesting he had been dead for years and guilty of numerous Sharia violations and other transgressions when still alive (e.g. in the 6th issue of its English-language magazine *Dabiq*), whilst describing Akhtar Mansour as a "liar" whom not even the rest of the Afghan Taliban trusted (*Dabiq*, issue 11). Irrespective of who was leader of the Afghan Emirate, however, Zawahiri's point is that the fact that al-Baghdadi as leader of ISI had pledged allegiance to bin Laden as leader of Al-Qaeda (which, Zawahiri argued, passed on to him as successor to bin Laden), who in turn had pledged allegiance to Mullah Omar, meant that al-Baghdadi's split from the fold was thus a violation of this oath. This is a major theme in Zawahiri's refutation of al-Baghdadi and the Islamic State.

15. An independent enclave declared by Dzhokhar Dudayev during the Chechen wars against Russia, which later became part of the Caucasus Islamic Emirate.

16. Chechen Islamist leader, president of Chechen breakaway Republic of Ichkeria 1996–7, killed in February 2004.

17. The formation of Al-Qaeda in the Indian subcontinent was announced in September 2014. The attack Zawahiri is referring to appears to be the attempted raid on a naval dockyard in Karachi shortly after the group was founded.

18. See note 12 in Part 1.

19. Jabhat Al-Nusra kidnapped twelve orthodox nuns in Maloula, a town in southwest Syria, in early December 2013 and held them captive for three months, before releasing them as part of a prison exchange.

20. Medieval Islamic commanders.

21. *Ahl al-Hal wal Aqd*—experts in Islamic jurisprudence qualified to elect or depose a caliph on behalf of the Muslim *ummah*. Cf. *The Oxford Dictionary of Islam*, ed. by John L. Esposito (Oxford: Oxford University Press, 2003).

22. A reference to Allama al-Hilli, a famous Twelver Shia jurist and scholar [d.1325 CE], a contemporary of Ibn Taymiyyah [d.1328 CE], a well-known Sunni scholar.

23. The 9/11 Commission Report.

24. See note 21, above.

25. An "interview" with Zawahiri published by Al-Sahab in December 2007.

26. Zawahiri uses the word *al-Rawafid* (pl.) for "the rejecters", which in this context is a derogatory Sunni way of referring to the Shia. Safavid if of course a reference to the Persian Safavid empire, so Zawahiri is effectively warning his Sunni audience against what he sees as transgressing Shia imperialists.

27. Zawahiri uses the word *al-Nusayriya* (pl.) to refer to the Alawi Shia sect, a (negative) reference to the founder of this school, a ninth-century (CE) religious leader called Mohammed ibn Nusayr. The Assad family and the political elite of Syria belong to this denomination of Shia Islam.

28. The attack on the *Charlie Hebdo* newspaper headquarters and other attacks in France in January 2015.

29. General Sir Percy Cox was a representative of the British colonial authorities in the Middle East and a key player in the formation of states and power elites in the region during the demise of the Ottoman Empire, including the emergence of the House of Saud.

30. Shah Ismail I (d.1524 CE), founder of the Safavid dynasty.

31. Probably a reference to the Egyptian Interior Minister.

32. President of Tunisia.

33. Pro-democracy Syrian opposition representatives met in Riyadh, Saudi Arabia, on 10 December 2015 to discuss ways in which to consolidate and cooperate in opposition to the Assad regime in Damascus.

34. An accord between Britain and Abdul Aziz was signed in 1915 which recognised the independence of the Kingdom of Najd. However, the Uqair Protocol was not signed until 1922, when the aforementioned General Sir Percy Cox [see note 29] represented the UK colonial authorities in drafting boundaries between modern-day Saudi Arabia, Kuwait and Iraq.

35. Former director of Saudi intelligence and later ambassador to the United States.

36. John Garang de Mabior, leader of the separatist Sudan People's Liberation Army in South Sudan, which became the country's state military following independence in 2011.

37. Inter-Services Intelligence, the main intelligence organisation of Pakistan.

38. Al-Suri, a leader of the Ahrar al-Sham opposition group in Syria who had close ties to Al-Qaeda, was killed in a suicide blast close to Aleppo in late February 2014. Al-Zawahiri reportedly appointed him mediator in the dispute with the Islamic

State, whose operatives were accused of being responsible for Al-Suri's death and killing other members of Ahrar al-Sham. Cf. Thomas Jocelyn, "Al Qaeda's chief representative in Syria killed in suicide attack", *The Long War Journal*, http://www.longwarjournal.org/archives/2014/02/zawahiris_chief_repr.php, accessed July 2016.

39. See note 2, above.
40. An attack in Idlib Province, Syria, in July 2015 which killed scores of alleged Al-Nusra members.
41. An attack by a member of Takfir wal Hijrah targeted worshippers at a mosque in Omdurman, Sudan, in December 2000, inflicting two dozen fatalities.
42. Abu Bakr al-Baghdadi was born Ibrahim al-Badri.
43. *Al-Hajjaj* means "the pilgrims". But here, as becomes clear a little later in Zawahiri's speech, this is a reference to al-Hajjaj ibn Yusuf (d.714 CE), an Umayyad governor of Iraq and Persia known for his harsh tactics and brutal treatment of adversaries.
44. Conferences involving Syrian opposition figures.
45. The new leader of the Afghan Taliban. Akhtar Mansour, his predecessor, was killed in a US drone strike in May 2016.

INDEX

bin Aashour, Mohammed al-Taher: Sheikh of al-Zaytouna Mosque, 125
Ibn Abbas: 223, 228
ibn Abbas, Abdullah: 235
Abbas, Mahmoud: 103
Abbasid Caliphate (750–1258): 127, 197, 228; fall of, 228
Abdulhalim, Tarik: 198
ibn Abdullah, Mohammed: 228
Abdullah of Saudi Arabia, King: 255
ibn Abdulsalam, Izaddin: 228–9
Abdurrahman, Omar: 176, 202, 213, 223
bin Abi Taleb, Ali: 60
bin Abdul-Muttalib, Hamza: 25
Abdullah, Abu: 22, 25
Abu Bakr (Al-Sadiq): 109, 220, 222, 224; death of, 227
Abu-Zubair, Mukhtar: death of, 186–7
al-Adnani, Abu Mohammed: 12, 153; 'Your Lord is Ever Watchful' (2014), 8, 10
Afghanistan: 27–8, 31, 37, 44, 66, 76, 100, 127, 129, 160, 180, 192–3, 196, 199, 202, 207, 210, 215, 217, 222, 234, 256, 270; Jalalabad, 255; Kabul, 30, 37–8, 48, 66, 255, 272; Kandahar, 31, 194, 255; Operation

Enduring Freedom (2001–14), 5, 27, 30–1, 37, 42, 52, 101–2, 127–8, 131, 192, 194, 232, 240, 266; Shahi Kut, 30; Soviet Invasion of (1979–89), 2, 61, 99, 105, 206, 271, 273; Tora Bora, 28, 30; Wardak, 37
Ahmad, Imam: 220
Ahmadinejad, Mahmoud: 128
Alawites (religious group): 208, 220, 237, 240, 257, 265
Algeria: 38, 52, 67, 190, 266; Civil War (1991–2002), 99, 251; French Invasion of (1830–47), 173
bin Ali, Zayn al-Abdin: sheltered by Saudi Arabia, 255
Allenby, Lord: 179
Amin, Abu Abd al-Rahman: 259
al-Andalusi, Sofian al-Maghrebi Abu Essam (Abdulkarim Hussein): 247
al-Ansari, Zaid bin Thabet: 267
Anwar, Hassan: 174
al-Aqsa Mosque: 186, 228, 248, 261, 265
Aqis, Sheikh Hassan: 28
Arab-Byzantine Wars: Battle of Yarmouk (636), 64
Arab Spring: vii–viii, 3, 11, 21, 73, 254, 264; Egyptian Revolution (2011),

27, 29–30, 34, 36, 41, 77, 84, 110, 122–3, 177, 251–2; Libyan Civil War (2011), 29–30, 77; Syrian Civil War (2011–), vii, 5, 11–12, 21, 29, 110, 135, 203, 206, 208–9, 242, 260; Tunisian Revolution (2010–11), 27, 29–30, 77, 177, 251–2; Yemeni Revolution (2011–12), 29–30

Arab Youth Survey: 7
Arabic (language): 38, 173, 183
Armed Islamic Group: 38
Ashoush, Ahmad: 176, 213
al-Assad, Bashar: 107, 142, 240; regime of, 96, 128–9, 154, 201, 253
atheism: 71, 78
Atta, Mohammed: 249
Attiya: 106, 131, 137–9
bin Auf, Abdulrahman: 224–6
Australia: 41, 155, 164
Awlaqi, Anwar: 244
Al-Aws wal-Khazraj: 171
Azzam, Abdullah: 233

Baath Party: 105, 143
al-Badri, Ibrahim: 264
al-Baghdadi, Abu Bakr al-Husseini: x, 12, 105, 135–40, 142–3, 185, 190–2, 194–5, 197–9, 207–8, 239, 241; declaration of Caliphate (2014), x, 6–8, 148, 220, 263; supporters of, 144
al-Baghdadi, Abu Umar: 136, 229, 234
Bahrain: 245
Balfour, Lord Alfred: Balfour Declaration (1917), 179
Bangladesh: 194, 199; Liberation War (1971), 40
Bani Shihr (tribe): 245
al-Banna, Hassan: 79
al-Barhimi, Yasser: 113–14, 118–20

Basayev, Shamil: 74
Bi-lah, Al-Mustansir: 228
Bonaparte, Napoleon: Egyptian Campaign of (1798–1801), 3
Bonn Conference (2001): 48
Bosnian War (1992–5): Srebrenica Massacre (1995), 43, 91
British Broadcasting Corporation (BBC): 74
Burma: 160, 194, 199
Bush, George W.: 31

Canada: 155
Catholicism: Inquisition, 91, 178
Caucasus Islamic Emirate: 195–6, 199
Ceuta: 48, 84
Chechnya: 29, 40, 48, 61, 66, 71, 73–7, 83, 96, 195, 200, 210; Grozny, 66, 249
China, Imperial: 172
China, People's Republic of: 160, 175, 209; East Turkestan, 48; Kashgar, 249, 252, 272–3
Christianity: 42, 55, 80, 96, 171, 181; Bible, 93, 114, 153; conversion to, 83; Coptic, 34, 39–41, 73, 90–2, 172
Clinton, Bill: 179
Clinton, Hillary: visit to Egypt (2011), 27
Constantine, Wafaa: 42, 91, 94
Cox, Sir Percy: 244
Cuba: Guantanamo Bay, 27, 44, 132, 173

Daghistan: 77
Daghistani, Abu Mohamed: Amir of Caucasus Islamic Emirate, 199
al-Dakhel, Abdulrahman: 197
al-Dandani, Turki: 244
David: 77

Dudayev, Dzhokhar: 74–5; death of, 75–6

East Timor: Independence of (2002), 40
Egypt: 33, 42–3, 45, 67, 78–9, 82–3, 90–1, 94, 100, 109–10, 124, 127, 153, 160, 174, 247; al-Azhar, 40; Cairo, 2, 28, 62, 66; Constitution of (1971), 113–19; Consultative Council, 85; Coptic Christian population of, 34, 41, 73, 90–1; Council of Deputies, 117; Military Council, 36, 39, 41, 87; Ministry of the Interior, 84; Parliament, 85; Revolution (2011), 27, 29–30, 34, 36, 41, 77, 84, 110, 122–3, 177, 251–2; Supreme Court of State Security, 117
ElBaradei, Mohamed: 80
Erdoğan, Recep Tayyip: 126
Euphrates, River: 233
European Union (EU): 83

Fahd of Saudi Arabia, King: 255
al-Faisal, Turki: 255
al-Faruq, Omar: 210, 217, 249
fatwa: 40–1
al-Filistini, Abu Qatada: 176, 198, 213
al-Filistini, Abu al-Waleed: 176, 213
First Chechen War (1994–6): 74–6; casualties of, 75
First Opium War (1839–42): 172
First World War (1914–18): 40, 83; belligerents of, 206, 254
France: 39, 131–2, 249; *Charlie Hebdo* Attack (2015), 169–71, 178, 180, 210; Paris, 125, 178, 180; Revolution (1789–99), 90
Free Syrian Army: 260

Garang, John: 255

Geneva Conventions: 27, 45
Ghamid (tribe): 245
al-Ghannouchi, Rached: 124, 126, 251
Ghazi bin Faisal, King (King Ghazi of Iraq): 255
Giap, Vo Nguyen: 74–5
God, Atiyah: 272
al-Golani, al-Fatih Abu Muhammad: 105, 143
Goliath: 77
Gomaa, Ali: 89–90
Groupe Islamique Armé (GIA): 99, 258

Hadi, Abd Rabuh Mansour: 255–6
al-Hadrami, Abu Saad: 260
Haibatullah, Mawlawi: 270, 273
al-Hajj, Khalid: 244
Halim, Tariq Abdul: 176
ibn Hanbal, Ahmad: 95
Hania, Ismael: 28
Harb (tribe): 245
al-Harithi, Abu Ali: 244
Hasan, Nidal: 210, 249
al-Himsi, Abu: 196
Hinduism: 54–5, 160, 209
Hizb al-Nour al-Salafi: 112, 114
Hizbollah: 249; members of, 129
Holbrook, David: x–xi
Houthis: 164, 170, 243–4, 253
Hussein, Mohammed al-Khadar: 125
Hussein, Saddam: removed from power (2003), 31

Ibrahim: 164
Ibrahim, Mohammed: 251
improvised explosive device (IED): 163–4, 166
India: 40, 48, 160, 175, 194, 196, 199
Indonesia: 40, 160, 195; Bali Bombing (2002), 249

Inqaz Court: funding provided to, 84

International Criminal Court (ICC): 27

Iran: 105, 127–8, 130, 196, 213, 239, 242, 245–6, 250, 257; *Wilayat e Faqih*, 128

Iraq: vii, 4, 6, 28–9, 39, 48, 100, 130, 144, 153, 159–60, 171, 190, 199, 202–3, 207, 209–11, 214, 239, 250, 255; Baghdad, 66, 159, 242; Erbil, 159; Karbala, 25; Kurdish population of, 166; Mosul, x, 8, 147; Operation Iraqi Freedom (2003–11), 4, 27, 31, 42, 52, 71, 127–8, 131, 158, 240, 242, 266

Islam: 2, 27, 34–5, 38, 48–9, 53, 55, 63–4, 66, 68, 76, 80, 85, 92, 105, 110, 118, 123–6, 132, 141, 144, 161, 164, 170, 172, 181, 189, 197, 206, 209, 211, 217, 237, 242–3, 245; Ismaelis, 54; Qadiyani, 54; Quran, 10, 22–3, 34–5, 39, 61, 78, 85, 91, 93–4, 102–4, 106, 114, 130–1, 148–51, 154–6, 161, 163–4, 172–3, 181–2, 193, 209, 216, 221, 230, 237, 243, 247–8, 256, 260, 263–4, 269, 274; Ramadan, 37, 47, 147–9, 187; Sharia, 7, 28, 30, 33, 42, 48–9, 56, 70–1, 73, 75, 78, 80, 83–4, 86–7, 93, 95, 100, 104, 108, 110, 113–19, 122–3, 126, 129, 132, 149, 181–2, 186, 188–9, 199, 201–2, 205–7, 209–12, 214–15, 220–1, 230, 242–4, 251–2, 256–7, 265, 272–4; Shia (Rafida), 52, 54, 129, 143, 154, 160, 162, 170–1, 186, 227–8, 237, 239, 242–3, 249, 253, 260–1; Sufism, 54; Sunna, 85, 193, 204, 242, 260, 272–3; Sunni, 54, 95, 128–9, 142, 162, 204, 246, 260

Al-Islami, Al-Amal: 103

Islamic Salvation Front: 173, 266

Islamic State of Iraq and Syria (ISIS): vii, ix–x, 4–6, 8, 10, 12, 21, 27, 51, 106, 135, 138–40, 142–3, 147, 153–4, 157, 160–1, 165, 185, 192–3, 203, 208, 219–20, 231, 239, 253, 257, 263, 266, 269; capture of Mosul (2014), 147; Consultative Council, 195; emergence of (2013), 6–7; propaganda systems of, viii, 7; territory occupied by, 147

Islamism: 5, 11–12, 77, 124; militant, 6, 12

Israel: 36, 43, 52, 84, 88, 103, 125, 130, 175, 179, 186, 249, 251, 256, 264; Acre, 179; Independence of (1948), 179; Jerusalem (Quds), 123, 186, 247–50, 252, 254, 265, 272; Occupied Territories, 48, 255; recognition of, 48; Tel Aviv, 61

Jabhat Al-Nusra: 141–3, 263

Al-Jamaat Al-Islamiyya: 105

Al-Jamiat-e Islami (Islamic Society): 194

Jammu and Kashmir: 29, 40, 48, 54, 83, 194, 210, 272

Japan, Imperial: 172

Ibn Jarir: 228

Jayed, Nazheer: 40, 42–3

Al-Jihad: 2, 233–4

jihadism: vii–viii, 2, 22, 25, 28, 37–8, 52, 68, 202, 236

Jordan, Hashemite Kingdom of: 162

Judaism: 53, 61–2, 64, 66, 68–9, 71, 158, 162, 166, 170, 179, 235, 248; Torah, 114, 232

Jyllands-Posten Controversy (2005): 172, 180

Ibn Katheer: 250; *Beginning and the End, The*, 64–5

Kenya: Nairobi, 61; US Embassy
Bombing (1998), 61
Kerry, John: 161
Khalis, Yunus: 255
Khan, Mohammed Sidiq: 210
Kharijites: 160–1, 253, 258–9
Khatami, Mohammad: 127
al-Khattabi, Mohammed Bin Abdul
Karim: 77
Khorasan: 233
al-Khurasani, Abu Djanah: 71, 102
al-Khurasani, Abu Muslim: 204
Kifaytullah, Mufti: 28
Kitchener, Field Marshal Herbert: 92
Kurds (ethnic group): 166
Kuwait: 245

bin Laden, Osama: x, 1–3, 11, 21–3,
26–8, 44, 106–7, 127, 131, 135–7,
169, 172, 176–7, 179–80, 183,
196, 212, 229, 232–3, 243, 248,
252, 259–60, 270; assassination of
(2011), vii, xi, 5–6, 21, 25, 37, 102,
137–9, 255; 'Inciting Jihad' (2003),
176–7; move to Afghanistan (1996),
232; pledge of allegiance to Mullah
Mohammed Omar, 257–8; pledges
of allegiance to, 273
Laith, Sheikh Abdul: 37
al-Layth, Abu: 272
Lebanon: 28, 61, 129; government of,
201
al-Libi, Abu Anas: 96
al-Libi, Aby Yahya: 131, 272
Libya: 21, 79, 83, 92, 96, 122, 153, 160,
164, 189; Civil War (2011), 29–30,
77; Misrata, 38; Tripoli, 37
Linguassist: translation efforts of, 10

Mali: 102, 197, 199
Malila: 84

Mamluk Empire: 62
Mansour, Mullah Akhtar Mohamed:
271–3; death of (2016), 269, 271;
pledges of allegiance to, 228
Mao Zedong: 77
al-Maqdisi, Abu Mohammed: 176,
198, 213–15, 233, 260
Marah, Mohammed: 249
martyrdom: 59; operations, 65, 69–71,
131, 180; permissions for, 64
Marxism: 88
al-Masiri, Dr Abdul Wahab: 88
Maskhadov, Aslan: 74–5
Mauritania: 37
al-Mawardi, Imam: 221
Melilla: 48
Mindad, Ibn Khwariz: 229
al-Misrati, Sheikh Abu Abdul Rahman
Jamal Ibrahim Ishtwai (Sheikh
Atiyyatullah): 36–7
Mohammed, Abd al-Ghafaar: 115
Mojaddedi, Sibghatullah: 255–6
Morjan, Salem: 176
Morocco: Tangiers, 249, 252, 273
Morsi, Mohammed: 84–5, 94–5, 260;
removed from power (2013), 73,
173, 256
Moses: 34
Mousavi, Mir-Hossein: 128
Mubarak, Hosni: 39–40, 90, 95, 119;
regime of, 40, 80–1, 87, 89, 120;
removed from power (2011), 85,
110, 123
al-Muhajir, Abu Hamza (al-Karoumi):
136–7, 208, 229, 233–4, 272; family
of, 45, 200–1
al-Muhajir, Hasna: family of, 45,
200–1; imprisonment of, 45
Muhammad, Prophet: 22–3, 31, 34,
45, 49, 57, 60, 65, 69, 77, 91, 94,
130, 135, 148, 152, 155–6, 159, 165,

167, 169–71, 176, 178–83, 185, 200, 204, 215, 220–1, 237, 243, 246, 251, 261, 267; Companions of, 227, 269–70; descendants of, 55; family of, 151; *hadith* of, 189, 223, 241

mujahidin: 27–9, 36–7, 52, 54–6, 64, 70, 77, 96, 102, 104, 106–7, 109, 112, 124–5, 129, 143, 151, 158, 161, 171–2, 178, 180–1, 188, 191, 196, 199–200, 206–7, 212, 219, 234, 237, 240–2, 254, 257, 264, 273; *fitna* between, 135, 143, 211, 214–16, 234, 250–1, 256; sects, 208; support for, 127; targeting in media, 131

al-Mukarram, al-Aziz: 136

ibn Muljam, Abd al-Rahman: 258

al-Muqrin, Abdulaziz: 244

al-Murjan, Salem: 213

Muslim Brotherhood: 2, 92, 118, 122, 126, 205; Egyptian branch of, 73, 130, 256

Al-Mustansir: 228

al-Mutanabbi: 100–1; poetry of, 43, 65, 78–81, 87–8, 102–3

al-Nadhari, Harith bin Ghazi: 171, 190

al-Nahda: 124, 126

al-Nahhas, Mustafa: targeting of Muslim Brotherhood, 79

Najjar, Dr Zaghloul: 42

Nakoula, Nakoula Basseley: *Innocence of Muslims*, 172

Naqib, Mullah: 194

Nasir, Sayed: imprisonment of, 44

Nasrallah, Hassan: 108; leader of Hizbollah, 129

Nasser, Gamal Abdel: 2, 87, 122

National Party: 40

nationalism: 35, 89, 92; Arab, 88

Netanyahu, Benjamin: 178

Nigeria: 160, 232

al-Niqrashi, Mahmood: 79

Noah: 153–4

North Atlantic Treaty Organization (NATO): 30, 38, 192, 240

North Vietnam (Democratic Republic of Vietnam): People's Army of Vietnam, 74–5

Nour Party: 113, 115, 120, 123

bin Nurhasyim, Emrouzi: 249

Al-Nusra Front: 188, 201, 209, 240, 254, 265–6

Obama, Barack: 27, 30–1, 45, 100–2, 158–9, 173

Omar, Imam: 220, 225, 227

Omar, Mullah Mohammed: 8, 28, 192–5, 198, 208, 212, 222, 232, 241, 255, 266, 271; pledges of allegiance to, 234–6, 257–8

Oslo Peace Process (1993): 53

Othman, Imam: 220, 225–7

Ottoman Empire: 92, 127, 249, 254, 261, 273

al-Oufi, Salih: 244

Pakistan: vii, 2, 5, 27–8, 38, 40, 44, 52, 79, 83, 102, 192–3, 196, 199, 231, 255; Abbottabad, 21, 25; American aid programmes in, 44; borders of, 37; Islamabad, 180; Peshawar, 2, 259; Waziristan, 186, 192, 194, 210, 215, 219, 231, 239, 247

Palestine: 3, 21–3, 25, 29, 33, 35, 61, 66, 79, 83, 92, 160, 173, 175, 185, 193, 210, 248, 250–2; Arab Revolt (1936–9), 255; borders of, 264; Gaza, 28, 44, 84, 94, 123, 178, 192–3, 195; Jerusalem, 66; Rafah, 92

pan-Arabism: failure of, 2

Payev, Zalim Khan Yandar: 74–5; as-

sassination of, 76; *Chechnya: Politics and Reality*, 76; visit to Moscow (1996), 82
Peru: 83
Philippines: 29, 84, 195, 207, 272; Manila, 28
Portugal: 127

Qaddafi, Muammar: 30, 38
Al-Qaeda: ix–xi, 11, 43–5, 47–9, 56, 99–100, 107–8, 127, 139, 171, 177, 185, 196, 198, 208–9, 212–13, 231, 233, 235, 247, 258, 265; affiliates of, 45, 232; Jamaat Qaeda Al-Jihad: 136–7, 141; Majlis Al-Shura, 138–9; members of, vii–viii, 1, 3, 5, 12, 140, 182; Al-Sahab, 3, 95, 99–100, 107–8, 121, 185, 210, 233; 'Support for Islam', 49, 51
Al-Qaeda in the Arabian Peninsula (AQAP): 169, 210; al-Malahim Foundation, 210; members of, 190
Al-Qaeda in the Islamic Maghreb: 207
Al-Qasir, Heela: 201
Qatar: 76
Quincy Agreement (1945): 120, 130; political impact of, 255
Qurasyh (tribe): 109, 222–3
al-Qurtubi, Imam: 229
Qutb, Sayyid: theories of, 2, 89

Radiev, Salman: 74
Abd al-Rahman, Umar: imprisonment of, 133
al-Rahman bin Awf, Uthman Abd: 109
Rahman, Sheikh Omar Abdul: 44
al-Rajam, Abd al-Razzaq: 258
Rashid, Abdullah: 244
al-Razeq, Ali Abd: *Islam and the Principles of Governance*, 125
Rif War (1920–7): Battle of Annual (1921), 77; casualties of, 77

Riyadh Conference (2015): 253–4
Roosevelt, Franklin D.: signatory of Quincy Agreement (1945), 120, 130, 255
Rushdie, Salman: 179; fatwa issued against (1989), 172
Russian Empire: 39
Russian Federation: 40, 48, 175, 195, 202; Dagestan, 200; Moscow, 82

al-Sabaaee, Abu Karim Hani: 136, 176, 198, 213
Sabahi, Hamdeen: 80
Sacking of Baghdad (1258): 127
Sadat, Anwar: 2, 122, 196; assassination of (1981), 115
al-Saeed, Mohammed: 258
Salafism: 64, 80, 120–1, 251
Salafist Group for Preaching and Combat (GSCP): 207
Salama, Sheikh Hafiz: 28
Salih, Ali Abdullah: 30
Al Saud, Abd al-Aziz: 254; signatory of Quincy Agreement (1945), 130, 255
Al Saud, Prince Abdullah: 255
Saudi Arabia: 82, 119–20, 126, 130, 254; borders of, 245; Damam, 245; Jeddah, 2; Mecca, 66; Medina, 66, 220, 223, 225, 228; Najran, 245; Qatif, 245; Riyadh, 265
al-Sebssi, Badji Kaid: 251, 256
Second Opium War (1856–60): 172
Second World War (1939–45): 48, 130; Atomic Bombing of Hiroshima and Nagasaki (1945), 172
Secret Fifty: 80
secularism: 35, 71, 92, 112, 123–4, 207; Arab, 88–9
Al-Shabaab: 191
Shaiba, Ibn Abi: 224
al-Shami, Abu Hamam: 240

Shehadeh, Camilla: 94
Shenouda III, Father: 40–2, 90, 93
al-Shihri, Saed: 244
Shining Path: influence of, 83
Siddiqui, Aafia: 201; imprisonment of, 45
Sikhism: 55
al-Sisi, Abel Fattah: 80, 87–8, 120–1, 163, 251; regime of, 84, 119; rise to power (2013), 81, 92, 110, 123, 173, 256
Six-Day War (1967): territory occupied by Israel during, 255
socialism: 63
Somalia: 28, 44, 52, 54, 61, 71, 102, 160, 185–6, 195, 202, 207, 210; Mogadishu, 249
Somali Civil War (1992–): 101
South Sudan: 43
Soviet Union (USSR): 2, 99, 105, 206, 271, 273; collapse of (1991), 61
Spain: Anadlucía, 40, 90–1, 178, 197, 272; autonomous cities of, 48; Madrid Train Bombings (2004), vii, 249
Sudan: 2, 28, 37, 39, 92, 255; agricultural sector of, 232; Khartoum, 259; Second Civil War (1983–2005), 255
al-Suri, Abu Khalid: 207, 258; death of, 258–9
al-Suri, Abu Musab: 44, 249; imprisonment of, 77
Switzerland: 173; Geneva, 265
Sykes-Picot Agreement (1916): 3, 39–40, 208, 212
Syria: 53, 71, 96, 103–7, 122, 127, 129, 141–4, 153, 160, 169, 190, 197, 199, 207, 210–11, 214, 231, 237, 239, 245, 249–50, 260, 264, 267; Aleppo, 228; borders of, 147; Civil War (2011–), vii, 5, 11–12, 21, 29, 110, 135, 203, 206, 208–9, 242, 260; Damascus, 66, 161, 253; Hama, 196

takfir: 108, 201, 212, 251, 258–61; Khawarij, 264
Talib, Abli ibn Abi: 258
Taliban: 31, 44–5, 77, 109, 127; Afghan, 7–8; affiliates of, 45
Tamorod Front: funding provided to, 84
Tanwir, Shahzad: 210, 249
Tanzania: Dar el-Salam, 61; US Embassy Bombing (1998), 61
tawheed: 120–1, 129
El-Tayeb, Ahmed: Sheikh of al-Azhar, 40–1, 89, 125
Ibn Taymiyyah: Sheikh of Islam, 226
terrorism: viii, 1, 160
Theodoros II, Pope: 90
Tigris, River: 233
Tsarnaev, Dzhokhar: 210, 249
Tsarnaev, Tamerlan: 210, 249
Tunisia: 33, 79, 83, 124–5, 153, 160, 164; Revolution (2010–11), 27, 29–30, 77, 177, 251–2
Tukrmenistan: 196, 207

al-Uairi, Yusuf: 244
Ullah, Abu Suleiman al-Nasser al-Deen: 137
Umar, Abu Obaida Ahmed: 188–9
Umayyad Caliphate (661–750): 197, 205
ummah: 22, 26, 29, 102, 106–7, 109, 129, 136, 157, 175, 178, 180, 186, 197–8, 203–5, 208, 217, 225–6, 239–40, 250–1, 261; efforts to incite, 108, 111, 207, 213, 232, 245; operations focusing on, 112
United Kingdom (UK): 39, 43–4, 79, 130, 172, 244, 254; 7/7 Bombings, vii, 249; London, vii

United Nations (UN): 272; Charter of, 48; General Assembly, 48; Security Council, 39–40, 47, 175, 265

United States of America: 4, 23, 29, 33, 39, 49, 82, 103, 111, 119–20, 125–6, 132, 157, 159, 201, 231, 244; 9/11 Attacks, vii, 1, 6, 8, 26, 52, 59, 61, 64, 66–7, 102, 128, 182, 233, 245, 249; Central Intelligence Agency (CIA), 71, 96, 173; Congress, 102; economy of, 25; government of, 142; military of, 62, 120–1, 126; New York, vii, 26, 41, 61, 64, 66–7, 102; Pentagon, 26, 245; State Department, 83; US Agency for International Development (USAID), 79; Washington DC, vii, 26, 61, 64, 66–7, 102, 125

Uqair Protcol (1915): 254

Uzbekistan: Bukhara, 272; Samarkand, 272

Vietnam War (1955–75): 27, 74, 102, 172; casualties of, 75, 101

War on Terror: 60

Warsaw Pact: 75

Weinstein, Warren: kidnapping and death of (2015), 44, 201

World Islamic Front: creation of (1998), 2–3

al-Wuhayshi, Abu Nasser: 190–1

Yahya, Abu: 106, 142

al-Yazid, Mustafa Abu: 272

Yeltsin, Boris: foreign policy of, 82

Yemen: 21, 28, 44, 102, 126, 130, 153, 160, 170, 185–6, 190, 210, 243; Aden, 61; borders of, 245; Civil War (2015–), 253; government of, 126; Revolution (2011–12), 29–30; Sanaa, 164, 244

Yousef, Ramzi: 210, 249; imprisonment of, 44

bin Yusuf, Hajjaj: 204, 264

Zahawi, Mohamed: 189

Zahran (tribe): 245

al-Zaid, Mustafa Abu: 106, 131, 137

bin Zaid, Osama: 230

al-Zarqawi, Abu Musab: 4–5, 231, 233, 269, 272; death of, 234

al-Zawahiri, Ayman: vii–xi, 2–4, 6, 8, 10–11, 34, 48, 59, 73, 95, 99–100, 105, 135, 139–41, 147, 153, 169, 176, 185, 203, 212, 219, 231, 241, 247, 253, 263, 269, 274; background of, 2–3; declared leader of Al-Qaeda (2011), vii–viii, 5; 'General Guidelines for the Work of Jihad', 51, 93, 106; imprisonment of, 2; 'Islamic Spring, The', 11, 171; *Knights under the Prophet's Banner, The*, 3, 200; media presence of, 10–11, 21–2, 73; 'Messages of Hope and Glad Tidings' 11, 33–4; 'Scent of Paradise', 69, 131

al-Zawahiri, Mohammed: 85–7, 213

al-Zayyat, Montasser: 2

Zionism: 36, 53, 60–1, 82, 86, 93, 106, 111–12, 121, 128, 133, 178, 211

Al-Zour Party: 118–21

bin al-Zubair, Abdul Aziz: 60

bin al-Zubeir, Abdullah: 24

ibn Zuhair, Abu Kaab: 170